LIGHTSTONE
— PUBLISHERS —

THE ZARDARI PRESIDENCY

NOW IT MUST BE TOLD

Farhatullah Babar

LIGHTSTONE
— PUBLISHERS —

Published by
Ameena Saiyid S.I., Chevalier des Arts et des Lettres, OBE

Lightstone Publishers

Plot no. B-103, Sector 6/F, Mehran Town, Korangi Industrial Area

Karachi 74900, Pakistan.

First Edition published by Lightstone Publishers 2025.

ISBN: 978-969-716-304-5

Printed in Pakistan by Le Topical (Pvt.) Ltd., Lahore.

Dedication

-To my parents, who, through unwavering perseverance and sacrifice, nurtured five sons and six daughters under the most challenging circumstances—providing us the foundations to stand on.

-To my wife, Musarrat Babar, and our children, for their unceasing persuasion, encouragement and support in turning this memoir from an aspiration into a reality.

-To Shaheed Benazir Bhutto, who taught people the courage to dream and the strength to pursue those dreams. Her ability to inspire and motivate lives on in the hearts of all who were privileged to know her.

-To Munir Ahmad Khan (Chairman, Pakistan Atomic Energy Commission, 1972-1991) for enabling me learn commitment to excellence and guiding me towards the power of knowledge and the word. His legacy continues to uplift and inspire.

-To LBK Babar, my father-in-law, for his assistance in transforming my profession into a hobby, and to my friend Abdul Wahid Yousafi (Chief Editor, Publisher *Daily Aaj*, Peshawar) for his most invaluable help and advice in critical times.

-And to the innumerable noble souls, known and strangers, who illuminated the paths of my life and left imprints that have guided me.

CONTENTS

Section Three

IMPEACHING MUSHARRAF

Section Four

FACE-OFF WITH THE JUDICIARY

Section Five

ZARDARI AND THE OSAMA BIN LADEN FIASCO

Section Six

THE RAYMOND DAVIS AFFAIR

Section Seven

THE FATEFUL MEMOGATE

Section Eight

SOME EPISODES

Section Nine

SOME MYSTERIES

Section Ten

ZARDARI BOUNCES BACK

Acknowledgements

As I reflect on the journey of writing this memoir, I acknowledge that this work is not mine alone. It is the product of countless hands, hearts, and minds who, in ways both large and small, guided, supported and inspired me. The debt I owe is vast, and even if it may not be possible to name each person individually, I acknowledge their contributions with appreciation.

I wish to express gratitude to my wife and children, whose unwavering love, patience, and understanding have been my anchor.

To my extended family, and to the innumerable friends, colleagues, political activists, and well-wishers who walked beside me, whether mentioned here or not – I am grateful.

Many of those who enriched my life are no longer alive; their memories live on, and I honour them.

I am indebted to countless strangers who crossed my path, often unknowingly imparting lessons and insights that have helped me navigate the broader course of life. They added layers of understanding.

A special mention of Shaheed Benazir Bhutto, who shortly before her assassination had asked and motivated me to document life's experiences through multiple works, beyond one memoir. Her wish was a command and a responsibility, one that I will endeavour to fulfil with sincerity.

To my colleagues in the media offices – both in the Presidency and within the Pakistan People's Party – for making my task lighter. By doing the daily work diligently, they gifted me the time and space to prepare for writing work in the future. They thus allowed me to stand on their shoulders, and for that, I am deeply thankful.

I also extend my appreciation to the Photo Branch of the Press Information Department, whose archival contributions have enriched this work, allowing the visual history to compliment the written word.

Lastly, I am profoundly grateful to Lightstone Publishers, its managing director Ameena Saiyid, publishing director Nadia Ghani and the team, whose guidance, dedication and support made this endeavour possible.

Farhatullah Babar

President Asif Ali Zardari conferring the Award of Hilal-e-Imatiaz upon Farhatullah Babar during the Investiture Ceremony held at the Aiwan-e Sadr on Pakistan Day, 23 March 2012.

Preface

This book is my memoirs of the Zardari Presidency (2008 – 2013), when I served as presidential spokesperson. It is a personal recollection of a witness and participant, from a privileged vintage point, of the momentous events that shaped the Zardari Presidency and impacted the nation. Some of these events may be summed up as: the deep state breathing down Zardari's neck; a partisan Chief Justice hounding him; fabrications and intrigues like Memogate post-OBL disaster to make Zardari the scapegoat and pushing him to the brink; and of the troops of 111 brigade thudding in the Presidency at night to browbeat a defiant Zardari.

It is an attempt to catalogue some cat-and-mouse games played in an imbalanced power structure, marked by the de-jure, and accountable government ceding and space ceaselessly to the de-facto but unaccountable deep state.
It seeks to delve into the extraordinary Presidency of a man who defied the odds, endured jeers and ridicule and navigated a treacherous course in dealing the ambitious elements within the state apparatus distrustful of democracy and democratic institutions. It also seeks to offer a peep into Zardari's mind about issues — both profound and mundane — and to breathe life into history by offering insights into the persons, events and decisions taken at the time.

In September 2008, after militants had assassinated his

wife, captured parts of Khyber-Pakhtunkhwa and a fragile democracy was teetering, Zardari stepped into his late wife's shoes, too big for him, with an emotional pledge: "Democracy is the best revenge." Many at the time — the author of this memoir included — were apprehensive whether the man who had accidentally catapulted into the high office would even complete the term. It describes how history indeed unfolded differently.

Zardari went to not only complete his term, he was elected yet again to another term — a feat never achieved before by any civilian President in the country's history — rife with army coups, judicial activism, social and political upheavals and militancy and extremism.

The Zardari Presidency was also marked by stretching political reconciliation a bit too far. He thought it necessary to bridge Pakistan's deep political and ethnic divides. The 18th Amendment, aimed at parliamentary supremacy and transferring powers from the Presidency to the Legislature was passed under his watch. Yet democrats were disenchanted when the fundamental principles of the party — the PPP — of which he was also the head, were compromised, allowing the deep state to enlarge its footprint.

It also explores some paradoxes of the Zardari Presidency: a President who voluntarily ceded his constitutional powers to the Parliament to strengthen it — a trait rarely seen in Pakistani politics-yet allowing the hybrid system to become entrenched. It reflects on missed opportunities to overhaul the unaccountable intelligence apparatus sustaining the hybrid, even when opportunities came his way.

Zardari's Presidency also witnessed the U.S. Navy Seals raiding the compound in the military cantonment in Abbottabad and went back with the booty of the dead body of world's wanted terrorist Osama bin Laden (OBL) hiding in Pakistan for nearly a decade. The fight with the Chief Justice, the Memogate scandal, rocking the Presidency, the Raymond Davis affair and much more have also been described in detail in the memoirs.

Behind the public persona of a calculating politician who easily allowed pragmatism to trump principles also lay a deeply human side of Asif Ali Zardari. He was a father who bore the grief of his children's loss with quiet strength and a friend whose loyalty often defied political logic.

Personal anecdotes bring this dimension to life. From his self-awareness about his being no match to his wife to standing by friends to ignoring with contempt media criticism, Zardari emerges as a man who defied stereotypes.

This is the story of a leader who grappled with extraordinary challenges and left behind a legacy that warrants deeper understanding. Readers will encounter not just the politics of Asif Ali Zardari but the person behind the headlines.

This account does not ask readers to see Zardari as a white washed hero. It invites them to see him as he was: a leader - more sinned than sinning. Readers' criticism is most welcome.

Farhatullah Babar

Prologue

I worked with Mohtarma Benazir Bhutto—the Muslim world's first and Pakistan's twice directly elected woman Prime Minister—for nearly two decades, from 1986, when she returned home from exile, until her assassination in December 2007. I was present when she was lowered into her grave in Garhi Khuda Bakhsh.

During her first stint as Prime Minister (1988-90), I served as her official speech writer. In her second term (1993-96), I was her spokesperson. When her governments were dismissed, she took to the streets, travelling from city to city to attend court cases, visiting Zardari in jail with their young children in tow, leading the Party from the front, and serving as leader of the opposition in the National Assembly. Throughout this period, I remained her spokesperson.

Naturally, apart from working sessions in the office, I frequently visited her residences—both official and private—in Islamabad, Karachi, and later occasionally in Dubai, where she lived in exile. I also accompanied her on tours within Pakistan and abroad. Her spouse, Asif Zardari, was invariably part of her entourage during foreign visits.

Crossing paths with Zardari during these foreign travels and in working sessions at her residences was inevitable. However, despite our frequent encounters, my acquaintance with Asif Ali Zardari remained nominal. Our interactions were limited to exchanging greetings; he showed little interest in prolonged conversation, and I did not attempt to engage him further. It was a relationship of "hello, hi" and no more.

Zardari had the reputation of pursuing hobbies typical of wealthy businessmen. He tended to his farms, engaged in business activities, played polo, kept ponies, looked after pet animals and birds in a small private zoo, and socialised with friends—some of whom appeared rather eccentric. His wife had not encouraged him to play any high-profile role in either running the Party or the government.

In private conversations, party leaders did not speak highly of him. Rather, they spoke about him in unflattering ways. Their opinions were far from charitable. Critics often said he was not cut out to be the spouse of Benazir Bhutto. The media painted a negative image of him, but Zardari's attitude towards media criticism was one of indifference. If some of the mud thrown at him seemed to stick, he appeared unconcerned, taking it all in his stride.

Some of Zardari's friends were also tainted with corruption allegations. He was loath to distance himself from them, which did not earn him any laurels, especially when some appeared to throw their weight around rather menacingly.

Zardari's own style—casual, unostentatious, a sincere friend, and always wearing a broad smile—was not enough to overcome the negative perceptions about him.

He had been elected to Parliament. As a minister in his wife's cabinet, he introduced institutional mechanisms for the protection of the environment at a time when climate change and environmental degradation were not yet recognised as existential threats. However, he was reluctant to publicise these achievements.

His disdain for media coverage and refusal to appease media barons earned him the ire of powerful media houses and influential journalists accustomed to pandering by the high and mighty. A sustained media campaign had painted him as a corrupt and a street-smart money-maker rather than a political leader.

A Party leader, who was also a lawyer, refused to defend Zardari in court cases against him, throwing Benazir Bhutto into a rage.

On one occasion, Chief Justice Sajjad Ali Shah came to visit Zardari in his office at the Prime Minister's House.

Wearing shorts and brandishing excitedly a racket in hand, Zardari arrived late, keeping the Chief Justice waiting in a side room.

During a visit to an important Gulf country with his wife, Zardari was momentarily unaware that he was sitting with legs crossed, the sole of his shoe pointed towards the royal host—a gesture not appreciated in the Middle East.

Zardari was known to be extremely generous, almost to a fault, towards his friends. He stood by a friend in the media, a highly intrusive and disliked individual, without caring for the backlash it provoked. He took personal charge of the fight against the opposition's no-confidence motion against Benazir Bhutto and triumphed. He was also known to have played a behind-the-scenes role in formulating energy sector policies during Benazir Bhutto's second term as Prime Minister.

On the whole, Zardari then came across as someone adept at smart negotiations, a go-getter, a friend to friends ready to bend the rules to help them, and possessing the courage to live in his wife's shadow, unruffled and at peace.

I was working with Benazir Bhutto and was detached from Zardari, who hardly impressed me.

One day, Zardari's secretary approached me. He said that "saab" (Asif Zardari) wanted a particular journalist included in the media team for an upcoming foreign visit. The secretary insisted that the Prime Minister should not be told it was Zardari's recommendation, instructing me to find a way to do it without informing her. It was too tall an order for me. Once the Prime Minister had finalised the list, I couldn't alter it without informing her. Despite the secretary's insistence, I declined.

Later that evening, Benazir called, saying, "FB, I hear you were rude to Asif today." Surprised, I replied, "Bibi, I haven't even met him today. It must be some miscommunication," and recounted what had actually transpired. She appreciated that I had done the right thing by not adding another journalist to the list but also cautioned, "No one should be rude to Asif."

Being very brief and perfunctory, my encounters with Zardari did not allow me to know him well. As long as I worked exclusively with the Prime Minister, he did not appear to me as a bright star on the horizon.

It never occurred to me then that someday he would be the President and I would be his spokesperson. The thought that there were other dimensions to his personality did not cross my mind. Working closely with him as a spokesperson, I discovered how underrated and misunderstood he had been.

Detached academic studies by scholars and the media watching important events from a distance during his Presidency are available in abundance. The pages that follow contain an account of the Zardari Presidency from the perspective of a witness and a participant—in short, from inside the ring.

Historians also need to immerse themselves in the mood, the temper, the attitudes, and the atmosphere when momentous decisions are taken. They need to hear the ambience quietly sing into their ears to be able to do justice to their subject.

This is thus an account of the dynamics of power play, of the hopes, fears, and machinations of major power wielders as revealed by their body language and conversations at the time. It is an eyewitness account of Zardari's high and low moments and of the strengths and weaknesses of his Presidency.

Farhatullah Babar
April 2025

President Asif Ali Zardari with the author
and Malik Asif Hayat, Secretary to the President.

Section One

ZARDARI AS A PERSON

Chapter 1

The accidental President

Born on 26 July 1955 to Hakim Ali Zardari, a Sindhi politician and head of the Zardari tribe, Asif Ali Zardari was little known outside his tribe before he married Benazir Bhutto, the daughter of Pakistan's President and Prime Minister Zulfikar Ali Bhutto, in 1987. His identity among his tribe was no more than that of a landowner and businessman fond of playing polo. The spotlight shone on him only after his marriage.

Few, if any, would have imagined that Zardari would one day become the President of Pakistan. Fewer still believed that he would complete his term and hand over the reins to another President in a peaceful and orderly manner. No one believed that he would go on to be elected President once again and attain a distinction no other civilian President had achieved before.

When he first became President in 2008, he was called an "accidental" President, having been catapulted into the office by the tragic assassination of his wife. A millennium before, Louis VII of France, initially destined for a different role in life, became king after marrying Eleanor of Aquitaine, one of Europe's wealthiest and most influential women. Similarly, Zardari first acquired prominence by marrying Benazir Bhutto and ended up as the President as a result of her assassination.

Shafaq chuphi tau sitaron nai roshni paai
Kisi ki mout kisi ki hayat banti hai

(It is only after the sun has set that the stars shine. The death of one becomes the life of another.)

In Larkana, on Benazir Bhutto's Soyem, I tendered my resignation, thinking that it was best to resign as the Party's spokesperson instead of being shunted out. Zardari declined, saying, "Continue for the time being; we will see later."

When he became the President in 2008 and asked me to work as his spokesperson, it was not due to any special attributes or great mutual admiration. Perhaps he wanted to send a signal of continuity with his wife's legacy and policies by retaining the staff who had worked with her.

I felt honoured, although there was a little serpent of doubt: Would I survive as the spokesperson for more than a few months—indeed, would Zardari survive as President?

I did not make a new business card as spokesperson to the President and continued using the old one as the Party's spokesperson. Why make a new business card when the business was not going to last long? Indeed, I never had a business card as a "Spokesperson to the President" for the full five years.

So I was no less an "accidental" spokesperson, offered the job only for "the time being".

The "accidental President" Zardari not only completed his five-year term but, fifteen years later, went on to be elected once again as President in 2024. As the "accidental spokesperson", I also not only completed five years in his first term in the Presidency but also went on to become the Party's secretary general and chairman of the Parliamentary Commission on the South Punjab Province, marvelling at the accidents of history.

During his five years in the Presidency, I worked with him and witnessed his way of working even more closely. Whether he presided over important meetings in the Presidency or Party meetings in Zardari House when he was not the President, I was around like a shadow. I also travelled extensively with him, both within the country and on his over two dozen foreign trips, eight or nine of which were to China alone.

A spokesperson's position is highly privileged. Engaging almost daily with the President one-on-one on important news enabled me to peep into his mind. Those interactions' spontaneous and not-so-spontaneous responses provided rare insights into Zardari's thinking. I began to understand more clearly his hopes and fears, as well as the motivations behind decisions that sometimes earned admiration and, at other times, disbelief and condemnation.

I have been in the newspaper world for decades. A nose for news and an irresistible urge to write instinctively compels a newsman to keep his eyes open and ears to the ground. Although I was a spokesperson for "the time being", there was a realisation that someday I would have to write an account of the Zardari Presidency for whatever little time I served him. So, I kept a diary as well.

Zardari appeared aware of the less-than-flattering images I had about him from the days I worked with his wife. When I congratulated him on the day he took oath in 2008, he cryptically commented: "*Tumhara khial tha keh main koi leader nahi hun.*" (You thought I was no leader.)

On another occasion, he told me: "Farhatullah, you have worked with Shaheed Bibi. I know you did not think much of me, but I wanted you to work with me."

When elected for the second time, I went to congratulate him, this time in Zardari House instead of the Presidency. A small crowd had already gathered around him. On seeing me, and before I could felicitate him, he said with a broad grin,

"*Haan, kuch log humai leader hi nahi samajhte.*" (Yes, some people do not consider me as a leader).

I wished that those gathered did not understand the context of Zardari's seemingly off-the-cuff remarks.

During Zardari's first Presidency, momentous events took place that shook both the country and his person.

It was during his period that Osama bin Laden was found hiding in a military cantonment; the army and ISI chiefs knocked at the Supreme Court, accusing the supreme commander of the armed forces of treason, and a military dictator was charmed out of the Presidency to eventually flee from the country; doors to CPEC opened; Mumbai was attacked by militants launched from Pakistan; the Taliban took over Swat; the judiciary was on a war path; and the deep state was conspiring against democracy at every step.

"Tumultuous" is the word that describes his Presidency.

As spokesperson, I was both a participant in and a witness to the decision-making processes in the Zardari Presidency.

The following pages contain an account of the tumultuous Zardari Presidency from the perspective of a spokesperson who witnessed the breathtaking dramas that played out and how a besieged President fought back.

Accidental leaders face unique challenges but also have opportunities to leave a mark in equally accidental ways. Zardari also faced unique challenges. Whether he left any mark is for the people and history to judge. This account might help a historian in making that judgment.

Chapter 2

Defying any single definition

It is challenging to fit Asif Ali Zardari into one single definition. People have described him variously depending on the lens through which they view him. In an editorial, the national Urdu Daily *Nawa e Waqt* called him "Mard e Hurr", likening him to the legendary commander Hurr, who defected from Yezid's army to join a vanquished Hussain, valiantly fighting until his death by Hussain's side. His detractors, however, vilified him as "corrupt", "Mr Ten Percent", "a wheeler-dealer", and worse.

Benazir Bhutto publicly admired him. In an article on the eve of one of his birthdays, she wrote: "Asif's life is full of interesting stories. In 1989, a corps commander met him with a message from the armed forces. He was asked to become the Prime Minister of Pakistan in place of his wife. The excuse was that the military could not salute a woman. In 1993, an Arab prince made the same offer to him." On another occasion, she likened him to the iconic leader of South Africa, Nelson Mandela, who spent 27 years in jail but, when released, left behind his anger and went on to end apartheid and unite his country in a great reconciliation. In casual private conversations, she spoke critically of some of his friends whom she did not like and did not want them to frequent the Prime Minister's House. He was known to be "a friend of friends" and did not care if some of them were suspicious-looking and threw their weight around.

A few exaggeratedly ranked him with his father-in-law, Zulfikar Ali Bhutto. No one denied his humane qualities, courage, resilience, and down-to-earth persona, with no pretensions to be above human failings. He was frank to admit, "I am no match for Bibi (Benazir Bhutto)."

Though not educated at prestigious institutions like Oxford and Cambridge, he ultimately acquitted himself no less honourably than any highly educated contemporary leader. He kept his cards close to his chest and tended to be secretive in decision-making. He sometimes made decisions like an "all-wise" and "know-all" wizard. If this made the people around him uncomfortable, he quickly disarmed them with a smile, guile, and charm.

During a foreign visit, a frustrated ambassador once barged into my room and sarcastically said, *"FB, yaar tumhara boss apne aap ko aql e kul samajhta hai."* (FB, your boss thinks he is all-wise).

I never saw him lose his temper or froth at the mouth.

Not many possess the craft, wile, and charm to neutralise detractors as Asif Zardari did. His wife, Benazir Bhutto, possessed charm and intellect but was not as adept at neutralising opponents. Indeed, she also leaned on him in times of crisis to neutralise her opponents. He was open to admitting mistakes and did not hesitate to retract his words and apologise for wrongs done. Once, he called a senior police officer in Karachi accused of hundreds of extrajudicial killings a "Bahadur bachcha" (brave son). But when he realised the mistake, he quickly acknowledged that he had misspoken publicly and retracted his remarks.

Zardari stood by his loyalists and friends like no one else. It is hard to imagine him throwing loyalists under the bus for his own safety. Sometime in November 2011, with some friends and coalition partners huddled around him, he offered a rare glimpse into his past:

"As a teenager, I was implicated in a case and was advised to name a servant to secure bail. I refused. How could I do that? It was against my conscience; the suggestion was insulting. I had to fight it myself."

He possessed the courage to endure hardships and torture. Once, in a private setting, he recounted an incident involving his jail doctor:

"My jail doctor was shocked upon learning that I was about to be shifted from jail to the notorious Attock Fort. He was almost shaking," Zardari said, recalling in some detail how he comforted his doctor at the time.

The doctor smiled. Realising that some improper words had escaped his lips when describing the incident, Zardari was quick to withdraw them.

"I was a macho in the past, but in this position now, I can't afford to be a macho," Zardari said. "I carry a burden and can't afford to act like a macho."

"No Sir, you are still a macho," a party leader from Khyber Pakhtunkhwa remarked.

Zardari was not amused. Placing his forefinger across his nose, he said, *"Allah muaaf karai"* (May God forgive me) in a gesture to disavow the words uttered.

On another occasion, he remarked, "Thank God I am not a gambler and don't gamble. I can't accept defeat. I would have persisted in gambling and perhaps lost everything."

A media baron once called on Zardari and complained that General Musharraf had ruined his media house financially, asking for compensation. Zardari explained that it was a court case and that he could not do much about it. Not expecting this response, the media baron became somewhat aggressive and warned of consequences. Smilingly, Zardari replied, *"Chalo dekh laitai hain."* (OK, we will see.) The meeting ended. The media baron must have regretted the encounter when the state-run television PTV launched its own sports channel, cutting into his private channels' huge profits.

Zardari is neither a Nelson Mandela nor a Hurr. But few will deny that if he had not stood by his wife's side, the future of Benazir and her democratic struggle might have been different. Zardari remained unchanged in the Prime Minister's and the President's Houses or jails. He had seen life from the depth of the valley as well as from the peak of the mountain. Power did not make his head dizzy, and adversity failed to crush his soul. Whether luxuriating in palatial houses adorned with plush carpets, antique chandeliers, and period furniture or thrown into dingy cells in jail, he took everything in his stride.

He was in jail when his mother passed away and could not hold her hand when she was dying. He was in jail when his children grew from infants into teenagers, missing the opportunity to play the role of a father as they were shaping up. An anguished Benazir, describing the agony, said that when Zardari came out of jail, the children had crossed the age to sit in their father's lap. Nothing could bring back those lost years, she lamented. He endured betrayal from some lifelong friends and rationalised it by saying that an animal's behaviour was predictable, but that of a human was not.

He was not bitter when PPP leader Rao Sikandar ditched the Party in the midst of the struggle by forming a forward bloc called "Patriots" against Benazir Bhutto in 2002. Rao later deeply regretted it. Zardari felt sorry when veteran Pashtun nationalist leader Ajmal Khattak fell into General Musharraf's trap and turned his back on his Party. "*Allah iman day qabar tak*" (May Allah give faith till the grave), he said when he heard about Khattak's betrayal. Like PPP's Rao Sikandar, the ANP's Ajmal Khattak also regretted it later.

When lifelong associate Zulfiqar Mirza betrayed him, Zardari was sad but was neither angry nor spoke ill of him. In a Party meeting, he fondly recalled that Mirza was a great childhood friend. Zardari did not regret making Mirza's wife Speaker of the National Assembly, preferring her over his own sister for the job.

"Mirza was so close to us, and when Shaheed Bibi advised him to leave the country for his safety, Mirza refused to go into exile, saying he would not abandon Zardari in jail," he recalled with gratitude.

"*Kuch log pehchanai tau gai*" (Some people have been exposed), he said lamentingly. "I trusted him," Zardari said and recalled with sadness how Zulfiqar Mirza once came to him saying: "I will always follow you even though I cannot quite understand you."

Some have called Zardari an enigma, others a paradox, and still others "an enigma inside a paradox". Zardari has defied any single definition to describe his person.

Chapter 3

Reconciliation – stretched too far

South Africa's iconic figure Desmond Tutu once said: "Forgiving is not forgetting; it's actually remembering—remembering and not using your right to hit back. The remembering part is particularly important. Especially if you don't want to repeat what happened."

"Forgive yes, Forget not," Tutu had said.

Whether he forgot or not, Zardari was not only quick in seeking reconciliation and forgiving but also in stretching it too far.

Among his early actions on returning to Pakistan was to visit the graves of the family members of MQM leader Altaf Hussain in a bid to reach out and reconcile with the political party dominating the politics of urban Sindh.

When Benazir Bhutto was assassinated, riots broke out in Sindh. People came out onto the streets, raising slogans against the federation and demanding revenge. Zardari responded with "Pakistan Khappay" (Pakistan First).

Zardari recalled to me that he could have taken on General Musharraf and settled scores with a few generals, but it would have resulted in bloodshed and a "disaster for the institution and the country."

Fifteen years later, another President, Arif Alvi of the PTI, publicly acknowledged this. In an interview with Hamid Mir in March 2023, during the height of political polarisation, Alvi said that the country would have been dismembered if Zardari had not said "Pakistan Khappay. I belong to Sindh, and I know it well," he said in the interview.

Zardari reached out to those who had harmed him and even invited them to the Presidency for tea or lunch.

A senior government functionary who had relentlessly chased Zardari while serving in the NAB and had become a federal secretary came to the Presidency for an official meeting relating to his new assignment. Zardari reached out to welcome him. He also invited for lunch a former army officer who, while serving in the NAB, had roughed him up.

He ordered a moratorium on the death penalty.

Zardari did not react angrily to any provocation, saying that a hateful reaction generated even more hatred and vengeance. The consequences of a reaction can be more harmful than the provocation, he used to say.

Newspapers, quoting Wikileaks, reported some highly uncomplimentary remarks allegedly made by the Saudi monarch about Zardari. He did not react angrily. Instead, he asked that a statement be issued saying that the President profoundly respected the Saudi monarch and dismissed the newspaper reports as an attempt to drive a wedge between the two countries.

This reminded me that Benazir Bhutto had also ignored Iranian President Rafsanjani's uncomplimentary remarks about her in an interview he gave to a foreign journal in October 2007, recalling his meeting with her in Tehran in 1995. Heeding the advice of Ambassador Zafar Hilali to ignore it, she had sent him a text message: "I agree. There will be time to set the record straight" and copied it to me. The difference was striking. While Benazir kept quiet, saying that the time to respond would come, Zardari responded that he respected the Saudi monarch and would not let it drive a wedge between Pakistan and Saudi Arabia.

Zardari did not chase his foes but only avoided them. A former Chief Justice and some senior bureaucrats who had wronged him sought to meet him after he was no longer in power. Zardari was not bitter, but he did not meet them. He got along easily with people of diverse interests and ambitions and was adept at threading the beads together.

When the dice were loaded against him, the military acted as a state within a state, and coalition partners demanded their pound of flesh; he only had a smile and guile to navigate the course. Without a parliamentary majority, he kept the coalition government of PPP afloat for a full five-year term. When some party leaders appeared impatient and talked of launching political agitation against the PTI government, he counselled restraint. "Wait at least until the honeymoon period is over," he advised, giving examples of how Zulfikar Ali Bhutto and Benazir Bhutto waited for opportune moments.

Zulfikar Ali Bhutto lived in Larkana until he sensed that the moment for action had arrived to launch his political campaign, he once recalled. On another occasion, he said Benazir Bhutto had only 17 seats in the National Assembly and lay low in Karachi until the issue of Kalabagh Dam provided her with an opportunity to come out into the open. She travelled to the border of Sindh and Punjab and made a historic speech that galvanised the people and breathed new life into the party.

Benazir Bhutto wanted to reopen the judicial murder case of Zulfikar Ali Bhutto, but the time was not on her side, he said. A reference could be filed only by the President, and with Ghulam Ishaq Khan as President, it could not be done. The Party was able to reopen it only when he became the President, he said.

"Trust me, I will come out at the right time," he advised as he often did.

He was too generous in building consensus. In 2008, at the time of government formation, he decided to let the ANP form the government in Khyber Pakhtunkhwa with PPP as a junior partner. Many in the Party were unhappy. But he had his eyes on restoring the 1973 Constitution. He needed the support of all parties and was ready to go far to meet their demands. He thought that Pakhtun nationalism needed to be strengthened against militants and to empower the ANP in Pakhtunkhwa province. The Party reluctantly agreed.

He believed in incentivising people instead of adopting coercive measures. When the finance managers recommended legislation against informal and non-banking channels of money transfer, he refused. "Let us incentivise foreign remittances by giving market rate and come back to me after three months." Remittances multiplied after that.

During a visit to Nawaz Sharif in Raiwind, Nawaz Sharif said that Musharraf must be punished for treason. Pointing towards a stuffed lion, Zardari said, "*Aap shair hain ye kaam aap karlain.*"

(You are a lion, please do it.) When the time came to show General Musharraf the door, he allowed him to quit gracefully and did not object to the army giving him a guard of honour.

He stretched reconciliation far too far. Zardari had labelled PML-Q as the "Qatil (Murderer) League," alluding to the alleged involvement of its patron, General Musharraf, in the assassination of Benazir Bhutto. But he had no qualms in co-opting it into the coalition government and later even agreeing to the unconstitutional demand of its leader, Chaudhry Parvez Elahi, to be nominated to the nonexistent Deputy Prime Minister post. It cost the PPP dearly in Punjab, but he believed it was the best way forward.

Chapter 4

Zardari and corruption allegations

Asif Ali Zardari has been mired in corruption allegations and alternated between power and prison on corruption charges even before he entered the Presidency. Fanciful stories of corruption were woven around him. Housewives shopping in Islamabad, complaining of price rises, were told by shopkeepers that Zardari had a share in the profits they made.

A senior journalist claimed that Zardari had tied a bomb to the leg of a businessman in Karachi to extort money from him. This turned out to be false. Senior editors of the media outlet later confided that an intelligence agency planted the report. Zardari was accused of feeding jam and marmalade to his horses in the Prime Minister's House, but when Benazir, as leader of the opposition, rubbished the allegations demanding proof, no one came forward with any evidence.

Zardari was the first to be arrested soon after the dismissal of the first Benazir government in 1990. He was accused of stashing tons of gold in the Governor's House in Lahore and killing political opponents. Charges were filed under the watch of President Ghulam Ishaq Khan. When no charges were proved and he was released, the same Ghulam Ishaq Khan administered the oath to Zardari as a federal minister. Benazir Bhutto cherished handing the President a spectacular rebuff. When Benazir's second government was dismissed in 1996, he was arrested again on corruption charges. General Musharraf also jailed him on charges of corruption. But nothing could be proved against him in the courts.

When General Musharraf's political face, Pakistan Muslim League-Quaid (PML-Q), failed to get a majority in the 2002 elections, the ISI began negotiations with the PPP, creating false hopes that corruption cases would be withdrawn. Benazir Bhutto knew that it was a ruse. She allowed the senior PPP leader from Sindh, Makhdoom Amin Fahim, to continue negotiations to explore whether the exiles would be permitted to return and whether the politically motivated cases would be withdrawn. The media was abuzz with reports of Makhdoom becoming Prime Minister even as behind-the-door secret negotiations continued. Makhdoom Amin Fahim let it be known privately that Musharraf was unlikely to give any assurances to withdraw cases, and after taking oath as Prime Minister, he would have to find a way around it. When Benazir Bhutto learnt about this, she directed that as her spokesperson, I make a statement that the Party had not yet decided on the name of its parliamentary leader in the National Assembly and that the media reports of the nomination of Makhdoom Amin Fahim as the future Prime Minister were premature.

Geo Television's blaring headline said: "*Makhdoom Amin Fahim ke ghubarai se hawa nikal gaie.*" (The wind has been taken out of Amin Fahim's balloon.) The talks failed. The deep state only wanted to split the Party by dangling a carrot to Makhdoom. Exposed, the negotiators of the deep state backed off from talks, leaving Makhdoom fuming. Makhdoom never lost his composure and kept his cool in public. Sympathising with him, some Party stalwarts sought to provoke him against the spokesperson. Makhdoom simply told them, "I know the spokesperson cannot issue such a statement on his own." Not even once did he complain or talk to me about it.

A judge of the Lahore High Court, Justice Malik Qayyum, sentenced him and Benazir Bhutto for corruption. Later, it transpired that the judge regularly received directions on the phone from the accountability czar Saifur Rehman during Nawaz Sharif's government. When the tapes of conversations surfaced, the Supreme Court censured the judge, saying 'the bias of the judge floated on the surface of record' and remanded the case back to the trial court. Both the Judge and the Lahore High Court Chief Justice resigned, but no action was taken against them.

Zardari spent 11 years behind bars without conviction. His nemesis, Saifur Rehman, later publicly admitted that he had wronged Zardari. When the two had a chance encounter during recess in a courtroom, Saifur Rehman fell at his feet to seek forgiveness.

However, while the corruption allegations against Zardari remained unsubstantiated, he tolerated reports of corruption by his friends and Party people. I also served as convener of the Party's Ethics Committee for a few months. When reports of alleged corruption by a federal minister were brought to his attention, he, naming the minister, said, "He is our Party leader. I cannot humiliate him in public. I will speak with him." Privately, he admonished the minister, thinking that it was enough.

He acknowledged that not all reports of corruption were untrue. Referring to corruption allegations against some specific individuals, he once said, "They are behaving as if it is their last day in office, and tomorrow shall never come." He also admitted, "During our previous government, some corrupt people made money but named me as their partner." Federal ministers, senior Party officials, and high public functionaries going on foreign visits were required to seek permission. A minister, however, travelled to Dubai without seeking the President's permission and tried to keep it secret. When Zardari learnt about it, he remarked, without naming the minister, that some smart people secretly travelled abroad to check whether kickbacks had been credited into their bank accounts. "They think nobody will come to know," he said. Towards the end of 2009, a state minister in a TV talk show said that politicians, too, had a right to corruption, and it was wrong to single them out. It provoked both laughter and criticism, but no overt action was taken against him. Subsequently, the minister not only reiterated his comments but also declared in a press talk in Quetta that there were corrupt elements both within the judiciary and the security establishment. He accused Chief Justice Iftikhar Chaudhry of being from Faisalabad but using a domicile of Balochistan to become a judge. Why single out the politicians? He asked. Chief Justice Iftikhar Chaudhry called Prime Minister Yousaf Raza Gilani on the phone: "*Ab hum kia karain*?" (What should we do now?) He asked. Instead of issuing a contempt notice, Chaudhry wanted the Prime Minister to take action.

The minister who had got away with remarks on corruption and made Zardari look pale now could not get away. Prime

Minister Gilani called the minister in Quetta, "Will you resign on your own, or should we send you a sacking order?" The minister resigned.

Zardari rejected allegations of corruption against him. "I learnt earning money in business from my father. I did not make money; I earned it. There is a difference. I used to buy plots long ago. At the birth of every child, I bought a plot."

He called out NAB (National Accountability Bureau) for destroying business and the economy, saying that it was for political witch-hunting. He was criticized for making such statements, accusing him of protecting corruption. Some big names in the media who fanned the poisonous narrative against him were also secretly seeking favours from him. During a media briefing session, Zardari once disclosed that a journalist had come to invite him to the marriage of his child. The journalist made it known that he expected a high-value Pajero for his son as a gift. Zardari did not disclose what gift he gave to the bridegroom. It is widely known that the Information Ministry and the Intelligence Bureau (IB) have long been operating secret funds to influence media projection. A PPP Parliamentarian was known for doling out hefty handouts to some media persons using secret funds, attracting criticism.

Corruption charges against Zardari were never proven, but he bore the brunt of the indiscretions of others. In a newspaper column, noted columnist Suhail Waraich said he would be the last person to call Zardari a thief or corrupt even if the world called him corrupt. Zardari maintained that intellectual dishonesty was worse than financial corruption. "I will ignore financial corruption if there is intellectual honesty in the person," he said to me once. If some mud stuck on him partly because of his worldview of corruption, partly due to his tolerance for it, and partly due to a vicious campaign, he did not care.

Chapter 5

Some snippets from Zardari's life

These snippets help define, albeit vaguely, Zardari's character.

(i) *On arrival from Dubai to bury Benazir*

Zardari and his children were in Dubai when Benazir Bhutto was assassinated in Rawalpindi on 27 December 2007. They arrived on a special flight from Dubai at around 9 P.M. that night.

Her body lay in the lounge of Nur Khan Air Base, Islamabad, awaiting transfer to Larkana. Clad in a grey shalwar-kameez and donning a chaddar, Zardari alighted from the plane and walked towards the lounge. Grim-faced and with a firm gait, he approached me.

The few words he uttered were, "Be firm, Farhatullah. I want you to tell everyone to be firm. No one should be seen shedding tears, and no one should show any weakness. The children are also standing very firm. This is an occasion to convert grief into strength."

I informed him that General Kayani, returning from Karachi, had spoken with me in the lounge shortly before and offered any necessary assistance. Zardari did not dwell on it. "No, everything has been arranged," he replied.

Some close associates had already gathered at the airbase to receive the family. A C-130 aircraft of the Pakistan Air Force was ready to take the body to her hometown for burial.

The few grief-stricken people who had managed to arrive at the lounge stood motionless. Zardari walked up to greet them individually as every gaze turned to his face.

He spoke clearly. His body language and facial expressions were those of a distressed person, but bore no signs of panic.

That day, history had not only taken a turn; it was also in the making. Zardari seemed conscious that his words and gestures would be closely watched and recorded at that moment, even if only as a footnote in history.

(ii) *On reports of contracting another marriage*

Sometime in 2010 or 2011, rumours began circulating that Zardari had secretly married a woman of Pakistani origin in New York. The woman, a doctor by profession, also spoke ambiguously, fuelling suspicions. Media outlets asked questions. An Indian media outlet claimed to have "credible" evidence and sought only the Presidency's viewpoint. Others offered incentives to me to break what they believed was a "huge story".

Instead of discussing it in the usual morning "media brief" meeting in the presence of other staffers, I requested an exclusive meeting. Instantly, he called me to the office. "*Khair, kia ho gaya. Akailai milna chahtai ho?*" (What's happened that you want to see me alone?). He asked as soon as I entered the office.

I told him about the circulating rumours and the questions the media was asking.

He was aware of the media reports and gave a hearty laugh.

"Farhatullah, even you believe it? At least you shouldn't have thought so. You know me so well. You worked with her (Benazir Bhutto)." He then paused.

"Farhatullah, I am the son-in-law of Zulfikar Ali Bhutto." he said. "That has become my identity. The world knows me by this association. History will remember me by this association. I am part of this historical legacy."

Then, with disarming candour, he said, "The people and the Party respect me because of it. Do you think people would even talk to me if I were no longer Bhutto's son-in-law and had become someone else's son-in-law?"

He added, "Even you would abandon me if I took another wife and ceased to be known as Bhutto's son-in-law or Shaheed Bibi's spouse."

(iii) *When Benazir was angry*

In January 2019, when Zardari was in an expansive mood, he related an incident:

"TFT (*The Friday Times*) published a false report in *Such Gup* about my contracting another marriage," he said. "Somehow, Shaheed Bibi thought the report might be true. She was furious and fought with me for several days," he disclosed. "*Auratain haathon se larne ki bajaay zuban se zyada sakht larti hain.*" (Women fight more with their tongues than with their hands), he added.

"After some time, when the report turned out to be false, I asked her to file a defamation suit against TFT," he continued.

Naming a woman lawyer of repute who was also a friend of Benazir, he said, "Bibi approached her, but she advised against it, saying that the media would only splash more dirt."

Zardari regretted that, ignoring his suggestion, Bibi did not engage another lawyer.

I asked why he regretted it when Bibi herself did not want to pursue it, and he himself did not care about the media maligning him.

"*Samjho* Farhatullah, history must be corrected," he replied.

(iv) *When given wrong advice*

In February 2009, the Supreme Court disqualified Shehbaz Sharif from being elected as an MPA, forcing him to quit the office of Chief Minister.

Taking advantage of this, Zardari swiftly sacked Shehbaz Sharif's provincial government and imposed Governor's Rule in Punjab. It was a colossal mistake that sent the Sharifs into a tailspin, as they believed Zardari was behind the verdict. Punjab was their power bastion. Seeing it slipping out of their hands, they were up in arms and latched onto the lawyers' protest movement to restore Chief Justice Iftikhar Chaudhry.

Soon, Zardari realised the mistake and asked the government to support appeals against the disqualification.

This reversal embarrassed the PPP during the first year of Zardari's Presidency, and an internal blame game started. Many demanded that those who advised the President to tread this perilous course be identified and held accountable.

No one accepted responsibility in the core committee meeting for giving the President the wrong advice. As the public face of policy shaping in the Presidency, I tendered my resignation, although I was not among the advisors giving the ill-fated advice.

With disarming candour, Zardari said that no one but he alone was to blame for the blunder. "I was given wrong advice," he admitted but did not name who had advised him. "*Lekin yeh to meri ghalati thi ke mai ne ghalat advice ko maan liya*" (But it was my mistake to have accepted the wrong advice), he said, ending the internal controversy by accepting total responsibility for the fiasco.

(v) *Lambasting the Army Chief*

In June 2015, the tribal chapter of the PPP brought together hundreds of tribesmen from all over the tribal areas in Islamabad to discuss advancing the reform process in the region. Zardari, the Party head, was also scheduled to address them.

As usual, before leaving Zardari House to meet them, Zardari reviewed the draft of his address several times, noting some points in his own hand.

At the venue, Zardari set aside the prepared text of the speech. Instead of discussing the issues and policy reforms in tribal areas, he lashed out at the Army Chief, General Raheel Sharif.

Warning "*eent se eent baja doon ga*" (I will respond with brickbats and stones), he declared, "The day our Party takes to the streets, not only Sindh but the entire country will be shut down."

"Army Chiefs come and go every three years, but the politicians are here to stay. We know the country and how to run it better than you think you do," he said, leaving everyone wondering what the provocation was.

There was not a word in his speech about the issues faced by the tribal people. He even forgot to welcome the tribesmen to Islamabad before launching his salvo against General Raheel Sharif.

Everyone was stunned. Did he speak impulsively, or was there some provocation before he left Zardari House for the venue? I was the last person to interact with him before he came for the meeting with the tribesmen. No one had whispered anything into his ears that might have changed his mind. While discussing the speech points barely an hour before, there was no hint of anything weighing on his mind. He had also not spoken with anyone before the meeting.

Did Zardari keep his cards closest to his chest, or had he acted impulsively? What provoked him to lambast the Army Chief publicly is hard to say. He used to say that of all creatures, man is the most unpredictable and prone to err at any time. Today, he proved that he was not immune from this human weakness. He, too, was capable of being the most unpredictable and prone to blundering grievously.

Reacting to his remarks against the Army Chief, Prime Minister Nawaz Sharif cancelled a luncheon invitation to Zardari the next day, leaving Zardari embarrassed and isolated. In response, Zardari called a meeting of his political allies the following day at Zardari House, hoping to send a message of unanimity among his allies. However, the front-ranking leaders of the allied parties did not attend the meeting, apparently to distance themselves from what he had said about the Army Chief; only the second-tier leaders attended. Zardari took it in his stride and did not complain.

Section Two

FORAYS IN FOREIGN POLICY

Chapter 1

A peep into Zardari's foreign policy

Zardari attempted to make some highly significant forays into the realm of foreign policy. His approach differed starkly from that of his wife, Benazir Bhutto. While Benazir discussed policy ideas with close aides in closed-door sessions to fine-tune and calibrate policy choices, largely relying on institutional mechanisms while confronting bureaucrats with hard questions, Zardari was open to making far-reaching decisions independently.

Some of Zardari's ideas on relations with neighbouring countries, China and Russia, were profound. However, except in relations with China, he did not achieve much success in other areas, due mainly to the resistance of entrenched institutional interests. Great ideas and enthusiasm alone do not guarantee success unless backed by a degree of synthesis among various stakeholders.

Selecting a woman as foreign minister for the first time was a breath of fresh air. The optics indicated a desire to break from the past. Hina Rabbani Khar rose to the challenge and acquitted herself honourably. But individuals no matter how competent, and optics however appealing, are no substitute for strong institutions. As an institution, the foreign office had been undermined by the security establishment. In a newspaper article around the time Zardari took over as President, former Foreign Minister Sartaj Aziz publicly lamented the undermining of the foreign office and the shrinking of its space in the formulation of policy in critical areas.

Through the 18th Amendment, Zardari strengthened Parliament and transferred Presidential powers to it. Thus, he was best placed to empower the foreign office and enable it to reclaim some of the space ceded to the security establishment. However, the vigour he demonstrated in strengthening Parliament was lacking in the government's efforts to bolster the foreign office and help it regain its lost space. Had this been done, Zardari might have achieved much more.

A few great opportunities had come his way to revamp the security and intelligence apparatus and curtail their role in foreign policy: the Mumbai attack in November 2008, the U.S.

operation to take out Osama bin Laden in May 2011, and the court verdicts to make legislation for determining the mandate of the intelligence agencies. Failing to seize these opportunities and strengthen the foreign office, there was little chance of success for his bold and imaginative initiatives.

Some policy statements and initiatives launched by Zardari described here provide a peep into his foreign policy. They illustrate the issues he was concerned about and how he envisioned resolving them.

Zardari decided to invite the unfriendly Afghan President Karzai to his swearing-in ceremony. A few months before, on 27 December 2007, Karzai had met Benazir Bhutto and expressed his belief that the mistrust between the two countries under Musharraf would end when Benazir came into power. In the past, Karzai had accused the ISI of backing the militants attacking Afghanistan and attempting to assassinate him.

The optics of inviting Karzai signalled a desire to turn a new page in bilateral relations and was widely applauded. Karzai was absolutely delighted by the gesture and hoped that Pakistan's state agencies' support for the Taliban would soon end.

As the ceremony concluded and the two walked back, I was in tow. Karzai said that the militants could be reined in if President Zardari really wanted. Later, talking with me in Pashto, he wondered if President Zardari would be able to act against the wishes of the powerful and headstrong security establishment.

The gesture of inviting Karzai did not go down well with the proponents of the "strategic depth" policies, which treated Afghanistan as the fifth province of Pakistan. Soon after that, Taliban militants stepped up attacks inside Afghanistan, and tensions increased further.

Chatting informally with some newsmen on the eve of his oath-taking, Zardari also hinted at taking initiatives to improve relations with India. He did not explain how. In one of his off-the-cuff remarks on the eve of Karzai's visit, he expressed optimism about resolving outstanding issues, including

Kashmir, with India. He seemed to exude confidence, and it appeared he was in a hurry, wanting to achieve big results quickly.

Like Benazir, Zardari saw great opportunities in energy pipelines to India from Iran and Central Asia across Pakistan, as well as opening new trade and transit routes. He was even more ambitious than her. He dreamt of opening a new route to Central Asia through the high mountains of Wakhan in Afghanistan. Karzai wondered how this could be made possible before opening the normal trading routes that were often disrupted by militants.

Zardari believed that to fight the militants in Khyber Pakhtunkhwa, the secular Pashtun nationalists like ANP in the province must be empowered against the religious extremists.

With powerful institutions not on board, Zardari's dream to reach Central Asia and Russia through the narrow strip of mountainous Wakhan turned sour. His enthusiasm was great, but he had no control over the non-state actors whose power projection beyond national boundaries undermined all regional peace initiatives.

Chapter 2

Offering "No-First-Use"

A few weeks into assuming office in November 2008, President Zardari called me to his office. He announced his intention to give an interview to prominent Indian journalist and anchor, Karan Thapar, instructing me to coordinate the modalities.

Formal interviews with the foreign media, particularly Indian outlets, by Presidents and Prime Ministers are normally decided with input from the ministries of foreign affairs and information. Benazir Bhutto sought institutional advice but made final decisions on media interviews herself. She was a darling of the media and possessed consummate skills in handling even the most hostile journalists. Later, input from the security establishment also became necessary for foreign media interviews.

Karan had directly approached the President, bypassing the normal channels. Zardari, surprisingly, agreed without seeking advice from anyone. This unusual decision caught many off - guard.

Before the interview, Zardari had not hinted at what he would say to Karan, let alone sought any advice. There was no brainstorming session with relevant institutions on anticipated questions and suitable replies. Karan was not even asked to indicate the parameters of the discussion in advance.

In the satellite interview with the sharp-witted anchor on 22 November, President Zardari made a startling announcement: "Pakistan is ready to talk about 'No-First-Use' of nuclear weapons with India," he declared. The interview instantly made headlines worldwide.

For the first time, a civilian Pakistani leader sought to reboot the peace process between Pakistan and India. No-First-Use (NFU) was offered to an arch-regional rival for the first time. Although not a reversal of deterrence, it was a giant leap forward, sweeping in depth and breadth.

Walking back from the makeup studio, he asked me what I thought of the interview.

"It is very far-reaching and will hit the headlines. But it will backfire if the GHQ was not on board," I said, and asked if what he had announced also had GHQ's approval. He was not amused and asked why I thought the stakeholders were not on board and that it would backfire.

As we were walking, I told him about a significant announcement on a strategic matter made by Army Chief General Aslam Beg in 1990 when Benazir Bhutto was Prime Minister.

I recalled that Soviet Foreign Minister Shevardnadze was due to visit Pakistan in February 1990 to work out a political settlement for post-Soviet Afghanistan. Benazir Bhutto wanted to explore peace proposals and welcomed the visit. The military did not want it.

Just on the eve of Shevardnadze's arrival, General Aslam Beg announced the test firing of short-range missiles. It was messaging that Kabul was within the army's latest missiles' range and indicated that it did not favour peace talks. It was a far-reaching announcement on a strategic issue made by the Army Chief and not by the Prime Minister.

The President listened. "So what do you mean?" he asked.

Continuing, I said that later I travelled with her to Beijing. Sitting with her in the cabin, I asked her whether General Beg had made this announcement with her approval. She laughed and asked for her Special Assistant, General Naseerullah Babar, who was also on the same flight. When General Babar came, she said to him, "Look, General, what your cousin is saying. He asks if I permitted General Beg to make that important announcement." Before General Babar could respond, she said:

"*Inn logon ke mun ko khoon lag giya hai*" (These people have tasted blood), and then added that the generals think they know everything and do not heed civilians and Parliament on strategic issues like peace in Afghanistan. Later in her memoirs, she also stated that the army and intelligence services did not want peace in Afghanistan.

I explained that Army Chiefs had made important strategic announcements without consulting civilian governments. The army's reaction to this far-reaching strategic announcement was highly unlikely to be favourable.

The President was not impressed.

"Trust your leader," he said. "I don't talk off my hat."

I trusted Zardari not to talk "off his hat", but I trusted Benazir Bhutto even more.

Zardari's offer of NFU talks was a bold initiative for ushering in peace without giving up the nuclear option. But all hell broke loose in the media.

Important state functionaries scathingly criticised him on state television, including renowned nuclear engineer Dr Samar Mubarakmand, who was working in the planning commission at the time. A chorus of orchestrated voices dismissed Zardari's offer of NFU as highly irresponsible and unworkable. Such pointed criticism in public by state functionaries could not have been made without a nod from the security establishment. Indeed, it may have been planned and orchestrated.

Within four days of the interview, on 26 November 2008, gunmen launched coordinated attacks for three days in Mumbai, targeting two hotels, a Jewish centre, a tourist restaurant, and a busy train station, killing 166 people. Pakistani investigators found that the attackers were launched from Pakistani soil.

It brought the two countries the closest to war in years and dashed all hopes of peace.

The warmongers shattered Zardari's dream of peace with India by offering talks on No-First-Use.

Chapter 3

I-P gas pipeline and CPEC

Zardari refused to be deterred by setbacks in his pursuit of economic development for Pakistan.

The prospects of cheap Iranian gas for running industries in Pakistan aligned with his vision of geo-economics as the basis of foreign policy. At the end of his Presidency, he laid the foundation of the Iran-Pakistan gas pipeline despite U.S. sanctions against Iran and Washington's stiff opposition to the project. He aimed to build strong relations with Iran and was confident he could overcome resistance to it.

The foreign office, treading a cautious path, was not enthusiastic about the project. Sartaj Aziz, foreign minister during the subsequent PML-N government, later told the Senate Committee on foreign affairs that the decision to lay its foundations was Zardari's.

Zardari also vigorously pursued his favourite project, the currency swap agreement with Iran, despite the reluctance of the State Bank of Pakistan. He saw an opportunity to reduce dependence on the dominant U.S. dollar in currency swaps and barter trade.

Developing strong relations with Iran was challenging, as both the United States and Saudi Arabia were at loggerheads with Iran, but Zardari had decided to proceed nonetheless.

CPEC

China's drive into the future was motivated by geoeconomics rather than geostrategic considerations. Its phenomenal rise owed much to its emphasis on economy, trade, and business. China was rapidly becoming a giant economic and military superpower. Its upward trajectory was not tainted by colonisation, hegemony, or the subjugation of other nations. Zardari's personal fortunes were also founded on successful businesses.

If all roads to human progress led to any single world capital, it was Beijing, not Washington.

Impressed with China's development model, Zardari visited

the country nine times, exploring a different province each time to "learn about the Chinese model of development," as he put it.

Early in 2013, President Xi announced his Belt and Road Initiative (BRI), also known as the New Silk Road. It was an ambitious infrastructure project initially intended to connect East Asia with Europe. The Karakoram Highway (KKH) already connected China with Pakistan by a land route. The BRI envisaged amplifying this connection to the sea through Gwadar in Balochistan.

Zardari's first term was coming to an end in September of that year. He quickly embraced President Xi's vision.

He hung a large world map in the conference room and enthusiastically explained to every visitor how opening up Gwadar would benefit Pakistan, China, and the world. For China, it offered the shortest route to markets in the Middle East, while for Pakistan, the mere transit of oil and goods through it promised an enormous economic bonanza. To the world, it also offered new economic opportunities. Zardari claimed ownership of the China-Pakistan Economic Corridor (CPEC) project, owning it as his brainchild.

However, to implement CPEC, the existing port at Gwadar, built by the Chinese in 2007, needed to be expanded and fully developed. It was central to CPEC and BRI, without which the project could not take off.

A contract for the development and operation of the port had been signed with Singapore five years before CPEC was envisioned. However, Singapore had made no progress, and the contract needed to be taken back and given to China.

Exiting from the contract with Singapore was highly challenging for three reasons:

1. It posed a diplomatic challenge complicated by the sanctity attached to international commercial deals. The Chinese had stated that they would not ask Singapore to relinquish the port; Pakistan had to handle this delicate task.
2. Various issues relating to the Gwadar Port were mired

in legal battles, with numerous court stay orders halting work. Relations between Zardari and Chief Justice Iftikhar Chaudhry's court were tense. The Chinese did not want to become entangled in litigation they had not caused in another country.

3. The port expansion required land. Nearly 600 acres were in the possession of the Navy, which refused to vacate them. Defence forces often cite "national security" reasons to protect real estate and commercial interests. The Navy initially cited national security reasons to hold on to the land.

During one of his visits to China, Premier Wen Jiabao expressed concern about these issues impeding CPEC's progress. The President reassuringly said, "I will do it in my own way." He urged the Chinese premier to give him some time.

Zardari's tenure was ending, and he was in a hurry. The Chinese also wanted an early clearing of the obstacles. There would be no CPEC without a functional Gwadar Port capable of handling millions of tons of cargo annually. Singapore had done nothing in five years to make it functional or expand it. There would be no jewel in Zardari's crown without CPEC.

He set out to address these issues. Getting the land vacated by the Navy was not very difficult. Although a civilian President may have no real powers over defence services, the Constitution conferred the title of "Supreme Commander of the Armed Forces" on him. Even a mere title can be a lever of power. The Navy was persuaded to vacate the land.

However, persuading Singapore to give up the port operations without damages and without fuss, and getting the stay orders vacated by Chief Justice Iftikhar Chaudhry (whose reinstatement Zardari had stoutly resisted) posed formidable challenges.

Zardari relied on two competent and reputable senior bureaucrats for this task:

He asked his secretary general, Salman Faruqui, renowned as a skilful negotiator and go-getter, to negotiate with the Singapore authorities. He tasked Foreign Secretary Jalil Abbas

Jilani with speaking to Chief Justice Iftikhar Chaudhry to get the stay orders vacated. As foreign secretary, Jilani was well aware of China's concerns and the impact on Pak-China relations. He was also a nephew of former Chief Justice Tassaduq Jillani. Zardari, adept at using different approaches to get things done, thought that Jillani's understanding of the issue, credibility, and indirect connection with the judiciary would be helpful. Jillani, a non-political patriot, readily agreed.

Singapore relinquished the port without fuss. The Chaudhry court vacated the stay orders.

How the two bureaucrats accomplished their assigned tasks is a different story. It was a triumph of patriotism, dedication, and commitment by all those involved.

When Faruqui informed the President about their success, Zardari rose from his seat as a mark of respect and admiration. He then picked up the phone and called Premier Wen Jiabao. One can imagine that he might have said, "Didn't I tell you that I would do it in my own way?"

A few months later, when his term ended and a military guard of honour saw him off from the Presidency, the jewel of CPEC was studded in the crown he wore.

Chapter 4

The proxy war in Yemen

After ceasing to be the President, Zardari, as the head of the Pakistan People's Party, discussed and brainstormed important foreign policy issues with Party leaders in his own peculiar way and style of consultations.

In early 2015, violent fighting broke out between the Iran-backed Houthi rebels in Yemen and Saudi Arabia. Saudi Arabia claimed it was fighting Al Qaeda hiding in Yemen. A few days later, it also announced that it was fighting the war with the support of ten coalition partners. The national flags of the countries that it claimed were included in the coalition "fighting Al Qaeda in Yemen" fluttered at the Saudi news conference making this announcement. It also included Pakistan's national flag.

The disclosure by Saudi Arabia that the Pakistani army was fighting Al Qaeda in Yemen was far-reaching. It shocked many.

The war in Yemen was actually a proxy war between Iran and Saudi Arabia. The revelation that Pakistan was also involved perplexed many. It was too serious a foreign and security policy issue. Friendly Saudi Arabia felt threatened by another friend and neighbour, Iran. Pakistan was still reeling from the war in Afghanistan. That it had been drawn into a proxy war in the Middle East without debate in the Parliament raised serious concerns among thoughtful people.

Zardari was in Karachi. Though no longer the President, he decided to call a meeting of Party leaders within a few days to discuss it.

Curiously, even before the Party meeting, former interior minister Senator Rehman Malik read a statement to the media in Islamabad declaring "all-out support of PPP to Saudi Arabia in the war." Reading from a prepared text, he claimed that it was a "policy statement of PPP Co-Chairman Asif Ali Zardari."

It came like a bombshell. A spokesman for Bilawal House denied any knowledge of the "policy statement". Questioned by the media, I also said that policy statements are issued by the media office and that it had not been issued by our office.

As soon as the denial was broadcast, Zardari called me from Karachi.

"Farhatullah, why did you deny without consulting me?" he asked.

"Sir, I really did not know. It was too far-reaching. The media office had no knowledge of it. I only said that I was not aware," I replied.

"The statement by Rehman Malik is the official party line," he said. He also asked me to come to Karachi for a meeting with leaders of other opposition parties whom he had already invited for the next day. The exclusive PPP meeting had not yet been called.

The few political leaders who met him opposed committing Pakistani troops to fight in Yemen. "We have already burnt our fingers in Afghanistan," Asfandyar Wali, President of ANP, said and asked, "Is that not enough to draw a lesson from?" Zardari quipped that Asfandyar had been briefed by me. The ANP leader retorted that he did not have to be briefed by anyone. It was clear as daylight to him that Pakistan should not send troops for a proxy war in the Middle East, he said.

All the opposition leaders proposed that a joint session of Parliament be convened to discuss the issue and that in no case should troops be sent to Yemen without Parliament debating it.

A few days later, he proposed calling a meeting of the Party's Central Executive Committee (CEC) in Karachi.

Zardari set the tone of the Party meeting by declaring, "We need to help Saudis at this critical hour," and invited the PPP leaders to express their views. The few who spoke on the occasion opposed sending troops to Yemen.

Zardari then signalled Rehman Malik to speak.

"Mr President, should I disclose all the facts?" Malik asked.

Without waiting for an answer, he announced, "But I will not speak out about everything."

Malik claimed to possess "some facts" on the basis of which he was convinced that Saudi Arabia should be unconditionally supported and troops sent to Yemen. "Unfortunately, my friends do not know all the facts," he said without disclosing what they were.

Turning towards Zardari, he said, "Sir, you had the vision to foresee the trouble coming." Naming a friendly Muslim country, he said it was secretly luring our people for war in Syria, he said almost authoritatively.

Pleading that Pakistan should send troops to Yemen, he also proposed that Zardari undertake a visit to the Gulf countries and meet their leaders to defuse the situation.

Malik's proposal was met with initial silence from the other CEC members. Someone pointed out that Zardari might have close relations with some Gulf leaders, but as a private citizen, it would not be easy to meet them.

Zardari agreed. "I am no longer head of the state, and arranging my meetings will take a long time," he said. He proposed that a Party delegation be first dispatched to the Gulf countries to prepare the ground for his meetings with their leaders.

"Who will lead the Party delegation?" someone asked.

"Let Rehman Malik and a few others go first," Zardari said.

"Power in Iran rests with the Rehbar and in Saudi Arabia with the royal family," he explained.

"Foreign Minister Zaeef will not be able to do anything even if I met him."

He then explained why he was keen to support the Saudis in the crisis.

"Non-state actors gaining strength in Yemen or anywhere else in the world will empower the non-state actors in Pakistan," he said. A military conquest by the rebels in Yemen would, therefore, threaten Pakistan's peace and stability. He had rejected calls for the inquiry and accountability of the army and intelligence leadership in the wake of the raid on the OBL (Osama bin Laden) compound, saying that it would strengthen the militants. Today, he was making similar arguments.

He then said, "Okay, I will accept the responsibility and talk to the leadership of the Kingdom of Saudi Arabia, Syria, Iran, Iraq, and Yemen, but first let Rehman Malik prepare the ground for my visit."

He then discussed the implications of the Middle East

situation for Pakistan. He disclosed that he had told President Obama that destabilising Hafez Al Assad's government in Syria would have serious consequences. Turkish and Qatari leaders once told him that he was "on the wrong side of history," to which he responded, "Only time will tell who is on the wrong side of history," Zardari told the meeting.

"I was right on how to handle the Syrian situation. Now you see a huge human tragedy is in the making in Syria," he said.

He said, "I first went to Iran's Khamenei, then to Saudi Arabia and Bahrain. But the dialogue process was sabotaged, and I knew that a disaster was in the making." Due to the worries on his mind and the pressure on him, he had fallen sick at the time, he said, while making a case to support Saudi Arabia in the fighting in Yemen.

Zardari's logic for supporting the Saudis was not framed in the usual jargon of "duty as Muslims" or "protecting the Haramain Sharifain" (the Holy Mosques in Makkah and Madinah) or protecting a friend in need. His logic rested on the premise that the triumph of rebels and militants anywhere was a triumph of militants in Pakistan as well.

Chapter 5

Mediating between Iran and Saudi Arabia

Little is known publicly about President Zardari's efforts to play a mediatory role and seek a rapprochement between Iran and the Kingdom of Saudi Arabia.

In January 2011, the Iranian President's special envoy invited Zardari to a conference on the global war against terror in Tehran. Despite advisors suggesting Pakistan participate at a lower level, Zardari readily accepted and decided to attend personally.

During his visit to Tehran in June 2011 for the conference, Zardari met with Rahbar Ayatollah Khamenei. After initial pleasantries, Zardari asked his delegation members to leave him alone with Iran's supreme leader.

The contents of their discussion remained undisclosed. A press release from the Rahbar's office merely reiterated the usual diplomatic language about "historical, cultural and religious bonds" and the need to "strengthen Tehran-Islamabad relations in all areas."

Unusually, Zardari revisited Tehran the following month, meeting the Rahbar one-on-one for a second time in less than 30 days.

I gained more insight into the June meeting with the Rahbar when Iran's foreign minister, Ali Akbar Salehi, visited Pakistan and met with the President at Bilawal House in Karachi that September. I was present throughout the meeting.

Salehi first summarised his visit's achievements, mentioning signed agreements and reiterating the need to earnestly pursue the Iran-Pakistan gas pipeline project.

He then broached the subject of Iran-Saudi relations, saying, "Mr President, I wish to convey my President's deep appreciation for your efforts." Speaking in hushed tones and glancing over his shoulder, Salehi appeared uncomfortable with my presence. As I rose to leave, Zardari gestured for me to remain seated.

Zardari's face brightened as Salehi disclosed, "Necessary elements are falling into the right place, and it is proceeding in the right direction." The cryptic nature of these "necessary elements" and the direction of progress intrigued me.

After a pause, Salehi continued, "As we started on your advice and took the first step, a storm erupted in Parliament. They even called for my impeachment."

Zardari interjected, "No, I did not give any advice. I only made a request." This exchange further piqued my curiosity.

Salehi elaborated on his response to the Iranian Parliament: "I asked them, what did they expect from me? As foreign minister, is it not my responsibility to talk with everyone, even our enemies? Indeed, it is my job to pursue peace. So why criticise me? Why condemn me merely for seeking to open a window?"

He explained that he had reasoned with Parliament that seeking peace was Iran's own desire and initiative, not driven by external forces.

Salehi then revealed that the Iranian Ambassador in Riyadh had received a message from the Saudi government stating, "We expect some progress next month," though he didn't elaborate further. Zardari didn't press for details but instead smiled and called for refreshments.

President Zardari informed Salehi that during his recent trip to Urumqi, he had already briefed the Chinese vice premier about these developments. He explained that this was to enable Chinese leaders to play a role if needed.

Salehi listened intently, eager to learn about the Chinese reaction. Zardari noted, "The Chinese vice premier did not respond to my comments," adding that the premier may have avoided commenting without President Xi's approval.

Pleased that Iran had accepted his mediatory role, Zardari continued, "When I met the Rahbar, I told him that I would sit in his office and not leave until he agreed. We have no choice but to seek peace and pursue rapprochement. We are all in serious turmoil. Pakistan cannot afford a war between Iran and Saudi Arabia."

His thoughts seemed to flow rapidly as he jumped from one subject to another.

"Economies are falling apart. I fear this will result in wars. I've seen how small mistakes and miscalculations can be disastrous. I witnessed Shevardnadze (then Soviet foreign minister, later President of Georgia) visiting Pakistan. He wanted to discuss Afghan President Najibullah's offer for a peaceful power transfer. Najibullah was willing to seek a political solution, and the Soviet Union supported this. It was a great opportunity. But our people insisted on a military victory. Egos came into play. They wanted to tell our people that we could win wars. Some were obsessed with a military victory. We all know what happened then. We were misled when they told my wife, 'Madam Prime Minister, Jalalabad will fall within a week.'"

Zardari also recalled U.S. Ambassador Oakley once telling him that the U.S. was unaware Najibullah possessed MiGs and other sophisticated weapons. "Oh, a serious lapse on the part of our intelligence," Oakley had admitted.

"The Americans do not have a plan A, let alone plans B or C," Zardari remarked.

As he continued speaking, Salehi listened without interruption.

Past midnight, the President requested the draft press release of the meeting. He reviewed it, deleting references to currency swap and banking cooperation agreements with Iran and diluting mentions of the Iran-Pakistan gas pipeline project.

While Zardari may have thought the Americans incapable of executing even plan A, he was careful not to offend the U.S. by publicly acknowledging the growing Pakistan-Iran cooperation.

Iran's Bank Melli had been on the United Nations watch list since 2008 for its alleged involvement with Iranian nuclear and missile programmes. The UN had also imposed sanctions on states opening Iranian bank branches in their countries.

The President removed references to banking cooperation.

However, the next day's newspapers quoted a statement from the Prime Minister's office, which was front-paged with reports that "despite UN restrictions on the Iranian banking sector," Pakistan had signed a banking cooperation agreement with Iran. Zardari was displeased.

Thus, in 2011, Zardari mounted a serious bid to seek Iran-

Saudi rapprochement. He was prepared to sit in the Rahbar's office until the supreme leader agreed. Zardari also informed Chinese leaders about his efforts.

Some speculated that Zardari might have undertaken this initiative at the behest of Chinese leaders, but there was no evidence to support this claim.

It remains debatable whether the Chinese encouraged Zardari to undertake this mission in 2011 or were inspired to broker peace between the two nations after Zardari informed them about his secret mediation efforts.

A decade later, in April 2023, the world was stunned to learn that Saudi Foreign Minister Prince Faisal bin Farhan Al Saud met his Iranian counterpart, Hossein Amir-Abdollahian, in Beijing for the first time in seven years. They agreed to reopen embassies and consulates.

The peace process between Iran and Saudi Arabia was on track. Zardari did not have to sit in front of the Rahbar after all.

Chapter 6

Meeting Suu Kyi

Myanmar's iconic leader, Aung San Suu Kyi, rose to prominence during what is known as the 8888 uprising. On 8 August 1988, she became the General Secretary of the National League for Democracy (NLD), the party she had formed to bring democracy to the country.

In the 1990 elections, her party won over 80% of the parliamentary seats but was robbed of victory as the military junta refused to hand over power. She was subsequently detained and, till 2010, had remained in detention for 15 years. She had also survived an assassination attempt in 2003.

Time magazine named her one of the "Children of Gandhi". In 1991, she was awarded the Nobel Peace Prize. Benazir Bhutto admired her.

Some dates and events in Suu Kyi's political journey evoked memories of events in Benazir Bhutto's life. Military dictator General Zia ul-Haq perished in an air crash in August 1988. It was in August 1990 that Bhutto's first government was sacked. Benazir Bhutto had also survived an assassination attempt in October 2007.

Like his wife, Asif Ali Zardari also admired Aung San Suu Kyi and had been exchanging messages with her through intermediaries.

In his first address to the UN General Assembly in 2008, President Zardari demanded the release of Aung San Suu Kyi from house arrest: "Today, as we meet here in New York, the democratically elected leader of Myanmar, Aung San Suu Kyi, continues to be imprisoned in Yangon. She has suffered year after year under house arrest. The world should demand that this great woman finally be freed."

In a public address in Garhi Khuda Bakhsh on Benazir Bhutto's martyrdom anniversary, he did not forget to pay tribute to Suu Kyi.

He also announced plans to confer the Mohtarma Benazir Bhutto Shaheed Award for Democracy upon Suu Kyi and wanted to present it in person. He requested that a bilateral visit to Myanmar be arranged.

They initially refused when the Myanmar government

learned he also wanted to visit Suu Kyi. Earlier, they had not allowed the Thai Prime Minister to meet Suu Kyi during a bilateral visit and had asked her to return to her country and then come again on a private visit for the purpose. The Myanmar government wanted President Zardari to follow the same procedure.

However, they later relented and allowed President Zardari to call on Suu Kyi without having to interrupt his bilateral visit.

The President arrived in the capital, Nay Pyi Daw, on 24 January 2012 and returned the next day. He held bilateral meetings with the rulers in the capital, travelled to Yangon to meet Aung San Suu Kyi, and visited the mausoleum of the last Mughal King Bahadur Shah Zafar, also in Yangon.

No minister accompanied him. Only his son Bilawal and daughter Aseefa were with him. Dr Asad Majeed, the head of the foreign office desk in the Presidency, and the President's personal staff also accompanied him. A distinguished diplomat, Dr Asad Majeed later became Pakistan's Ambassador to the U.S. and was at the centre of what is known as the "cypher controversy". The small delegation travelled by a special aircraft.

From Nay Pyi Daw, Asad Majeed and I went to Yangon ahead of the President to discuss the modalities of the ceremony at Suu Kyi's residence and his visit to the mausoleum of Bahadur Shah Zafar.

Daw Suu lived in a spacious yet unpretentious house. In Myanmar, Aung San Suu Kyi is reverently called Daw Aung San Suu Kyi. "Daw", meaning "aunt", is not part of her name but an honorific akin to "Madam" or "Mohtarma". Her personal staff officer showed us around the sitting room where the two were to meet and the lawn where the award ceremony was planned to be held.

The meeting room was small and contained a few chairs and a medium-sized round table. The furniture and fixtures seemed to have been in place for a long time and were not brought in hurriedly from outside for the meeting.

The ceremony details were worked out to the minutest

detail: the entry point of cars, the location where Daw Suu would receive the President, the photo opportunity, walking up to the meeting room, the note-takers, the citation reading, and the like. There would be no interaction with the media, keeping in view the sensitivities of the Myanmar junta.

As they arrived at midday, Daw Suu was waiting in the car porch to receive the President who was accompanied by Bilawal and Aseefa. Attired in a simple dress and beaming, she looked like nobility personified. The main entrance to the house opened onto the car porch. After the handshake and family photo, she led the guests to the meeting room.

President Zardari and Daw Suu were seated at the main table, Zardari on her right and Bilawal and Aseefa on her left. Ambassador Qazi Habibullah and the President's personal staff were also in attendance. A young man and a woman seated behind Daw Suu were taking notes.

Chapter 7

Zardari's conversation with Daw Suu Kyi

President Zardari presented Daw Suu Kyi with a painting of her late husband, Michael Aris, a British historian who had passed away during her incarceration. She had not been allowed to attend his funeral. Suu Kyi admired the artwork, and Zardari remarked that he was unsure if the painting faithfully reproduced the image of Michael Aris. He mentioned that he was looking for a statue of Buddha to present to her.

Continuing, Zardari said he was keen to meet her and pay respects for her struggle for democracy. He said that democracy-loving people were inspired by her leadership and sacrifice. He said she brought to mind the struggle of his wife, Shaheed Mohtarma Benazir Bhutto. He congratulated her on her peaceful and successful political struggle and for following the path of reconciliation, saying that his late wife also chose that path.

Reciprocating, Suu Kyi thanked the President for his generous remarks. She did not dwell on her democratic struggle or her personal misfortunes but simply remarked, "Destiny has strange ways." She spoke about the need for peace and reconciliation in general. About her country, she said that Myanmar's democracy was very fragile and needed the healing touch of reconciliation.

"But it's not so easy," she confessed. "It is very, very hard." She explained this by saying that it was not easy to satisfy those who had been wronged and sought revenge. They want the injustices done to them and the wounds inflicted on them to be at least acknowledged. "I have found that the perpetrators did not want to even acknowledge that they had wronged some people," she said. Suu Kyi found this "the most difficult part in working out reconciliation."

Zardari responded that he, too, believed in reconciliation. "I have redefined revenge," he said.

Suu Kyi replied, "Yes, it was your wife who first said democracy is the best revenge." She also admired Benazir Bhutto for her struggle.

Suu Kyi's admiration for Benazir made Zardari reminisce

about his wife emotionally.

"I owned a cinema. She (Benazir Bhutto) had come to see a movie. I liked her. Later, I witnessed her political struggle. I was impressed. No one thought what she would become in the future. I did not know she would become the Prime Minister one day. It was a marriage by choice. I loved her."

He then reminisced: "I used to play polo. I was playing polo when I learnt about the vote of no-confidence against her. I immediately rushed to her rescue. I became her force multiplier." Continuing, he said, "I have a conversation with my wife every day. I live in that environment. I don't know whether you also have some similar experience."

Suu Kyi seemed surprised that Zardari had daily conversations with his wife. She did not have that kind of relationship with her husband and made no secret of it.

She said that her relationship with her husband was very different and not comparable to the relationship Zardari had with his wife.

"No, no. In my case, it was totally different," she said rather candidly.

"You were committed to your wife and her struggle. In my case, my husband just allowed me to do what I wanted to do. He was not political. My husband's involvement was different. He was totally uninvolved." Suu Kyi was surprised but did not ask how Zardari was still communicating with his late wife.

Reverting to reconciliation, she said, "I wish all these generals long life so that they see for themselves how well democracy works."

Appreciating her remarks, Zardari said, "I have gone a bit further. I retained all the former employees who worked for Musharraf in the Presidency. Not one has been removed from his position. I have not taken it in a personal sense." He said that some in his own Party did not like it.

Suu Kyi admired Zardari for not avenging the harm done to him by his detractors.

They also talked about the media and democracy. She said that the media had maligned her, but this was nothing compared to the media trial Zardari endured.

Responding, Zardari said: "They gave me a bad name. I was accused of murdering my own brother-in-law, of murders, of drug peddling and whatnot."

"It was really hard," he said. "To be tried for political offences is one thing, but to be tried for killings, drugs, and criminal charges is very hard. The whole family was maligned, and it made things very, very difficult for us. The media should not dictate a political agenda," the President said. "It is the right of the people and not of the media barons to make and unmake governments in a democracy."

Endorsing the remarks about people's right to make governments, she said, "We can also learn from your experience."

Zardari said that he refused to be provoked by the media and had adopted a different approach. "I have simply ignored them. I have not cared. They just do not like me. One has to be thick-skinned."

"But not too thick-skinned," Suu Kyi said.

Suu Kyi once again talked about reconciliation, describing how far she had gone to pursue it. The extent to which she went to reconcile with the generals seemed to baffle Zardari as well. When she said, "I am not too worried about the seats reserved for generals in the elections," Zardari looked at me.

"I am worried about the things they have inserted in the Constitution," she said.

"Our major problem is that the Constitution provides that the military has a right to intervene," adding, "It is worse than the 25% reserved seats for them in Parliament."

That she saw no harm in uniformed generals in the elected Parliament was most surprising. She then spoke of "winning over" instead of resisting the generals.

"We have to win over the military; we have to win over the cooperation of the army. We have to convince them that it is not good for the country and the army itself."

"We are quite pragmatic and prepared for it."

In allowing serving generals to sit in Parliament, she saw

reconciliation and pragmatism. This was a far cry from the image of Suu Kyi that had stuck in people's minds about her iconic struggle for democracy. Her "pragmatism" indeed went too far when, later, she defended the military on international platforms against allegations of genocide and massive rights violations. She bent over backwards to appease the generals who struck again and again. Her silence on unspeakable atrocities against Rohingyas in her country disappointed many. There were calls for the Nobel Peace Prize awarded to her to be withdrawn. She had pushed reconciliation to the farthest limits even as democracy remained elusive.

She won a landslide victory in 2015 but was not allowed to become President. An arbitrary legislation had rendered ineligible those with foreign national children to hold that office.

Elections were last held in Myanmar in November 2020, but the civilian set-up was toppled a few months later, plunging the country into deep turmoil from which it is still reeling. She was jailed for inciting dissent and breaking Covid rules.

Pakistani politicians have admired Suu Kyi. Few, valuing reconciliation, have tried to pursue it vigorously. Fewer still, like Zardari, have met her. But the lessons from Suu Kyi's experience have escaped them all: that appeasement and bending over backwards in pursuit of reconciliation do not bring democracy any closer; they may make it recede even farther away.

Before the meeting ended, Zardari said to her, "I got your message through some friend." He did not say who the messenger was or what message he had got from her.

He said, "Nominate anyone you may want to be in touch with me." He continued, "We will help you in whatever way we can." He quickly added, "We live with the fact that people will come to know of it soon."

Suu Kyi smiled and said, "We should expect that our conversation today will hit headlines tomorrow. We have to live with it."

When the meeting, which lasted over an hour, ended, they

moved towards the lawn, where Zardari conferred on her "The Benazir Bhutto Shaheed Medal for Democracy."

The citation read out on the occasion said in part:

"The life and work of Ms Aung San Suu Kyi is a source of inspiration for the people of Pakistan. Like Shaheed Mohtarma Benazir Bhutto, she is held in the highest esteem and respect as one who ardently espoused and struggled for democracy and human rights fearlessly and, by non-violent means, stood for and worked for the transformation that touches each heart and soul."

Section Three

IMPEACHING MUSHARRAF

Chapter 1

Showing the door to Musharraf

Musharraf took oath as a civilian President on 29 November 2007, and, as a result of elections early in 2008, a PPP-led coalition government was formed in Islamabad. Zardari was the Party's head, but his eyes were set on the Presidency. He, however, kept his cards close to his chest and did not let anyone know.

An early indication of his intent came to light when PPP's cabinet ministers were to take the oath from President Musharraf. Until recently, the PPP had denounced him as a fascist and a dictator, and they detested taking the oath from him.

"Sir, I will clean a gutter if you order, but don't ask me to take oath from this gutter," the late Chaudhry Ahmad Mukhtar said to Zardari. "I cannot bear it," he added.

"Do as I tell you. You don't know what I will do," Zardari replied. "I will not disappoint you," he reassured Mukhtar.

"Sir, what can you do after I have taken oath from him?" Chaudhry Mukhtar asked.

"Don't ask me what I will do," Zardari responded.

Zardari often told frustrated Party leaders, "Do as I say. I will not disappoint you."

The secret Memorandum of Understanding between Benazir Bhutto and Musharraf envisaged that the PPP would accept him as a civilian President in return for Musharraf shedding his army uniform. Musharraf had shed his uniform and been elected by the assemblies as well. The PPP had agreed to work with him as a civilian President.

The agreement was not merely between Musharraf and Benazir Bhutto. The U.S. had played a role in nudging the two to reach an agreement. In her memoirs, Secretary of State Condoleeza Rice recalled her active engagement in reaching an agreement on transition modalities. Brokered by the U.S., it had broader implications as well. Those who had brokered the deal also had to be taken on board.

Zardari was aware of this.

Although Zardari held no official position, U.S. Ambassador Ann Patterson in Islamabad and senior diplomats, including

Assistant Secretary of State Richard Boucher and other U.S. dignitaries visiting Pakistan in those days, met with him. I was not present in those meetings, but I learned about them from his remarks during Party meetings.

A few days after meeting a U.S. official, he told the Party's core committee without elaborating,

"*Mai dunya walon se negotiate kar raha hoon, laikin sab kuch nahi bata sakta*" (I am negotiating with the world but cannot tell you everything), and repeated his refrain, "Trust me."

Apart from the U.S., the army also had to be taken on board.

Years later, Zardari disclosed that to gauge reaction, he had asked Kayani what he thought about Musharraf being replaced. Kayani didn't object but suggested the name of Aftab Shaban Mirani as the next President, he said. Kayani, having no objection to replacing Musharraf, was reassuring. As to who should succeed Musharraf, Zardari told Kayani, "The Party will decide it."

Zardari was confident.

After concluding that the powerful military would not oppose it and taking the U.S. on board, he had firmed up plans to send Musharraf home peacefully by July 2008.

Moving step by step, Zardari then asked trusted members of the Provincial Assemblies to move resolutions demanding that Musharraf be impeached for corruption and other charges.

As the Provincial Assemblies passed the resolutions, it was leaked to the media that the government had decided to impeach Musharraf. Curiosity was aroused when the government did not contradict these reports.

A few days later, the government formally announced that it had decided to impeach the President.

Zardari formed a committee to prepare the impeachment charge sheet and asked it to meet daily. Media reports of its daily meetings and the orchestrated resolutions in Provincial Assemblies created hype, building pressure.

The heat was turned on Musharraf to resign or face impeachment. Shrieking newspaper headlines and blaring news and commentaries on television channels dramatised the battle of nerves between a commando and a wily politician.

When the situation reached a crescendo, Zardari decided to send a discreet message to Musharraf through the National Security Advisor, Major General (Retd) Mahmud Ali Durrani, to either resign or face impeachment.

Durrani had previously served as ambassador to the U.S. and was well known in the State Department and Pentagon. He also knew Musharraf very well.

Durrani conveyed a "polite message" to Musharraf that he had played a long innings and needed rest, offering him a "safe and honourable exit" in return.

Musharraf couldn't believe it. He scoffed at the idea. Durrani returned to Zardari House disappointed.

Overconfident, Musharraf had misjudged the situation and overestimated his possibilities.

Musharraf was mistaken if he thought the army would protect him against impeachment. General Kayani had not objected to sending him home. The army's corporate interests are not best served by a former chief, even as a civilian President. Musharraf was now an ex-Army Chief.

He was no less mistaken if he thought Washington would rescue him from a crafty politician because it had underwritten the "Memorandum of Understanding" with his wife or that he was a friend of President Bush.

The U.S. may have endorsed the agreement on power transfer with Benazir Bhutto, and President Bush may have called him "my friend" and "a courageous leader and a friend of the U.S.," but in taking it too seriously, Musharraf had blundered. He forgot how the Afghan Mujahideen commanders were first welcomed to the White House as "moral equivalents of George Washington" and later chased to death because "A good Talib is a dead Talib."

The dice were loaded against Musharraf as Zardari sharpened the knife.

Chapter 2

Musharraf blinked first

Zardari constituted a committee of senior politicians belonging to PML-N and PPP to prepare a comprehensive charge sheet. The Provincial Assemblies passed unanimous resolutions calling for impeachment, one by one. Musharraf declined to resign.

The committee included Ishaq Dar and Ahsan Iqbal from the PML-N and Raza Rabbani, Farooq Naek, Sherry Rehman, and me from the PPP. Sherry Rehman was the perfect host for the meetings held at her residence in Islamabad.

Different members were assigned the task of collecting documentary evidence against Musharraf. Several meetings, extending well past midnight, were held. Charges against Musharraf were discussed threadbare, and a rigorous selection of documentary evidence was made.

Impeaching a President is a numbers game in the Assemblies, but a credible charge sheet was essential as a force multiplier and to avoid accusations of malafide intent.

The Constitution permitted Musharraf to address Parliament in his defence against the impeachment motion. The charges against him had to stand scrutiny. If, during his address to Parliament, Musharraf was able to prove even a single charge wrong, he would be vindicated in the eyes of the public.

Therefore, nothing could be part of the charge sheet without scrutiny and verification. Collecting a trove of documents was easy, but their meticulous verification was not and took time.

Acting as the devil's advocate, a no-nonsense Farooq Naek would question every document until he was satisfied. He knew the perils of political statements placed as evidence in a court of law. He insisted that each document submitted as evidence against Musharraf be verified.

Several drafts were prepared and discarded before the final version was completed on Independence Day, 14 August.

Zardari did not interfere in the committee's work at any stage. He didn't ask even once that the drafts be shown to him as work on it progressed. Did he trust the committee completely? Or was he confident that Musharraf would soon blink first, and there would be no need actually to table the impeachment resolution in Parliament? Some such questions readily came to mind at the time.

However, Zardari was concerned about preparing the impeachment charge sheet in complete secrecy. Time and again, he stressed that it must not fall into the hands of the media. Perhaps Zardari visualised the impeachment charge sheet as a weapon of last resort, to be used only if Musharraf did not resign and, therefore, did not want it made public. No one, therefore, kept a copy of the final draft.

After the documents were collected and verified, Farooq Naek drafted the charge sheet strictly in legal parlance. Musharraf was doomed to be impeached, and only a miracle could save him. The thought that a military dictator would soon be impeached by an elected Parliament lifted our spirits. We liked to believe it would be the first of its kind in Pakistan.

Zardari, who had not asked to see the draft even once, only wanted to be informed when it had been finalised.

When informed on Independence Day that the charge sheet titled "Gross Misconduct" was ready, he asked that a formal announcement be made that it would be tabled in the National Assembly within a week. He still did not ask to see it. A flurry of activities in the National Assembly dramatised the setting into motion of the impeachment ball.

Within four days, Musharraf addressed the nation on 18 August: "After reviewing the situation and consulting legal advisors and political allies, with their advice, I have decided to resign."

"My resignation will go to the Speaker, National Assembly, today," Musharraf said, blinking first, while raising his clenched fists to chest height in a gesture of defiance.

Musharraf had blinked first. He had been chased out. Zardari did not ask to see the charge sheet. He never even looked at it. The nation finally saw the back of a military dictator.

Chapter 3

Confronting Musharraf

Musharraf had abrogated the Constitution twice and, under Article 6, was liable to be tried for high treason. There were indeed muted and not-so-muted voices calling for his trial on these grounds.

Before becoming President, during a meeting with Nawaz Sharif in the latter's expansive residence in Raiwind near Lahore, Zardari politely declined Sharif's suggestion to try Musharraf for treason.

If Zardari had considered other means to remove Musharraf, he did not share them with Nawaz Sharif then. He was ready for confrontation with Musharraf but did not want to confront the military. He knew well the difference between the two.

In democracies, high public office holders, such as Presidents and superior court judges, have occasionally been held accountable and removed from office through democratic processes known as impeachment.

At the back of his mind, Zardari entertained thoughts of impeaching Musharraf but never disclosed it to anyone.

Impeachment is a formal democratic and Constitutional process by which a sitting President accused of gross misconduct is removed through a parliamentary vote. The procedures involved may vary across countries, but they share a common structure involving charges, investigation, and trial. The specific grounds for impeachment also differ from country to country, but some common reasons include subversion of the Constitution, gross misconduct, and criminal acts.

In the U.S., for instance, impeachment is enshrined in the Constitution. The House of Representatives initiates the impeachment process by bringing formal charges and investigating them. A simple majority vote is required to impeach. The Senate then holds a trial, presided over by the Chief Justice of the Supreme Court. A two-thirds majority vote is required for removal from office.

The U.S. has impeached several Presidents. Donald Trump was impeached twice, but none was removed by the Senate.

In India, the President's removal requires a resolution from either house of Parliament. If a two-thirds majority in both houses passes the resolution, the President is removed.

In Pakistan, Article 6 of the Constitution of 1973 provides for a criminal trial for treason. In 2010, through the 18th Amendment, a new clause was added, barring the Supreme Court from validating any act of high treason.

Zardari, however, contemplated invoking Article 47 "Removal (or impeachment) of President" instead of Article 6 calling for a trial for high treason. Under it, the President may be impeached on a charge of violating the Constitution or gross misconduct.

A written notice signed by at least half the total members is required to be sent to the Speaker of the National Assembly or the Senate Chairman to move a resolution, citing also grounds for impeaching the President. A copy of the notice is then transmitted to the President, giving him at least seven days before a joint sitting of Parliament is summoned to investigate the matter. The President has the right to appear and be represented before the joint sitting. If, after investigations, the resolution is passed by a two-thirds majority of the joint session, the President shall cease to hold office.

Zardari quietly chose this route to remove Musharraf from office. The first step involved drafting a notice to move a resolution along with grounds for the impeachment of Musharraf.

Notice of impeachment

A committee had already been formed, and Zardari asked it to prepare the notice and the grounds for the resolution. It was a delicate task. It was critical that the grounds not only be credible but also appear so to the public. Advocate Farooq Naek was very conscious of this requirement.

The committee members set out to collect credible material, including office orders, press reports, and records of the proceedings in Parliament and the court that prima facie made strong grounds for impeachment. The committee worked overtime.

About twenty grounds were prepared. However, before the notice and the charges contained in it were sent to the National Assembly Speaker, Musharraf blinked first and resigned. Perhaps Zardari was confident that Musharraf would blink first, and that was why he did not bother to see the draft notice.

Musharraf could well have defended himself in Parliament, but he missed the opportunity and called it quits without giving a fight. He could possibly have made a forceful speech in his defence in Parliament and challenged the notice as malafide. But he did not. This is how tin-pot dictators and Bonaparte generals turn out to be in the end. Musharraf was no exception.

The grounds for impeachment stated in the notice included two most serious ones:

One, Musharraf first dismissed an elected government, subverted the Constitution on 12 October 1999, and again suspended the Constitution on 3 November 2007. It was undeniable. There was overwhelming evidence, and all records were attached to the notice.

Two, and no less serious, pertained to the proliferation of nuclear weapons under Musharraf, exposing Pakistan to serious harm. It had come to the surface only when, during a meeting with U.S. President George Bush in September 2003, he was taken aside by the U.S. President and told to meet the CIA director for an "extremely serious" matter.

According to Musharraf's own account in his memoirs *In the Line of Fire*, published in 2006, the CIA director showed him documentary evidence of proliferation, including blueprints, part numbers, dates, and signatures exported out of Pakistan. It was so overwhelming that Musharraf, by his own admission, was "flabbergasted". He also described his meeting with the CIA chief as "one of my most embarrassing moments". He claimed that, until then, he was unaware of the existence of the proliferation network.

In July 2000, well after Musharraf had taken over as the National Command Authority Chairman, the government published a full-page advertisement in *The News* inviting applications from vendors for the export of bomb-making material, including enriched uranium, plutonium, heavy water, nuclear power reactor, reactor pressure vessels, reactor control systems and frequency changers. The export of nuclear material was unlawful. All this also raised suspicions in the international community, and terms like "rogue nuclear state" began to be employed concerning Pakistan, the notice said.

Musharraf laid the blame entirely on one individual, Dr A.Q. Khan. However, according to his account, he had first noticed some "suspicious activities" even before the CIA brought more details to his attention. It's indeed surprising that one individual could run such a vast proliferation network single-handedly—lifting heavy centrifuge machines, passing through security cordons, loading the equipment into cargo planes, and transporting it to Libya, North Korea, and Iran – countries under intense international scrutiny. Musharraf's narrative strained credibility.

Musharraf had protected himself and probably many others involved in the proliferation network. The documentary evidence, including extracts from his memoirs and copies of statements of Dr A.Q. Khan and others, was annexed to the impeachment document. This indeed constituted a very serious ground for his impeachment. By exposing Pakistan's nuclear programme and assets to grave dangers, Musharraf had rendered himself liable for impeachment under Article 47 of the Constitution, the notice said.

Another ground for impeachment was the handing over of scores of Pakistani nationals to the CIA in violation of the law and without due process. It was not hearsay. In his autobiography, *In the Line of Fire*, Musharraf had admitted that Pakistan earned millions of dollars by the illegal handing over of terror suspects to other countries. Relevant pages from the chapter "Manhunt" from his memoirs were enclosed with the notice. Later, when Musharraf realised that he had blundered in making this admission, he deleted it from the Urdu edition of the biography, the notice read.

Musharraf's alleged involvement in the assassination of Benazir Bhutto was also a ground for impeachment. According to the book *The Way of the World*, Musharraf warned Benazir Bhutto in one of his taped telephonic conversations thus: "You should understand something: your security is based on the state of our relationship." The murder trial of her assassination was already in the court, and Musharraf also was an accused in it even though the trial had not yet been completed, it said. A component of the grounds contained some dubious financial decisions allegedly linked to Musharraf in one way or the other. Could Musharraf be held liable for it?

Farooq Naek flipped through the pages of the Constitution and the relevant laws to thread the various elements into a compelling narrative. The legal opinion said that even if evidence of direct graft to Musharraf was not available, he could still be held responsible for acts of omission and commission by functionaries under his direct watch.

Juxtaposing Article 90 of the Constitution with various articles of the rules of business and schedules, he painstakingly made a case that Musharraf could not evade responsibility.

This component included the sale of the Khoshgi Sugar Mill by the Fauji Foundation (FF) to a party other than the highest bidder in April 2005. The Parliamentary Secretary for Defence in the National Assembly admitted that the entity to which it was sold had not even participated in the bidding process and that a high-level inquiry had been ordered into it. The inquiry, however, was never held.

The Senate Committee summoned the foundation's managing director to answer questions, but he refused, claiming that the Fauji Foundation was a private body and could not be probed by Parliament. Instead, it placed advertisements in newspapers claiming innocence.

The MD of the foundation had been appointed by his friend General Musharraf after the former's retirement from the army. Brazenly refusing to appear before the Parliamentary

Committee, the MD claimed that General Musharraf acknowledged his integrity and declined to answer questions.

The notice said Musharraf was thus culpable. The complete record of the proceedings in Parliament and the MD's press interviews claiming friendship with Musharraf were attached to the notice.

The allotment of a residential plot measuring 1054 square feet to General Musharraf in September 1998 in Peshawar and its subsequent unlawful disposal by him was also made part of the grounds for impeachment. The plot had been leased to him for 99 years for a nominal amount. The lease terms said it was non-transferable, and a residential house had to be built on it within 24 months.

However, it appeared that Musharraf sold the plot against the law as the assets he declared on 1 November 1999 did not mention this plot. Documentary evidence, including the allotment letter and a declaration of assets released by the ISPR itself, was also collected to substantiate this.

The bid to privatise the Pakistan Steel Mills (PSM) and the privatisation of the Karachi Electric Supply Corporation (KESC) in 2005 under Musharraf's direct watch also figured among the grounds for impeachment.

The notice said that during the height of the sugar crisis in early 2006, NAB initiated a probe into the scam. But when a group of mill owners met General Musharraf in March 2006, NAB announced closing the probe, raising serious questions about Musharraf's role in it.

The notice, the grounds for impeachment, and the documentary evidence almost formed a complete book. However, even before it was submitted to the Speaker of the National Assembly and Musharraf was formally confronted with it, the commando had cold feet and resigned.

Chapter 4

Zardari succeeds Musharraf

Zardari had kept his intentions to become President a closely guarded secret. However, those who knew him well had sensed his ambitions even before signs appeared shortly after the general elections.

Yousaf Raza Gilani from Punjab was nominated for the office of Prime Minister after the February 2008 general elections. As a PPP loyalist from South Punjab, the scion of a reputed political family and a former Speaker of the National Assembly, he possessed strong credentials for the role. His nomination also sent positive signals to the people of South Punjab, who had long felt neglected. Zardari had been advocating for a separate Seraiki province, and this choice demonstrated his commitment to that cause.

However, there was more to Gilani's nomination than met the eye.

Makhdoom Amin Fahim from Sindh also possessed formidable credentials. Belonging to a highly respected family of spiritual leaders and a Bhutto loyalist, he was the most senior Party member after Benazir Bhutto. Following the 2002 elections, when various parties failed to form a government, Benazir Bhutto had allowed him to make a bid for the office of Prime Minister—a bid which ultimately failed. It was widely thought that Makhdoom Amin Fahim would be nominated for the office of Prime Minister in the coalition government.

Political correctness demanded that the two highest offices of President and Prime Minister be held by two different provinces. Zardari, like Amin Fahim, also came from Sindh. Thus, when Gilani from Punjab was nominated as Prime Minister, it signalled that the President would likely be from Sindh. Who else, other than Zardari, would be nominated by the Party for the Presidency?

During an informal chat, PML-N leader Mian Nawaz Sharif once remarked to Zardari, "*Meri party ka khial hai ke mai saddar ban jaoon.*" (My Party thinks that I should become the President.) Laughing, Zardari replied, "*Meri party da vee iwee khial ai ke main saddar ban jawaan.*" (My Party also thinks that I should become the President.) The conversation ended there.

Although Zardari said this in jest, it indicated that he may have already set his sights on the Presidency.

Having lost the race for Prime Minister, Makhdoom Amin Fahim began to be sidelined in the Party and gradually faded from prominence.

With Amin Fahim sidelined and Musharraf ousted, the path was cleared for the Party to nominate Zardari for the office of President. Known for his skills in uniting disparate groups, he managed to secure broad-based political support and easily won the Presidential election, becoming the 11th President of Pakistan at the age of fifty-three.

Zardari entered the Presidency on Tuesday, 9 September 2008, with a copy of the Quran held high over his head. He ensured that large portraits of his wife, Benazir Bhutto, and her father, Zulfikar Ali Bhutto, hung on either side as Chief Justice Abdul Hameed Dogar administered the oath.

Thunderous chants of "Jeay Bhutto" from party workers greeted him as he entered the hall, flanked by Prime Minister Yousaf Raza Gilani, acting President Muhammad Mian Soomro, and Chief Justice Abdul Hameed Dogar.

Witnessing the ceremony were Zardari's two daughters, Bakhtawar and Aseefa, and his son Bilawal, who had been named Chairman of the Party a year earlier, with Zardari as Co-Chairman. Distinguished guests, including Afghan President Hamid Karzai, parliamentarians, diplomats, high-ranking officials, and service chiefs also attended. Together, they witnessed the completion of the transition to democracy that Benazir Bhutto had envisioned and for which she had sacrificed her life.

Army Chief General Kayani may have agreed to Musharraf's ouster but did not want Zardari to replace him. Instead, he favoured Aftab Shaban Mirani, former Chief Minister of Sindh and defence minister, to succeed Musharraf in the Presidency. Zardari himself later disclosed this during a subsequent Party meeting.

The military did not welcome Zardari's ascendancy to the Presidency, as subsequent events would demonstrate.

Marriage of Benazir and Asif, 18 December 1987.

Bibi and Asif Ali Zardari with their children Bilawal, Bakhtawar, and Aseefa.

Bibi with Asif Ali Zardari, Ghulam Ishaq Khan and a visiting dignitary.

Bibi with Asif Ali Zardari at the Holy Mosque, Makkah.

Bbi and Asif Ali Zardari on arrival from a visit.

Bibi snapped on the gangway of a PIA aircraft with Asif.

Benazir and Asif with Nepalese dignitaries.

Benazir and Asif with General Babar and others.

Bibi honouring an artist as Asif Ali Zardari looks on.

Benazir with Asif at the Kamra Airbase.

A historic photograph of Benazir and Asif with the PLO leader Yasser Arafat.

Benazir and Asif with Iqbal Haider and Sajjad Ali Shah.

Benazir and Asif with the PLO Leader Yasser Arafat
at the Mazar-i Iqbal, Lahore.

President-elect Asif Ali Zardari on his arrival at the Aiwan-e Sadr, Islamabad, on 8 September 2008.

Chief Justice Abdul Hamid Dogar administering Oath of Office of President, Islamic Republic of Pakistan, to Asif Ali Zardari in Islamabad, on 9 September 2008. Prime Minister Yousaf Raza Gilani and Senate Chairman Mian Mohammad Soomro are also present.

President Asif Ali Zardari waving the photograph of Mohtarma Benazir Bhutto before delivering his address at the United Nations General Assembly in New York, on 25 September 2008.

President Asif Ali Zardari addressing a gathering on the first death anniversary of Mohtarma Shaheed Benazir Bhutto at Naudero, Sindh, on 27 December 2008.

President Asif Ali Zardari with Pope Benedict XVI and members of the Pakistani delegation in Rome, Italy, on 1 October 2009.

President Asif Ali Zardari greets PML-N Chief Mian Nawaz Sharif upon his arrival at the Presidency for a meeting, on 26 October 2009.

President Asif Ali Zardari with his daughters Aseefa and Bakhtawar, being received by the Chinese President Hu Jintao at the Great Hall of the People, in Beijing, China, on 7 July 2010.

President Asif Ali Zardari talking to a flood-affectee during his visit to a relief camp in Garhi Khuda Bux (Larkana), on 1 September 2010.

President Asif Ali Zardari accompanied by his daughter Aseefa before leaving for the Grand Reception hosted by the Kazakh President Nursultan Nazarbayev in honour of the visiting delegates, on the eve of the SCO Summit held in Astana, on 14 June 2011.

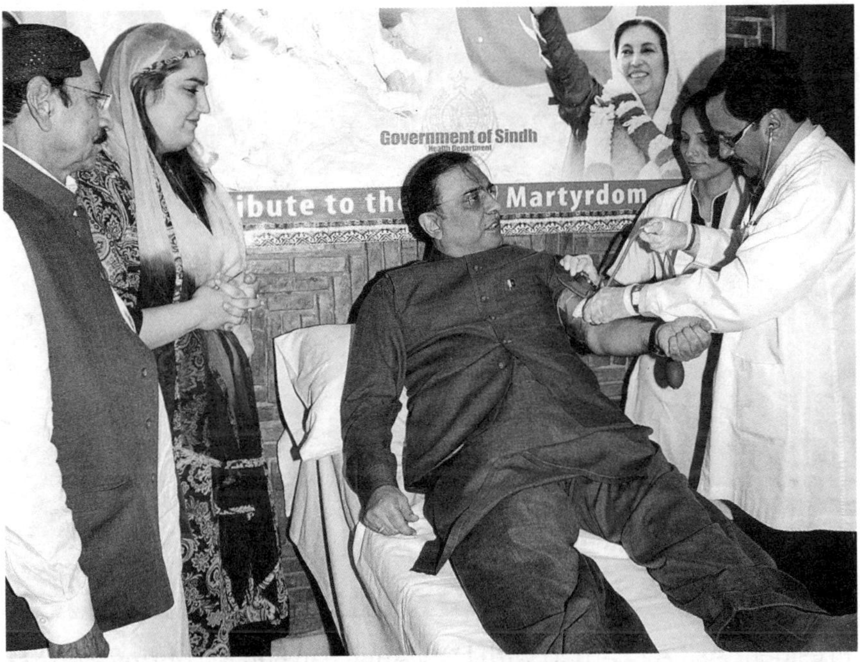

President Asif Ali Zardari donating blood on the 58th birth anniversary of Shaheed Mohtarma Benazir Bhutto in Naudero, Sindh, on 21 June 2011.

President Asif Ali Zardari with Daw Aung San Suu Kyi during a press-talk at the latter's residence in Yangon, on 25 January 2012. Aseefa and Bilawal accompany their father.

Aseefa Bhutto Zardari presenting the Shaheed Mohtarma Benazir Bhutto Award for Democracy to Daw Aung San Suu Kyi in Yangon, on 25 January 2012.

President Asif Ali Zardari with Bilawal at the Dargah of Hazrat Khawaja Moinuddin Chishti (RA) in Ajmer Sharif, India, on 8 April 2012.

Chapter 5

Resignation or a "deal"

In December 2013, Prime Minister Nawaz Sharif instituted a treason case against Pervez Musharraf for abrogating the Constitution on two occasions. The 11-page complaint detailed five charges of high treason to be tried in a special court under the law. By this time, Asif Ali Zardari was no longer the President of Pakistan.

As the case progressed and made headlines, former Prime Minister Yousaf Raza Gilani spoke to the media, criticising Musharraf's treason trial under Article 6. Gilani claimed that the trial was a breach of an agreement, stating, "An understanding had been reached with the establishment by his government for an honourable exit for General Pervez Musharraf, and the PML-N was also a party to it."

Gilani further asserted, "Musharraf had resigned under a deal reached with the establishment." He even defended Musharraf's controversial referendum to become President, arguing that it was endorsed by the Judiciary. "To agree to a negotiated resignation of such a President was really no small achievement. It was the result of a deal," he added.

While Gilani's personal opinion about the treason trial and his remarks about seeking a safe exit for Musharraf did not surprise many, his assertion about Musharraf resigning under a deal conflicted with what his Party, the Pakistan People's Party (PPP), had maintained all along. This revelation raised several questions: If there was indeed a deal, why did Musharraf stubbornly refuse the resignation option? Why did the assemblies pass resolutions one after the other demanding his impeachment? And why spend huge sums on a nonsensical issue at public expense?

Gilani's statement appeared to protect Musharraf from the treason trial. It embarrassed the PPP and strengthened the army's position.

Three days later, at an iftar dinner hosted by the Azad Jammu and Kashmir (AJK) Prime Minister, Gilani reaffirmed his stance. He reiterated that the deal for safe passage and no treason trial for Musharraf had been reached when he was Prime Minister and that the PML-N was also a party to this agreement.

Gilani is known as a great party loyalist. He had previously faced contempt charges and readily sacrificed the office of Prime Minister instead of writing a letter to the Swiss government against President Zardari.

Attributing Musharraf's resignation to a deal devalued the PPP's narrative that Musharraf had been forced to exit through political processes. Therefore, the statement about a "deal" surprised everyone, with many in the Party resenting it and a few fuming.

When Zardari learned of this, he asked that the Party's position on the impeachment be clarified. Accordingly, a brief statement issued by the Party reiterated its position: "It had been decided to impeach Musharraf, but he chose to resign."

Section Four

FACE-OFF WITH THE JUDICIARY

Chapter 1

The background of a relationship

To put the tense relationship between Zardari and the Chaudhry Court in perspective, it is essential to look into Justice Chaudhry's background.

Iftikhar Chaudhry became the Chief Justice of the Balochistan High Court in April 1999 and was subsequently elevated to the Supreme Court. General Musharraf appointed him as the 20th Chief Justice of Pakistan (CJP) on 30 June 2005, making him the youngest CJP who went on to lead the top court over three non-consecutive terms for the next eight years until 11 December 2013.

He was a judge of good standing but not reputed for breaking from the past mould to chart an independent course. As a judge of the Balochistan High Court, he was among those who took oath under Musharraf's Provisional Constitutional Order (PCO) in January 2000.

As a Supreme Court judge, Chaudhry sat on four pivotal benches between 2000 and 2005 that validated highly controversial and anti-democratic orders of a military dictator. Although he did not head any of these benches, he consistently voted with the majority to uphold the dictator's orders. These included:

1. Endorsing General Musharraf's coup in 1999, which sacked Nawaz Sharif's government
2. Validating Musharraf's referendum in April 2002
3. Endorsing Musharraf's Legal Framework Order (LFO)
4. Supporting the 17th Constitutional Amendment in December 2003
5. Allowing General Musharraf to contest elections for the office of President from the Assemblies while in uniform and as Army Chief

Critics have alleged, without proof, that he was one of two judges who urged President Rafiq Tarar to resign in June 2001 and allow General Musharraf to assume office.

While Chaudhry's judicial career was not tainted with corruption, his elevation to the top position and subsequent scrutiny in a political setting led to stories of corruption and misconduct.

Musharraf, who had elevated Chaudhry to Chief Justice, suddenly decided to sack him in March 2007. Chaudhry's admirers claimed he had undergone a genuine transformation into a democratic judge, which Musharraf feared. Whatever the reason, Musharraf wanted him out of the way. Reportedly, Chaudhry was privately confronted with a stinging charge sheet and asked to step down voluntarily. He refused.

It was widely believed that a faction of the military, led by ISI chief Lt General Kayani, encouraged Chaudhry in his defiance of Musharraf. General Kayani, next in line for promotion, aspired to take over the army command after Musharraf. Kayani's natural expectation to soon become the Army Chief may have motivated his support for Chaudhry's defiance.

Upon Chaudhry's refusal to resign, Musharraf "suspended" him in March 2007, accusing him of "corruption, violating norms of judicial propriety, seeking favours and misbehaving with senior lawyers." This was unprecedented, as there was no constitutional provision to suspend a Chief Justice. Justice Javed Iqbal, known for accommodating the establishment, readily agreed to replace the suspended Chaudhry as Acting Chief Justice.

Chaudhry had been wronged and gained sympathy from people who already disliked the military dictator. Countrywide protests, led by the bar, erupted. PPP leader Barrister Aitzaz Ahsan, the leading star of the lawyers' movement, drove Chaudhry around on a tide of mass approval. Chaudhry also relished the street power. Three months later, on 20 July 2007, the Supreme Court declared his suspension illegal, and he bounced back.

However, the reinstatement proved short-lived. On 3 November 2007, General Musharraf struck back with a vengeance, imposing emergency rule in yet another military coup and asking judges to take oath under the PCO once again.

Chaudhry hurriedly called a full court meeting and declared the emergency proclamation unconstitutional, forbidding all judges from taking oath under the new PCO, Musharraf's second. When asked why he refused to take the oath now when he had no qualms about taking such an oath in 2000, he said, "There is a time in one's life when one says that enough is enough."

Musharraf not only sacked Chaudhry and 60 other judges but also imprisoned them in their homes. Justice Abdul Hameed Dogar was sworn in as the new Chief Justice. Chaudhry was mistreated and roughed up by the police while defiantly breaking the siege around his house.

Chaudhry may not have been a charismatic judge, but the dictator's mistreatment aroused widespread sympathy for him. He was seen as a judge grievously wronged and appeared as a symbol of judicial independence. A photograph captured by an intrepid press photographer, feigning to be a labourer, showed police officials grabbing Chaudhry by the hair and shoving him into a car. This image, taken on 13 March 2009 in Islamabad, turned Chaudhry almost overnight into a larger-than-life figure, fueling the fire already ignited by Musharraf's sacking of judges.

The bar had already risen in his defence. Protests gained momentum as the public cheered him wherever he went. As masses chanting "*Terai jan nisar, beshumar, beshumar*" (Your fans ready to die are countless) swelled; he appeared like a hero defying a military dictator.

Elections held in February 2008 brought a coalition government led by PPP Prime Minister Yousaf Raza Gilani to power. He promptly lifted the barricades around judges' houses and set them free, raising hopes of their reinstatement.

Zardari replaced Musharraf as President in September 2008 while agitations for Chaudhry's reinstatement continued. He also opposed Chaudhry's reinstatement, ignoring public demonstrations. When Zardari was finally forced to reinstate Chaudhry in March 2009, it was not due to a change of heart. Party leaders around him developed cold feet as demonstrators became more rowdy. Claiming that protesters would besiege the Presidency, they feared a military takeover as a result.

After restoration, Chaudhry liked to believe he had a people's mandate to respond to public calls and correct anything that appeared wrong to him. He succumbed to populism and relished TV channels flashing his bench observations and comments as breaking news, often interpreted as declarations of guilt. In many cases, the media, itself a complainant, also acted as a cheerleader. He basked in the thunderous media applause.

His overdrive of a sense of purpose, unrestrained by any law and fuelled by media headlines, almost bordered on vanity. Inevitably, the seeds of confrontation with Parliament and the political government had been sown.

Chaudhry knew that Zardari had stubbornly opposed his reinstatement. In Zardari, he saw his nemesis. Zardari also did not conceal his dislike for Chaudhry. Their relationship was fated to be mutually hostile.

Chapter 2

Benazir Bhutto opposed judges' reinstatement

Benazir Bhutto was in London when the Supreme Court reinstated Iftikhar Chaudhry in July 2007 after his first sacking in March of that year. In an interview with the *Times of India*, she said, "I think this judgment will help defuse some of the frustration, if not all frustration, prevailing in Pakistan." However, she did not praise Chaudhry.

After the interview, she phoned me, saying that a copy of the interview should be kept for record and given to her when required. I did not quite understand why she wanted a routine statement kept in the record and given to her when required. There must have been a reason behind it.

Much later, I realised why she wanted her interview to be kept on record. While condemning Chaudhry's second sacking in November that year as an "attack on the majesty of justice," she did not demand his reinstatement nor praised him as a "symbol of independence of the judiciary"—a narrative assiduously built around himself by Chaudhry during the period he was on the road. Her position was consistent with what she had told the *Times of India* a few months before. Benazir Bhutto condemned the judges' sacking but did not demand their reinstatement.

To register a protest against the sacking of judges, she decided to pay a symbolic visit to the official residence of the Chief Justice in Islamabad in December 2007. I accompanied her in the car.

The police had already cordoned off the area and blocked the road leading to the judges' colony with barbed wire. She did not break the barrier and, popping out of the vehicle, addressed the crowd.

The police had already removed the national flag from Chaudhry's official residence. Condemning this action, she said, "*Hum Chief Justice kai ghar par Pakistan ka jhanda leharaaen gai.*" (We will hoist the flag of Pakistan at the Chief Justice's residence).

On the way back, I took a different car. Before we reached Zardari House, she called: "FB, tell everyone (in the Party) not to demand reinstatement of Iftikhar Chaudhry in statements and press talks."

"But Bibi, you just said that you wanted him reinstated," I replied.

"No, I only said that we will reinstate the majesty of the judiciary and the sanctity of the office of the Chief Justice," she said.

"I said we will restore the flag of Pakistan on the residence of the Chief Justice. I did not name Iftikhar Chaudhry as Chief Justice. I condemned the sacking of judges but did not ask for reinstatement of Iftikhar Chaudhry. Play the tape of my speech and listen again."

I first called Raza Rabbani to convey her instructions.

"But in the speech, she herself has demanded that she will fly the flag of Pakistan on CJ Chaudhry's residence. It is already in the news all over," a disappointed Raza said.

I told him about how Bibi looked at what she actually said.

"Oh no, FB, what is this?" a frustrated Rabbani said.

"If you have any doubts, call her," I said.

She had serious misgivings about Chaudhry.

In her meeting with Nawaz Sharif in Zardari House in Islamabad in the second week of December 2007, she broached the subject of the judiciary. She told Nawaz not to expect any justice from him if Chaudhry were reinstated. I was present at the meeting.

Nawaz Sharif appeared surprised but did not say anything.

She then continued, "Mian Sahib, Iftikhar Chaudhry should have at least sent a bailiff to the airport when you returned from exile."

"After all, you had returned to the country under orders of the court. If Chaudhry had sent the bailiff to the airport, it may not have saved you, but at least it would have sent a message that he had the spine and wanted to do justice."

Nawaz Sharif listened, nodding his head as if in approval.

Reminding him that Chaudhry had not sent the court bailiff

to the airport, she asked, "Mian Sahib, did he send the bailiff to you?"

"No, he did not, Mohtarma," Nawaz Sharif said.

"I had not even given a thought to it," he confessed.

Continuing, he said, "*Aap bilkul theek kehti hain Mohtarma, bailiff bhaijna chaheiy tha.*" (You are absolutely right, Mohtarma. He should have sent a bailiff.")

The conversation about the reinstatement of the CJP ended without any formal decision on what to do.

Nawaz endorsed Benazir Bhutto's view about Chaudhry, although he did not categorically commit to opposing his reinstatement. He was open to suggestions against reinstatement. Indeed, the conversation between the two that evening was of a general agreement against reinstatement.

A few days later, on 23 December 2007, Senator Taj Haider went to the just-retired Supreme Court Judge, Justice Bhagwan Das, to deliver a letter from Benazir Bhutto on his retirement. During the conversation, Justice Bhagwan Das wondered why the PPP did not categorically demand the restoration of the judges. He conveyed a message to Benazir Bhutto that political parties, particularly the PPP, should unequivocally demand the reinstatement of all the sacked judges.

Taj Haider conveyed this to Benazir Bhutto. She wrote back to him: "Taj, the PPP does not support the reinstatement of all judges. They are pro-PCO judges, and some of them are highly politicised. However, under a Parliamentary Committee, we will scrutinise their judgments and neutral judges will be retaken in. This is our position which we do not highlight now, being more apt to state that PPP will leave the issue to the next Parliament. Happy to discuss further with you when I get to Karachi at the end of the month. Bibi"

Unfortunately, she did not live beyond 27 December. She never got back to Karachi to be "happy to discuss further" with Senator Taj Haider.

Benazir Bhutto did not want political judges reinstated. She had in mind a Parliamentary Committee to decide who to take back based on the judgments delivered. Chaudhry had already become highly political and controversial. Asif Zardari was aware of this background.

Chapter 3

A grievous error

Zardari was confident he could weather the protests demanding Chaudhry's reinstatement and did not go out of his way to reach out to the leaders of the lawyers' movement. Chaudhry's successor, Justice Abdul Hameed Dogar, had been sworn in as the Chief Justice before Zardari became President. Reinstating Chaudhry meant that Dogar would have to be sacked. Zardari maintained that sacking Chief Justice Dogar would be unconstitutional. He knew that Benazir Bhutto had not wanted the reinstatement of all judges who had become politicised. While Zardari was right in refusing to reinstate Chaudhry, he made a grievous error that would tilt the scales.

Towards the end of February 2009, as the lawyers' movement was gaining momentum, the Supreme Court upheld an order of the Lahore High Court (LHC) disqualifying Nawaz Sharif from contesting by-elections due to his conviction in the 1999 plane hijacking conspiracy case. Almost simultaneously, in another case, the court also declared Shehbaz Sharif's election to a Punjab Provincial Assembly constituency "null and void". forcing him to step down as Chief Minister.

These court verdicts, coming in quick succession, shocked everyone.

In Shehbaz Sharif's disqualification, Zardari saw an opportunity to regain lost ground for the Pakistan People's Party (PPP) in Punjab. Without any discussion within the Party, he swiftly sacked the provincial Punjab government and imposed Governor's Rule in the province.

The decision to impose Governor's Rule was taken in complete secrecy. I learnt about it only when the Prime Minister came that evening to meet the President for a one-on-one meeting, causing a commotion in the Presidency. With files in hand, Law Minister Farooq Naek came to my office. He had already drafted a Presidential Proclamation imposing Governor's Rule in the province and given it to the President, who was in a meeting with the Prime Minister.

Drafted in great haste, the proclamation initially envisaged not only sacking the provincial government but also suspending the Provincial Assembly. Quickly realising the mistake, Naek dashed towards the President's office and returned with the file in hand. The President and the Prime Minister had yet to see the draft proclamation.

Farooq Naek corrected the draft proclamation to sack only the provincial government and not the Punjab Assembly. It read:

"WHEREAS I, Asif Ali Zardari, President of the Islamic Republic of Pakistan, on receipt of report from the Governor of the Punjab and other information made available, am satisfied that the situation has arisen in which the Government of the Province of the Punjab cannot be carried on in accordance with the provisions of the Constitution." "AND WHEREAS an unprecedented and unique constitutional void has been created in the Province consequent upon the decision of the Hon'ble Supreme Court of Pakistan on 25 February 2009 in the matter of disqualification/unseating of Mian Shehbaz Sharif as Member of Provincial Assembly."

"Now, THEREFORE, in exercise of the powers conferred by Article 234 of the Constitution of the Islamic Republic of Pakistan, I hereby

a) "Direct the Governor of the Punjab to assume on my behalf the functions of the Government of that Province;

b) Make the following incidental and consequential provisions which appear to be necessary or desirable for giving effect to the objects of this Proclamation:

i) The Chief Minister and Provincial Ministers of that Province shall forthwith cease to hold office;

ii) In the exercise of the functions which the Governor has been directed to assume hereinbefore stated, the Governor shall act to such extent and subject to such conditions as I shall, from time to time, deem fit to give or impose."

Thus, the Punjab government was brought under Islamabad's control.

The abrupt Presidential Proclamation convinced the Sharifs that Zardari was behind the Supreme Court verdict, unseating Shehbaz Sharif as a member of the Punjab Assembly. With prospects of losing their bastion of power looming large, their backs were to the wall, and they were up in arms.

Swiftly, Nawaz Sharif latched onto the lawyers' movement, turning it into a full-blown political crisis. He announced that he would personally lead the lawyers' march from Lahore to Islamabad and stage a sit-in before the President's House until Chaudhry was reinstated. The movement appeared to snowball menacingly.

Newspaper reports stated that U.S. Secretary of State Hillary Clinton telephoned both Zardari and Nawaz Sharif to defuse the crisis, warning that it could risk U.S. aid to Pakistan.

In hindsight, sacking the Punjab government turned out to be a huge mistake. It transformed the hitherto lawyers' movement into a political movement. It set in motion a series of setbacks for Zardari and PPP politics at the hands of a judge who was no less political. Without this provocation, Nawaz Sharif might not have gone that far. After all, not long ago, he had agreed with Benazir Bhutto that Chaudhry was a politically motivated judge who lacked the qualities of an independent jurist.

The caravan of opposition parties and lawyers, led by Nawaz Sharif, set out from Lahore on 15 March to stage a dharna (sit-in) in Islamabad "until Chaudhry was reinstated". PPP leader Aitzaz Ahsan was also among the leaders.

Zardari, however, had dug in his heels and refused to reinstate Chaudhry.

Chapter 4

Triple-One troops enter the Presidency

Some advisors of Zardari, known for their links with the establishment, had made it known that General Kayani wanted Chaudhry reinstated. Throughout the day on 15 March, they spoke, first in whispers and later loudly, that troops in Rawalpindi had been alerted in anticipation of some emergency. Zardari had never mentioned what Kayani wanted. Indeed, he did not heed any talk about it.

As the convoy of hundreds of vehicles led by Nawaz Sharif readied in Lahore to march on Islamabad for the "final push", the chorus by these advisors grew louder, and the push for Chaudhry's reinstatement stronger.

A few, painting a grim picture, even claimed they had heard about the takeover from the horse's mouth. Their refrain was that a military coup was imminent if Chaudhry was not reinstated immediately.

Whether they had cold feet or they sang on cue from some common music sheet, Zardari was not ready to budge. His attitude was that of "couldn't care less". He seemed convinced nothing would happen even if a few thousand protestors gathered in the capital. "Can't we control a few thousand people?" he asked more than once. "It's all drama," he said. He was unfazed.

"What, even if they (the army) came in, so what? Let them *sambhalo* (manage) if they want," he told me, astonished at the fears of a military takeover.

Amid such gloomy talk throughout the day, I went home in the evening, knowing that we would have to reassemble later that night as the caravan of protestors from Lahore arrived in Islamabad past midnight for a sit-in before the Presidency.

Around 10 P.M., I received a call to come to the Presidency urgently. Within minutes, I was on the road. No military vehicles were running through the streets, no unusual activity was occurring, and no sirens were sounding.

But as I drove into the main gate of the Presidency, I noticed dozens of gun-wielding troops guarding the entrance. Troops had usually been guarding the entrance, but tonight, they stood guard at the gates in unusually large numbers. Their mere number was daunting and served to convey a message, one felt.

A few metres inside the presidential complex, I noticed troops in pairs standing alert at different points from the main entrance to the rear gate of the Presidency opening into the complex of Parliament House. All lights in the main compound and car park were switched off. The Presidency was submerged in total darkness. This had never happened before. It was as if the warning sounded by some advisors earlier in the day was coming true.

In the darkness, the faces of the troops were not clearly visible. Only shadows strutted around in silence. I had been to the Presidency at night before. The darkness, the eerie silence, and soldiers in pairs standing like motionless statues were never witnessed before. The hissing sound of the wind breaking the silence made it dramatic.

While driving towards the Presidency, I passed by the Pakistan Television studios, the first building the troops of the Triple-One Brigade are known to conquer when they take over. There were no signs of troops at the PTV building. The contrast between the commotion in the presidential compound and its total absence on the streets was striking.

Did the commanders deliberately plan a manoeuvre only in the Presidency to exert pressure on Zardari to reinstate Chaudhry?

I grew suspicious. In the car park, I sat inside the car for some time, trying to figure out what was happening, and drew out my notebook and pen. Remaining seated inside the car, I watched how the troops moved in pairs more closely, strutting around with an air of assumed authority. I began noting my feelings and observations in shorthand.

The troops were armed, and their boots thudded heavily on the ground. In the darkness of the night, it was hard to see the expressions they bore on their faces. I assumed their faces must have been stern, and their eyes pretending to scan the area for any signs of trouble.

The soldiers who stood still seemed to gaze at something far away as if on guard duty, watching the area and ready to respond to a command signal. The silence was palpable, broken only by the hissing of the wind or the sound of boots scraping on the ground.

The soldiers' movements were synchronised. Their discipline was evident in the way they carried themselves. They moved with purpose, as if part of a larger, carefully orchestrated operation, while actually, there was none. Despite the darkness and the tension, a sense of order and control permeated the scene. Such signs of order are not witnessed in a real takeover. It was a sham and pretentious "takeover".

As the night wore on and they continued to patrol the Presidency, I was reminded of how, in the past, they had similarly waited for a nod from the top to take control at a moment's notice. The sight was ugly but not fearful. It hardly inspired love and admiration for the troops or their commanders. For me, it was déjà vu. The feelings it invoked were of extreme distaste if not revulsion. How small the commanders looked to me at the time.

I parked my car but did not come out of it for several minutes, which made some soldiers suspicious.

A pair of soldiers walked past me in measured steps. They pretended to look straight ahead as if not noticing me still sitting in the car. Even if they had glanced at me occasionally, I would not have noticed it. The lights had been switched off, and it was dark. I did not hear them speak with one another. They walked past me like still statues.

Their pretence that they had not noticed me seemed near perfect, but it conveyed that my not coming out of the car had been observed with suspicion.

Perhaps it was not their brief to come closer and ask questions.

The emptiness of the space, the darkness of the night, and the stillness exaggerated the shadows lurking behind the trees.

My mind swirled. I began to think of how troops swiftly took over important state buildings during coups since the creation of Pakistan. In army parlance, this was called "securing buildings" in times of turmoil.

I had been a witness to the Triple-One Brigade "securing" the Prime Minister's House twice when Benazir Bhutto was ousted from power through the army-backed presidential decrees in 1990 and again in 1993. The Triple-One Brigade laid siege around the PM's House whenever it was required to be "secured" in the past, the troops artificially wearing stern looks on their faces.

This time, it was different in the Presidency. There was no siege. The troops strutted around in pairs mysteriously but not menacingly. They also did not have dirty looks on their faces.

Later, when the ADC called the security in charge at the main gate, he learnt that fresh troops from outside had come and assumed security at the gate. They had come uninvited, believing they might be needed in an emergency they thought was likely. The ADC later told me he knew instantly that the 111 Brigade had moved in.

The manoeuvre may have created a perception of a military takeover, but it was not. It was optics for exerting pressure on Zardari to reinstate Chaudhry.

I thought of Zardari and irresistibly admired him. The distasteful spectacle made me think for a while about how our commanders liked to believe that they were indeed loved and idolised by the people. Strange indeed are the illusions by which humans are capable of sustaining themselves.

Amid such thoughts, I exited the car to take the elevator to the President's chamber on the 4th floor.

Chapter 5

Inside the President's chamber

As I entered the President's chamber on the fourth floor, Zardari was seated on a rocking chair. Surprisingly, he appeared unfazed. A few close advisors were already present. It was difficult to tell whether he had been informed of the shadows lurking in the compound below. Even if he was aware, he did not seem to care. The late-night meeting was held in the President's official chamber instead of the committee room where such meetings were typically conducted.

Twenty-two close associates and advisors had been invited to the huddle, but only thirteen turned up. One suspected they avoided coming at that hour, fearing an army takeover. Those who had been falling over one another for an audience with the President in the morning were conspicuously absent at night, even when asked to come.

Zardari inquired about those who had not turned up. No one had an answer. There was a hushed silence. Everyone pretended that he had not heard what the President had said. Zardari did not press for an answer. It was enough just to point out that several invitees had failed to appear. The message would reach those who did not come for the meeting.

"Sir, my information is that in a short while, the marchers will set out from Lahore towards the capital and lay siege to the Presidency and PM's House," a close advisor said with a drawn face.

Zardari responded, "Sometimes you have to take strong decisions and take a firm position and stand by your decision."

Regarding the threatened march on the Presidency, he said in Urdu: "*Ye logon ka samundar jo Islamabad ki taraf aaraha hai yeh chand gaarion ke siwa kuch bhi nahi hoga. Yeh sab drama hai.*" (The sea of people marching towards Islamabad will turn out to be no more than a few cars). "*Yeh sab drama hai*" (All this is a drama), he further emphasised.

He reassured the dozen advisors gathered around him, saying nothing would happen even if the demonstrators were allowed to camp in front of the Presidency for a few days.

The cabinet ministers, however, already had cold feet.

A federal minister expressed concern: "A serious law and order situation, even bloodshed, can result if the masses were allowed to converge at the 'D' Chowk."

Zardari remained unimpressed.

The huddle continued until past midnight. Almost everyone urged the President to reinstate Chaudhry to avert an imminent military takeover. A few who may have thought otherwise kept quiet. A minister occasionally called someone from the meeting room to ascertain whether the marchers had actually started from Lahore. Every time he made a phone call, he told the President, "Sir, the marchers will start off in a few minutes. They are led by Nawaz and will be joined by groups on the way. I am keeping watch."

The few minutes seemed like an eternity, never-ending.

Occasionally, a minister would rise and, coming closer, almost whispering into the President's ears. One guessed that the advice to reinstate Chaudhry and "save the system" was being whispered. Zardari remained defiant.

Everyone spoke about reinstating Iftikhar Chaudhry. No one talked about reinstating the scores of other sacked judges.

Surprised, the President asked why no one talked about reinstating the other sacked judges.

No one responded.

The President said, "In principle, I am not against the reinstatement of other sacked judges, but I don't want Chaudhry reinstated."

"Sir, if you agree to reinstate all other sacked judges, why not also reinstate Chaudhry," Prime Minister Gilani asked.

"Why, Sir?" another asked, endorsing the suggestion. "If it is right to reinstate other sacked judges, why would it be wrong to reinstate Chaudhry?"

Almost in chorus, everyone said that all sacked judges, including Chaudhry, should be reinstated.

As everyone stressed Chaudhry's reinstatement, Zardari once again said, "I know Chaudhry more than you do."

He explained that it would be wrong because to reinstate Chaudhry, he would have to sack the sitting Chief Justice, Abdul Hameed Dogar.

"I will not do it under any circumstances. Dogar has been appointed under the Constitution. I will not go against the Constitution."

He reminded the advisors around him that Shaheed Benazir Bhutto also didn't favour reinstating Chaudhry, although she protested the sacking of judges.

"We cannot ditch Dogar unceremoniously and unconstitutionally," he said.

Zardari then talked about Chaudhry and said that some people had brought messages from him that he would not cause any problems if reinstated. He did not name the messengers.

"His (Chaudhry's) methods were not like (that of) a Chief Justice," Zardari told the meeting.

At one point, Zardari blurted:

"*Wo qasmain kha raha tha key Saab ko meri taraf sai guarantee dai do*" (He swore to assure me that he would not cause any problem to me), Zardari recalled.

"I cannot talk more than this," he said, leaving everyone guessing.

He was surprised at how his close associates had ditched him at this hour and left him alone in the ring. He turned around to look closely at a go-getter federal minister as if saying to him, "*Et Tu, Brute*?"

Once again, he firmly said he would not sack Dogar to bring in Chaudhry, "come what may".

Gilani pointed out that Dogar would be retiring in a week, and Chaudhry could be reinstated after Dogar's retirement.

"Chaudhry will not mind waiting for a week," he said.

There was silence as all eyes turned towards Zardari.

Zardari was silent, signalling his agreement.

Chapter 6

Reinstated—but not before Dogar retired

The impatient ones and those who had cold feet were still not happy.

An advisor argued, "Chaudhry had declared Dogar an unconstitutional Chief Justice. He will not wait a week to replace him. It would imply that Chaudhry accepted Dogar as a legitimate Chief Justice and make him look small."

Another said, "Chaudhry going back on his public statements about Justice Dogar would make him look opportunistic. He will not agree."

"It would be '*gunah-e-belazzat*' (a tasteless sin) for Chaudhry," yet another remarked.

One advisor pressed, "Forcing Chaudhry into a corner will invite another crisis. If he is to be reinstated a week later, why not now?"

The President, however, was not prepared to allow any dishonourable exit for Chief Justice Dogar, come what may.

He blurted, "I don't care what Chaudhry thinks of himself. I don't care when Dogar retires, today or tomorrow or a year later. I will not sack Dogar illegally."

Reaching for the water bottle, he continued, "Chaudhry will have to wait for as long as it takes until Dogar has completed his constitutional term."

Once again, he lambasted Chaudhry: "I know him inside and out. You people don't. He will accept anything as long as he knows that he will be reinstated. He has been sending me messages. I know it. None of you knows about it."

Reiterating, "You don't know him," he said again, "I will not go against the Constitution."

Zardari may have been aware that troops had entered the Presidency as he spoke these words. He may have also known that Kayani wanted Chaudhry's reinstatement. He was disappointed that his close advisors had cold feet. "Nothing will happen," he had said repeatedly, trying to reassure them, but to no effect.

Prime Minister Yousaf Raza Gilani and Army Chief General Kayani arrived at around 2:30 A.M. and separately met with the President.

Emerging from his meeting with the President and seeing me standing in the corridor, General Kayani approached me and said,

"Agar das din bad karna hai tau abhi kion nahi karte?" (If it has to be done ten days later, why not reinstate him now?) as he tarried with me briefly. The constitutional niceties did not bother him.

That night, Zardari was as lonely as loneliness can be. Troops had arrived at the Presidency, and his close advisors had deserted him. There was no applause and no crowds to cheer him on.

It was one of his darkest moments. But in another sense, it was also one of his finest.

Finally, everyone agreed that Chaudhry would be reinstated, but only after Dogar formally retired, barely a few days away. It was already well past midnight.

A message was sent to the leaders of the marchers gathered in Lahore that Chaudhry had been reinstated. The Army Chief personally called one of the marchers' leaders. The marchers' leader, however, did not trust any assurance from the government and asked that the Army Chief reassure them personally. If there were any doubts about the drivers behind the hype, these were dispelled.

A particularly sad aspect of the wrangling that night was the insistence by some on a personal call from the Army Chief to assure them that it had been decided to reinstate Chaudhry. This may have been an indication of distrust in Zardari. But more than that, it also exposed some underlying power dynamics.

The protest march was called off.

Iftikhar Chaudhry readily agreed to wait until Dogar retired and made no fuss about the "unconstitutional" CJP Hameed Dogar continuing in office for a few more days.

Justice Abdul Hameed Dogar was not shown the door unceremoniously. After retirement, Zardari invited Dogar for dinner at the Presidency, sending one last signal of standing by him.

The decision to reinstate Chaudhry having been taken past midnight, Prime Minister Gilani addressed the nation around 5:45 A.M. on 16 March.

He set the tone of his address by beginning with a verse from the Holy Quran that reminded Muslims how God had saved them from disaster just when they were on the brink.

Gilani announced the restoration of the deposed Chief Justice and all other sacked judges "as the President and I had promised."

He recalled that soon after being elected as Leader of the House with a "heavy mandate by Parliament", he had released all detained judges and ordered their emoluments be paid.

He said the legislation would increase the number of judges in the apex court to accommodate the reinstated judges.

He explained that Justice Iftikhar Chaudhry would replace Chief Justice Abdul Hameed Dogar, but only when the latter retired on 21 March. "A notification to this effect is being issued now."

Chaudhry could not be reinstated earlier because there was already a Chief Justice who could not be removed unlawfully.

All political workers detained during protest marches would be released and the cases against them withdrawn.

Referring to last month's Supreme Court verdict disqualifying the Sharif brothers from holding public offices, Gilani announced filing a review petition "for the sake of reconciliation."

All issues would be resolved in accordance with the Charter of Democracy, he said.

Gilani further claimed that the decision had been taken in consultation with all allies.

Thus, Dogar was not sacked prematurely for Chaudhry's reinstatement. Chaudhry also did not question Dogar's continuing as CJP for a few more days. He waited until Dogar actually retired. The bravado that he did not accept Dogar as legitimate Chief Justice even for a day was no more than hot air.

Zardari remembered with anguish that his own advisors had

forced Chaudhry's reinstatement. In March 2015, in an informal chat with Party leaders in Zardari House in Islamabad, he recalled it once again succinctly:

"I was opposed to reinstating Chaudhry; you all know it. We could not have been forced to reinstate him. But some of my own ministers came running to me shaking. Our own government had cold feet," he said and lamented, "What could I do when our own ministers had cold feet and everyone was shaking?"

Chapter 7

Clash inevitable

Having been restored as Chief Justice by street power and tasting blood, Chaudhry saw himself as a messiah destined to correct all wrongs and injustices.

Chaudhry turned the constitutional principle of the trichotomy of powers, dividing state authority between the legislature, judiciary, and executive, on its head.

He overturned the ruling of the Speaker of the National Assembly and sent elected Prime Minister Yousaf Raza Gilani home, thus creating a precedent for sacking elected leaders through judicial processes.

While setting aside the Speaker's ruling in the matter, he conveyed the court's orders through a curt letter by the assistant registrar of the court. This angered the Speaker, who publicly called it "in bad taste and also against parliamentary norms", but Chaudhry remained unmoved.

He ordered the reopening of graft cases against the President, disregarding constitutional immunity. Stepping into the domain of the Election Commission, he changed the election schedule to the office of President to elect Zardari's successor in 2013. The Chief Election Commissioner, Fakhruddin G. Ebrahim, resigned in protest.

Chaudhry took judicial notice of the so-called Memogate case, disregarding that a parliamentary investigation had already been ordered into it, sending Zardari into a tailspin.

Acting like the sole arbiter of everything, he assumed all powers to appoint and sack judges. He appointed over a hundred and sacked scores of superior court judges, denying any role to the President, the Prime Minister and the bar.

Article 175-A, introduced in the Constitution by the 18th Constitutional Amendment, conferred a limited role on Parliament in selecting judges of superior courts.

Resenting it as interference in his domain, Chaudhry wanted it repealed. He sent discreet messages that if it were not done, he would undo the 18th Amendment, which had already been challenged before the court.

Members of the Constitution Committee, who took pride in

giving Parliament a limited role in judges' appointment in the 18th Amendment, appeared quick to appease him. None stood up to challenge him. They even pleaded that Chaudhry should not be antagonised. To please Chaudhry, the 19th Constitutional Amendment was passed by Parliament against Zardari's wishes.

Chaudhry was still not satisfied. He declared that the decisions of the Parliamentary Committee in the appointment of judges were subject to judicial review. By employing the mechanism of judicial oversight, he ensured that Parliament was made redundant in the appointment of judges.

He alone appointed more than 125 judges to the superior judiciary during his tenure. All eight recommendations made by the Parliamentary Committee were overturned, and it was thus consigned to the dustbin. In private, the Parliamentary Committee members grumbled before the President over their helplessness and said there was no use for it, but none was prepared to resign in protest. Zardari wished they would resign in protest but did not ask them overtly.

In the matter of sacking judges, the Chaudhry court also set new precedents. He sacked scores of judges for taking oath under Musharraf's second PCO but did not heed criticism that in doing so, he had invented a new mechanism not provided for in the Constitution.

By placing the fate of judges in the hands of one person—himself, Chaudhry undermined the judiciary's independence and rendered it a monolithic structure akin to a military unit. Over time, this would rob the judiciary of the glory of developing jurisprudence based on the diverse opinions of judges on benches.

The strident accumulation of power by the judiciary under him attracted adverse international attention, but he did not care.

In September 2011, a high-level mission of the International Commission of Jurists (ICJ) visited Pakistan and met serving and retired judges, members of the bar, and politicians.

The mission declared that the Supreme Court was "exceeding

the limits of use of suo motu powers" and that there was "no transparency and a laid down criteria in allocating cases to different benches".

A few months later, in 2012, the President of the International Crisis Group, Justice Louise Arbour, after visiting Pakistan, poignantly remarked that judges have become "intoxicated with their independence". She also warned that the current direction of the court "threatens to upend the very democratic order that restored them to the bench".

Acquiring more and more power, Chaudhry acted like the sole arbiter of national destiny.

Zardari was rendered utterly powerless in the matter of appointing judges. He wanted the matter placed before Parliament. He did not expect to get a constitutional amendment passed by Parliament and only wanted a comprehensive discussion and debate in public view.

The chairman of the Senate, Nayyar Bokhari, supported him in this, but most of the lawyers in the Party's core committee opposed it, saying it would only antagonise the Chief Justice. Several members of the 18th Amendment Constitution Committee also opposed him. They were appeasing the Chief Justice. They prevailed, too. Zardari was disappointed.

When Parliament did not take up the matter of the division of powers between state organs, Zardari, in December 2012, decided to file a constitutional reference before the Supreme Court seeking opinion on the proper role of the judicial commission, a Parliamentary Committee, the Prime Minister, the President and other stakeholders in the appointment of judges.

The reference essentially aimed to rationalise powers and restore balance among the different state organs in appointing judges. Once again, several party leaders and stalwarts of the 18th Amendment advised him against it, saying it would not go down well with Chaudhry.

When someone said that filing a reference against Chaudhry's powers before his court was useless, Zardari was adamant that he wanted to do it for history's sake.

Zardari said that the Constitution permitted him to file a presidential reference and seek an advisory opinion from the court.

"*Mai ne tau apne saarai ikhtiarat Parliament ko dai diye hain. Atharween tarmeem ke bad ab mai ye bhi na karoon? Mai tau Parliament ko mazboot kar kay hara hoon. Lekin ye samajhtai nahi*" (I have surrendered all my powers to Parliament. Why, even after the 18th Amendment, should I not do this [file a reference]? I am only strengthening Parliament. But these people do not understand), he said to me, disregarding the advice of the naysayers.

As expected, Chaudhry ruled that the Prime Minister and President's roles were no more than those of a post office.

He stretched to its limit the independence of the judiciary to mean its independence from the Constitution and the law. Instead of using his newfound power to repair the broken criminal justice system, he expanded his powers.

Obsessed with power, sound bites, and media headlines, Chaudhry refused Parliament's request to present the court's financial accounts to Parliament's Public Accounts Committee (PAC).

Later, his reckless verdict in cancelling international contracts involving a mining project in Balochistan and a power project in Karachi cost the country nearly 8 billion dollars in penalties.

Acquiring more and more power and using it injudiciously, Chaudhry, acting like the sole arbiter of national destiny, demolished constitutional structures.

Chaudhry stepped into the executive domain and ordered postings, transfers and disciplinary cases against senior government officials. It is a different matter that, in the end, he backed down when Zardari said that enough was enough.

Parliament tolerated Chaudhry's assault on it. Senior party leaders and legal luminaries around him were against doing anything that might displease him. His advisors prevailed on him not to make public the rise in the pay and perks of judges because Chaudhry did not want it. Zardari also had no love lost for Chaudhry. In opposing his reinstatement, he had gone as far as he could and failed. In private conversation, he revealed how dimly he regarded Chaudhry.

Zardari was wringing his hands against Chaudhry. An uneasy relationship leading to a clash was inevitable.

Chapter 8

Towards a head-on clash

Chaudhry frequently ordered transfers and postings of senior officials. Fearing him, senior bureaucrats complied with his orders, bypassing the Prime Minister. Initially, the government tolerated it, but by the end of July 2011, it had made the executive almost dysfunctional. On several private conversations, Zardari remarked that the government business could not be run like this.

Chaudhry had ordered the transfer of the police chief of Gilgit-Baltistan (GB). Complying with it, the establishment secretary issued transfer orders without even informing Prime Minister Yousaf Raza Gilani. The government responded by removing the establishment secretary and making him an Officer on Special Duty (OSD).

Simultaneously, the GB Chief Minister, who was from the PPP, also refused to relieve the police chief, defying Chaudhry's orders.

Not used to such rebuff, Chaudhry went into a tailspin and gave a 24-hour deadline to comply with the transfer orders.

Thundering to "defend the rule of law", he called a full court meeting on 27 July.

Zardari also dug in his heels.

A cabinet meeting was called for the same day. It declared that the cabinet would "defend the rule of law" and uphold the principle of separation of powers in accordance with the Constitution.

President Zardari was on a visit to Iran, Afghanistan, Saudi Arabia, and Dubai and was scheduled to return to Karachi. He sent a message to call an immediate meeting of all coalition partners in the Presidency and decided to return to the capital instead of Karachi.

The full court met in the Supreme Court building; the Cabinet in the Prime Minister's House; and the leaders of the coalition parties in the Presidency. They met separately on the same day, but the agenda was the same: the imminent Chaudhry-Zardari clash.

Zardari personally telephoned Sindh Governor Ishratul Ibad to ask about MQM's participation in the meeting of the coalition partners in the Presidency but received a cold response.

Eminent human rights defender and Supreme Court Bar Association (SCBA) President Asma Jahangir called me.

"I want to see you urgently," she said. "There is something very urgent and important."

"Can we talk on the phone?" I asked.

"Iftikhar Chaudhry has called me for an urgent meeting," she replied. She had just arrived from Lahore and wanted to see me before meeting Chaudhry.

I went to see her in the SCBA lodge in Islamabad. Two other lawyers were also with her.

She was concerned about the imminent head-on clash and advised restraint. She said campaigning for the Supreme Court bar elections had started, and the government's attitude towards the judiciary could be a game-changer.

"Confrontation with the judiciary will only increase the government's difficulties," she said.

She elaborated, "Every now and then, the bar will pass resolutions against the executive."

When I explained the background of the standoff, she was surprised by the judicial transgression: "Oh, Babar Saab, this is a serious violation of the principle of trichotomy of powers; I agree."

"So what do you suggest should be done? What should I tell the President?" I asked.

"Tell Zardari to hold his horses. I am going to meet Chaudhry shortly."

I informed the President about the conversation. He said, "OK."

After meeting Chaudhry, she told me she had conveyed concerns about the judiciary's interference in the executive. She said that she had impressed upon the Chief Justice that postings and transfers by the court were not consistent with the principle of the trichotomy of powers.

"What did he say?" I asked.

"*Uss nai bari ajeeb baat ki mujh sai.*" (He [referring to Chaudhry] said something highly unusual to me.)

She said the Chief Justice blamed the Attorney General (AG) for not arguing the case against the transfer of IG Gilgit-Baltistan that he had ordered. Chaudhry had told her the AG should have argued the case instead of hurriedly rushing to the Prime Minister with the court orders in hand.

"Isn't it strange that he issues orders and expects the attorney general to not implement them too readily and instead argue against them? Will it convince Zardari Saab to back off? The coalition partners are about to meet today," I said.

"You are right, Babar Saab, but you should know that public perception does not favour the government, and confrontation would not suit it. The bar will also not support the government."

She suggested that the Prime Minister make a strong statement on the floor of the house against the court's interference in the executive's functions. She also advised that any prolonged confrontation must be avoided: "Babar Saab, tell the President that the democratic system should continue."

Emphasising this, she disclosed that in the morning, the executive committee of the SCBA had drafted a strongly worded resolution against the government, which she had watered down with great difficulty.

She said there were "skeletons in the cupboard of the government, which was why the court was so aggressive and the government was helpless." She also mentioned the corruption case before the Supreme Court against the religious affairs minister, Hamid Saeed Kazmi.

Saying that the bar would endorse a strong statement by the Prime Minister on the house floor in support of the principle of the trichotomy of powers, she asked me to convey her message to the President before the coalition partners met.

The message in a nutshell was:

One, the court orders must be implemented, and the notification making the establishment secretary an OSD must be withdrawn.

Two, the Prime Minister should make a strong statement on the floor of the house about how the Supreme Court had been interfering in the day-to-day running of government business.

The bar would support the government in demanding this.

I rushed to the Presidency. The coalition meeting was about to start, and Zardari was on his way to the committee room. I conveyed Asma Jahangir's message. He listened intently.

"What other options are on the table? What else did she say? Is she sure that Chaudhry will keep his word and stop interfering?" He turned back, saying, "Let's go to the office and talk about it."

Back in his office, Zardari continued,

"*Mai Chaudhry ko janta hoon, wo iss ko itna nahi jaanti.*" (I know Chaudhry; she does not know him that well.)

However, the suggestion that the Prime Minister make a strong statement on the floor of the house against violation of the principle of the trichotomy of powers appealed to him.

On the matter of transferring the establishment secretary, the President said, "Let us see what others say," referring to the coalition meeting.

About "skeletons in the cupboards" and allegations against the religious affairs minister, he defended Hamid Saeed Kazmi.

He asked how much commission he (the minister) could have made on hiring Haj accommodation. It was not a dam building or power generation project, he said. Chaudhry Iftikhar is after Hamid Saeed Kazmi for other reasons; I know it.

"I know why he (the Chief Justice) is after him," he said. Zardari then briefed Prime Minister Gilani about it as the two approached the committee room.

Chapter 9

Coalition meets – warning: “enough is enough”

The mood in the meeting of coalition partners in the Presidency was sombre.

The President began by saying that he wanted to brainstorm some important issues. Waving a file, he said he had brought a summary of Chaudhry's transgressions and asked the law minister to brief the meeting. It read like a charge sheet.

The government faithfully implemented more than 50 Supreme Court judgments, even though these transgressed into the executive domain. The court verdict in a privatisation case caused multi-billion rupee losses to the exchequer. Apart from appointing over 100 judges on his own, Chaudhry also sacked 110 judges without giving them the right of defence.

Chaudhry wanted the five judges who had refused to be blackmailed and did not resign under pressure to be de-notified by the government. Gilani said that he had received a summary for their de-notification but was in a fix. If he removed them by an executive order, it would be unconstitutional, and later, he would be held accountable.

The meeting was informed that 54 secretaries, three FIA DGs, two NAB chairmen, and two of its prosecutor generals had been changed under Chaudhry's orders. Five law secretaries and two attorney generals also had to quit their jobs.

It was reported that the court even summoned Begum Nusrat Bhutto when she was already dead and there was no case against her.

"He wants to try the grave of Begum Sahiba," Zardari interjected at this point. "I will not permit it."

Works on the Rental Power Projects were stopped, and Chaudhry reversed the LNG contract. Court orders scuttled the power generation policy.

Regarding the implementation of court orders in the NRO case, the meeting was informed that the President was not named in it and that over ninety per cent of the court orders had been implemented.

The summary read out by the law minister said that Attorney

General Chaudhry Farooq's letter during the PML-N government requesting an inquiry by a Swiss magistrate against Zardari had been withdrawn by his successor, Malik Qayyum. Chaudhry maintained that while the letter by A.G. Farooq was legal, that by A.G. Malik Qayyum was not.

Saying that the NAB cases against him were still in the courts and not closed, Zardari asked, "What is the problem with Chaudhry? I really don't know."

The President then said that he had filed a reference in the Supreme Court to seek clarifications on the powers of executive authority, which was pending. Despite this, he said Chaudhry continued to order postings and transfers of officers whimsically.

The meeting was told that the court summoned the secretaries and forced them to issue posting/transfer notifications, and the Prime Minister only rubber-stamped them.

A senior FIA officer had complained in writing that he was forced to reverse the transfer of a subordinate who had served at the same station for over twenty years.

The President did not mention Asma Jahangir's intervention.

Some proposals were also made. The Rules of Business of the Supreme Court were deemed arbitrary and needed to be changed. The tenure of the Chief Justice and judges needed to be fixed, like that of the President, Prime Minister, services chiefs, and the chief election commissioner.

Zardari said that the Supreme Court had rendered the government dysfunctional, as senior bureaucrats threatened with jail looked up to the judges instead of the government. "This cannot go on. It must stop."

"*Hum isay inshaAllah aisa nahin rehnai daingai.*" (God-willing, we will not let it continue), he said emphatically.

Everyone concurred.

The meeting decided not to cede further ground to the Chaudhry court. It was time to stand up.

The President then asked, "How about raising the issue in Parliament also?"

Previously, the PPP legislators and legal wizards opposed discussing Chaudhry's conduct in Parliament. In today's coalition meeting, everyone agreed to call a joint session of Parliament. As time was short, it was decided that the Prime Minister would address the two houses separately and lay bare all the facts of judicial transgressions under Chaudhry.

Someone referred to Makhdoom Javed Hashmi's speech in the National Assembly soon after his release from jail, in which he made an impassioned plea to the judges not to transgress limits. Another said that Gilani was soft-spoken and that there should be an open debate where everyone should speak. "Chaudhry cannot question speeches in Parliament under the Constitution," yet another said.

Gilani smiled without commenting on the proposal. It was decided that the coalition parties' vocal leaders would "sing from the same music sheet" when using media platforms.

Zardari proposed that all Provincial Assemblies pass resolutions supporting Parliament's supremacy.

"The Pakhtunkhwa Provincial Assembly will be the first to do so," he said.

The Chief Minister Khyber Pakhtunkhwa asked that a resolution be prepared beforehand to be adopted in all assemblies. It was decided that the President would meet the Punjab PPP Parliamentary Party and take them into confidence.

The meeting upheld the decision to make Establishment Secretary Sohail Ahmed an OSD and asked the Prime Minister to stand by it. Inspector General of Police Gilgit-Baltistan, Hussain Asghar, would also not be relieved of his post, come what may.

A session of the National Assembly had already been summoned. The meeting asked the Prime Minister to make a hard-hitting speech.

It must be now or never. Enough is enough. The die had been cast.

Chapter 10

Chaudhry backs down

When the court reconvened the following day, Chief Justice Chaudhry adopted a more conciliatory tone. He refrained from demanding whether his orders to reverse the sacking of the establishment division secretary had been implemented within 24 hours, as he had previously insisted.

Attorney General Maulvi Anwarul Haq also took a diplomatic approach. Rather than asserting that postings and transfers fell under the executive's purview, he simply stated, "My Lord, I have not been able to meet the Prime Minister to discuss the matter and need more time for it."

Chaudhry was aware that his posting orders would not be implemented, but his ego had been sufficiently placated. He did not press the issue further, swiftly concluded the proceedings, and left Court Room One, feigning satisfaction that the government had agreed to comply with his orders.

Subsequently, the six-judge bench issued an order stating that the Gilgit-Baltistan Inspector General of Police, Hussain Asghar, should be reinstated in the Federal Investigation Agency (FIA) "whenever he was relieved from his current post." Notably, the order did not specify a timeframe, effectively deferring to executive authority. This allowed the Chief Minister of Gilgit-Baltistan to maintain his stance that he would not relieve the police chief based on the court's orders.

Regarding the establishment division secretary, the court retreated from its earlier demand for reinstatement within 24 hours. Instead, it merely stipulated that he should be given any other post within seven days. This concession acknowledged the chief executive's prerogative in matters of transfer and posting of senior government officers.

The court order, dictated by Chaudhry, also included elements of self-praise. It claimed that by declaring Musharraf's proclamation of emergency on 3 November 2007 and the subsequent order of 31 July 2009 unconstitutional, the court had safeguarded President Asif Ali Zardari's oath and protected the system. The order also expressed respect for Parliament as the law-making body, leaving interpretation to the courts, and commended Parliament for adopting the 18th and 19th Amendments.

The attorney general described it as "a beautiful order", momentarily flattering Chaudhry. However, the Chief Justice's satisfaction waned when the attorney general added, "It would go a long way in defining the domain of both the judiciary and the executive."

In the wake of the court verdict, President Zardari convened a meeting with provincial chief executives at the Presidency. Attendees included the governors of Punjab and Khyber Pakhtunkhwa; the Chief Ministers of Sindh, Khyber Pakhtunkhwa, Balochistan, and Gilgit-Baltistan; the President-elect and Prime Minister of Azad Kashmir; the leader of the opposition in the Punjab Assembly, and other executive authorities.

The meeting concluded that the Prime Minister no longer needed to deliver a forceful speech regarding judicial interference in the National Assembly. Notably, the chief executives deliberately refrained from praising the court as the final arbiter and custodian of the Constitution. Instead, the press release stated, "The meeting reiterated that Parliament reflected the will of the people and was the mother of state institutions and, therefore, supreme." This meeting effectively conveyed the message that postings and transfers of government officers remained within the executive's domain.

In a separate development, Chaudhry instructed all Supreme Court judges from provincial registries to return immediately to Islamabad and remain in the capital until further notice. This move evoked memories of similar posturing on 15 October 2010, when he had convened a 17-member full bench in response to false reports of government plans to reverse the 16 March 2009 order restoring superior court judges.

Questions arose about Chaudhry's motives: Was this a show of strength to deter the special National Assembly session scheduled three days later? Was it an attempt to mask his embarrassment? Whatever the reason, good sense ultimately prevailed, and a showdown was averted. An eerie calm settled over Islamabad.

Chapter 11

Chaudhry lobbied for reinstatement

Iftikhar Chaudhry had lobbied Zardari for his reinstatement but failed. Zardari said that Chaudhry's methods were crude and unbecoming.

The full extent of Chaudhry's efforts would not have come to light until he summoned Attorney General Latif Khosa to an open court hearing on 21 October 2009. Chaudhry called upon Khosa to answer some allegations of impropriety in a case during the tenure of former Chief Justice Abdul Hameed Dogar—Chaudhry's predecessor and nemesis. Khosa had been defence counsel for a sacked government officer who later turned against him.

Latif Khosa was deeply offended at having been summoned in this manner. He had expected to be called to the judge's chamber for a private explanation, given that no criminal case had been instituted against him. Chaudhry, however, was known for summoning people and dressing them down in open court, relishing the media headlines generated by his public observations. Khosa felt humiliated and was fuming.

In full view of the court, a furious Khosa reminded Chaudhry of a recent visit to his residence to seek a favour. He told Chaudhry that he had expected courtesy, not humiliation. Khosa did not specify what favour Chaudhry had sought from him.

Chaudhry was taken aback. No one had confronted him like this in open court before. He attempted to brush aside Khosa's pointed retort, saying, "It is an old story." Realising that he had almost blurted out a confession, Chaudhry tried to change the subject, but Khosa was unrelenting—the Baloch in him awakened.

"No Sir, No Sir, it is not a very old story," Khosa shot back. "After all, you came to my house on 1 March 2009 in the company of a civil judge in connection with your reinstatement." His remarks stunned everyone present.

"Never challenged in this manner before, Chaudhry was visibly uneasy, his face betraying the unease."

The encounter was indeed extraordinary. Khosa paused.

Later, I asked Latif Khosa about this incident. The account

of Chaudhry lobbying for his reinstatement was subsequently corroborated by Zardari himself, though not in such detail.

Allegedly, Chaudhry Iftikhar had visited Khosa in the Minister's Colony in Islamabad on 1 March 2009, accompanied by a former civil judge who had resigned in support of Chaudhry during the lawyers' protest movement.

"Chaudhry allegedly urged Khosa to intercede with Zardari for his reinstatement, promising also that he would create no problems for the government and asked Khosa to reassure Zardari on his behalf."

It is claimed that Chaudhry even offered to provide a signed resignation letter in advance in case he reneged on his commitment. The civil judge who had accompanied him acted as the intermediary. Chaudhry's primary concern was his own reinstatement; he did not appear to care whether other sacked judges were reinstated or not.

The message was conveyed to President Zardari, who declined to accept these assurances. Zardari did not want Chaudhry reinstated, believing he had become overtly political.

Chapter 12

A peep into Zardari's mind

Zardari provided a rare glimpse into his thoughts about the judiciary during a meeting with the Supreme Court Bar Association (SCBA) in August 2012 amid tensions.

In a 90-minute conversation with senior lawyers, he openly expressed his disappointment with some judges.

"I never wanted confrontation," he told the lawyers.

The SCBA President, Yasin Azad, acknowledged that the Chief Justice alone making all judicial appointments was problematic and expressed concern over the standoff with the judiciary. He offered to play the role of a mediator.

Yasin's willingness to intervene encouraged the President, who smiled approvingly.

"Why would we pick a fight with the judges whom we had released from house arrest?" Zardari said, attempting to reassure lawyers that he did not seek confrontation.

"I had told the Prime Minister to free the judges and not get involved in the fight between Musharraf and the judges. It was his [Musharraf's] fight, but Chaudhry turned it into a fight against democracy."

He continued, "Chaudhry might have thought he was making history, but actually, he was undoing everything. Even when Chaudhry made all appointments of judges, I did not react."

"He assumed my powers by shifting the President's powers to the Chief Justice. How could he do it? If I wanted, I really could have created hurdles. But I did not want any confrontation."

Without naming anyone specifically, Zardari said, "I know these judges inside and out. I have seen them in different situations. No one knows them as well as I do."

"How well do you know them? You are not a lawyer," a member of the delegation asked.

Provoked, Zardari responded scathingly: "As the Prime Minister's spouse, I have witnessed how some of them came running to me for appointment as judges. Most undignified I should say. Then I saw how vindictive they turned against me, only to prove themselves as independent in the public eye. I remember everything."

"I have seen them [judges] as an undertrial prisoner. I have seen how some have bent over backwards to please their masters."

"I may not be a lawyer, but legal education is not only taught in colleges and universities. It is also learnt in the courtrooms, whether one is a litigant or an accused. I have seen enough of it. I have some views based on my personal experience."

With anguish, he then recalled some instances.

"When I was given bail in the narcotics case, I was still kept in jail in the BMW [car] case," he said.

"This Chaudhry calls himself courageous and independent," he said laughingly. "It was the same Iftikhar Chaudhry who at that time dared not give me bail, saying every time that he had yet to study the case."

"But when we successfully negotiated the return to democracy, he readily granted me bail, and the order he wrote almost read like my acquittal," Zardari told the lawyers.

"The BMW car was not registered in my name, but I was kept in jail for two years for it."

Realising that he might have spoken rather too harshly, the President said, "Still, I did not take it as a personal affront. If I have to be in politics for larger objectives, I have to take such injustices in my stride. There is no complaint or grudge against any judge on this score."

He explained that he finally secured bail only after successful negotiations for the return to democracy and then left the country.

Admiring Law Secretary Yasmin Abbasi, who was present in the meeting, he said that he wanted more women judges because they were relatively fairer.

"As a sessions judge, Yasmin Abbasi also recorded correctly the statements of defendants. If she did not listen to everything I wanted to say, she also did not listen to everything that the prosecution wanted to say. That is fair enough. I have no complaints."

Zardari spoke about Chaudhry appointing all the judges by himself as if a serpent bit his soul. He also implied that

Chaudhry had made some promises but had reneged on them now, though he did not explain what those promises were.

"These things do not happen in a vacuum," he said with a tinge of regret.

"After Shaheed Benazir's assassination, Iftikhar Chaudhry came running to me."

"Maybe we had talked about all these issues and agreed upon some working relationship. Maybe I was taken for a ride. Maybe I wanted to test the waters. Maybe it was my patience to see how it would work out."

He seemed to suggest that he had discussed these issues with Chaudhry beforehand, and the latter had agreed but now had backtracked on his promises.

Continuing, he said, "Maybe there were some other reasons for it [Chaudhry appointing all judges]." As if accepting responsibility for how things panned out, he said, "But the fact is that I also let him fill all the vacancies. Maybe I should have resisted. Maybe I failed in that."

"But let me state that it was a result of dialogue that I allowed him to appoint judges. I wanted the democratic system to continue and for the sake of harmony between institutions."

"After Shaheed Bibi's assassination, when Chaudhry Iftikhar met me, he assured me that the judiciary would not disrupt the system," he told the lawyers.

The lawyers exchanged glances as Zardari spoke. No one interrupted him with questions or pressed him for more details.

This was the first time Zardari spoke of Chaudhry, assuring him of support if he were reinstated.

"But just look at what they [judges] did," he said, scratching his palm.

"I was going to meet [Russian President] Putin, planning to talk about new regional and international alignments. Just as I landed in Moscow and was still at the airport, the judiciary sent Gilani [Prime Minister] home, and I had to turn back immediately, cancelling the visit."

"A great opportunity had been lost," he said. "I had to talk with Putin about something and had great hopes. All of that came to nothing," he groaned.

"Now I will wait for Putin to visit Pakistan to talk. But there is a difference between talking with Putin in Islamabad and me travelling to Moscow especially to talk about the possibilities of new alignments."

"I cannot take from Putin in Islamabad what I could hope to get from him during my visit to Moscow," he said without explaining what "new alignments" he had in mind to discuss with Putin.

"But these people [judges] do not understand this."

He told the lawyers, "The Chief Justice calls grade 22 officers and threatens them with jail every now and then, not realising how demoralising it is for the bureaucracy and the functioning of the government."

"The IG has been summoned over a dozen times. The FIA has concluded that there is no case against Hamid Saeed Kazmi [Minister for Haj], but he has been denied bail. We all know very well that a sessions judge can't give bail when the CJP makes such remarks in the court."

"Take the case of my immunity. The Constitution has given me immunity. The international legal regime allows me immunity. The case [SGS Cotecna] is well known. The Supreme Court said that the bias of the trial judge floated on the surface of the record. The court did not say this about the investigating agency or prosecution, but it said that the judge was biased."

"If the judge was biased, the court should have taken action against him. But the Supreme Court only remanded the case to the lower court. It was a case of double jeopardy."

"Then came the NRO, and the same case was reopened. I endured it. The Swiss magistrate verdict is on the record."

Pointing towards law minister Farooq Naek, he said, "Naek will give you all the details. You can see it for yourself."

"Chaudhry Iftikhar stopped the investigation in the case of his son Arsalan but is insisting on an investigation in my case, even though it was a closed and past transaction, and I had constitutional immunity."

Zardari also discussed judges' suo moto powers. He said

denying the right to appeal in such cases was a denial of justice.

"Iftikhar asked us to remove Attorney General Latif Khosa. We accepted it. He promised that matters would be all right if Khosa was removed. But it did not happen. He did not keep his promise. We showed patience in this case also."

Zardari rarely shared his inner thoughts with anyone outside his close circle. Today was different.

Section Five

ZARDARI AND THE OSAMA BIN LADEN FIASCO

Chapter 1

Raid on the OBL compound

On Monday, 2 May 2011, the ADC (Aide-de-Camp) to the President called around 6:30 A.M., asking me to come to the Presidency immediately for a "very important and urgent meeting". The Presidency typically observed normal government timings for official business, with the President usually arriving at the office around midday. Being summoned so early was most extraordinary. I instinctively knew something had gone terribly wrong, but I didn't know what.

When I asked, the ADC said that Foreign Minister Hina Rabbani Khar and Foreign Secretary Salman Bashir were also being summoned to the Presidency and then hung up. Perhaps he knew but didn't want to discuss it.

I asked myself: Why so early in the morning? What had happened?

My thoughts turned to the meeting the previous night at the Presidency with the Chaudhries of Gujrat, which had continued into the early hours. No disturbing news had come from anywhere until then. If anything had happened, it must have been after the meeting ended. This meant that something serious had occurred between 1:30 and 6 A.M., I reasoned.

I tried to reach out to Hina Rabbani Khar and Salman Bashir but failed.

While driving to the Presidency, I received a phone call from journalist Mazhar Abbas in Karachi.

"*Assalam o Alaikum Babar Saab, mera khial hai ke Amreecion ko pata lag gaya tha ke Osama Abbottabad mai chupha hua tha*" (I think the Americans had found out that Osama was hiding in Abbottabad), he said, quickly adding, "*Lekin mujhe pata nahi hai.*" (But I don't know.)

As he said this, my mind swirled, and I swerved the car. Now I knew what the "urgent meeting" was about.

For a few moments, I was speechless.

For the past decade, Pakistan has been denying any knowledge about Osama. It had been caught on the wrong foot. Several years ago, Afghan President Karzai had talked of Osama hiding in Abbottabad. He was jeered at the time. Amid thoughts like these, I did not utter a word to Mazhar.

"Hello Babar Saab, *Awaaz aarahi hai*?" (Hello, Babar Saab, can you hear me?), Mazhar asked impatiently.

"*Haan, haan, Mazhar Saab, aap ki awaaz aa rahi hai. Mai Aiwan-e Sadr hi jaa raha hoon, phir baat karoon ga*" (Yes, yes Mazhar Saab, I can hear you. I am on my way to the President's House, will talk later), I said, pretending I knew about the cataclysmic incident, and hung up.

Mazhar wasn't sure about the OBL raid and wanted confirmation. Unwittingly, he had learnt from me that the President had called an early morning meeting at the Presidency. He may or may not have been the first journalist in the country to learn about the midnight raid, but he was the first to learn of this urgent meeting. As a journalist, he must have drawn some satisfaction from getting such an important clue.

Unknowingly, I had also learned from him that the U.S. had taken out OBL. I felt an eerie sense of satisfaction that I was armed with this vital piece of information while heading towards the Presidency for a fateful meeting.

My mind churned as I drove to the President's House.

Irresistibly, my thoughts turned to the mundane talks in the Presidency the previous night, occurring just as the world's most wanted terrorist, hiding in the military cantonment in Abbottabad, was being taken out by the U.S.

The meeting was about power-sharing between PPP and PML-Q. I, along with others, participated in it.

I couldn't help thinking that just when OBL was being targeted, the President, the Prime Minister, and a few others, oblivious to what was happening nearby, were wrangling over power-sharing. I also couldn't help thinking that no one in the nuclear-armed country boasting of the world's top intelligence network had the faintest idea—literally no one—not the President, Prime Minister, Army Chief, or the ISI. These thoughts were unsettling. A sense of guilt and shame was overpowering.

Later, I learnt that the President's ADC, Squadron Leader Jalal, who had also returned home after the meeting, was still awake. At around 2:30 A.M., he learnt that a helicopter had crashed just a while ago in Abbottabad.

As a PAF pilot, he instinctively knew something had gone wrong.

Why was a helicopter flying at night in hilly Abbottabad? Pilots don't fly helicopters at night, a life in PAF had taught him. It sounded unbelievable, negating his lifelong training and knowledge of the strict protocols of PAF helicopter flights.

If it wasn't a PAF helicopter that had crashed, whose was it? He asked himself. What was it doing in hilly Abbottabad, a military cantonment and home to the Pakistan Military Academy in nearby Kakul, at that odd hour?

Suspicious, he rushed back to the office. It was 3 A.M., and all was quiet. He started calling his contacts in the PAF and elsewhere to investigate. He was the first among the President's staff to learn about what had happened.

He still didn't break the news to the President. Perhaps the information he had gathered wasn't entirely accurate. He knew that bells on telephone hotlines between the decision-makers would soon be ringing, and the President would be informed if he hadn't already been.

He was right. The telephone bell rang. The switchboard operator of the Army House was on the line.

"The chief is on his way to the Presidency," the caller said, asking the ADC to inform the President. The authoritative information that the Army Chief had already left his house showed that Kayani had already spoken with the President on the direct hotline without ADC Jalal knowing it.

Jalal immediately informed the President that the Army Chief was coming to see him. The ADC learnt that the President was awake and hadn't slept till then after the late-night meeting when the Army Chief called him.

I arrived at the Presidency before 7 A.M. Except for ADC Jalal, none of the President's personal staff was around.

From the whispering tones of the attendants and guards, it appeared that they, too, had learned something unusual had happened.

I learnt that President Obama had also called Zardari.

As I sat in the ADC's office, I couldn't avoid thinking about the previous night's meeting and juxtaposing it with the U.S. Navy SEALs' daring operation in Abbottabad. I thought about intelligence agencies hunting for Osama and the claims that he was nowhere in Pakistan. I thought of Musharraf's false claims that Osama had died due to kidney failure. I thought of Benazir Bhutto saying at the time that Musharraf was not gunning for the militant but actually "running with the hare and hunting with the hound".

These thoughts haunted me then and haunt me today.

Chapter 2

Power wrangling in Islamabad

The defence forces and intelligence agencies were unaware of what was unfolding in the cantonment in Abbottabad. Meanwhile, in Islamabad, the two coalition partners, PPP and PML-Q, were engrossed in wrangling over a power-sharing formula, just as U.S. Navy Seals were eliminating Osama bin Laden.

The meeting in the Presidency commenced after dinner on 1 May. Presided over by Zardari, it was attended by Prime Minister Yousaf Raza Gilani, Makhdoom Amin Fahim and Raja Pervaiz Ashraf from the PPP side, and Chaudhry Shujaat Hussain and Chaudhry Parvez Elahi from the PML-Q side. Law Minister Farooq Naek, real estate tycoon Malik Riaz, and I were also present.

The discussions over power sharing, which continued until midnight, resulted in a broad-based agreement. The PML-Q would receive six federal ministries, five ministers of state, two advisors to the Prime Minister with the status of federal ministers, and some adjustments on a few seats to be made later in the next general elections.

However, its finalisation took time as the PML-Q continually sought more concessions.

They asked that one of their ministers, along with Makhdoom Amin Fahim of PPP, be designated senior minister. They also demanded that PML-Q have a say in appointing the secretaries of their ministries.

Both sides agreed. To ensure neither party reneged on the agreement over power-sharing, it was decided to formalise it in a "Memorandum of Understanding" (MOU).

It was around 11:30 P.M. on 1 May.

When the draft was ready, Chaudhry Parvez Elahi examined it and demanded that he be named deputy Prime Minister. The post did not exist in the constitutional scheme, so how could anyone demand it?

His cousin Chaudhry Shujaat had tasted glory as caretaker Prime Minister for a few weeks under Musharraf. Zardari, generous to a fault, listened as Elahi insisted that some way be found to accommodate his request. "Nothing is impossible," he said.

Zardari turned to Farooq Naek for advice.

Naek and Malik Riaz stepped out for consultations.

Naek returned with a handwritten note. It read: "PPPP and PML-Q covenant that the post of deputy Prime Minister of Pakistan will be created, if possible, after making necessary amendments in the Constitution of the Islamic Republic of Pakistan 1973, to accommodate PML-Q."

Without considering its implications, Elahi readily agreed. He may have assumed that the post of Deputy Prime Minister had thus been created and he would be appointed to it the next day.

Farooq Naek chuckled and glanced at me, as if to say, "Poor Chaudhry Parvez Elahi."

The power-sharing formula also envisaged PML-Q unequivocally supporting the federal government's policies and cooperating in the creation of the South Punjab province.

Parvez Elahi then asked that the creation of a separate province of Hazara be included as well.

Zardari refused, advising Elahi to speak with Asfandyar Wali Khan and the Awami National Party (ANP) before the PPP agreed. Elahi did not push the issue further. Perhaps he had raised it only to be able to claim later that he had advocated for the Hazara province, but Zardari had refused.

The draft memorandum was amended accordingly and brought back for signatures. It was already past midnight. Parvez Elahi made further demands.

As senior minister, he wanted to use the Prime Minister's helicopter and aircraft. Zardari looked to Gilani. Elahi also asked for an office for the Deputy Prime Minister in Lahore, preferably in the State Guest House. Zardari agreed to this as well.

"Who will oversee the implementation of the accord?" Elahi then asked.

After some discussion, it was decided that a two-member committee comprising Prime Minister Yousaf Raza Gilani and PML-Q President Chaudhry Shujaat Hussain would oversee the agreement's implementation.

"Who will arbitrate in case of disagreement between Gilani and Shujaat?" Elahi pressed.

Naek further amended the draft: "In the event of disagreement in the two-member implementation committee, the matter will be referred to Mr Asif Ali Zardari, President of Pakistan, whose decision shall be final and binding on both PPPP and PML-Q."

Naek ensured that Zardari retained the trump card.

Elahi then further requested that the memorandum also mention the perks and privileges he would be entitled to as Deputy Prime Minister. By this time, everyone was growing weary and eager to finalise the deal.

The agreement was finally sealed around 1:30 A.M. on 2 May, precisely when U.S. Navy Seals were infiltrating the country, raiding the compound, killing Osama bin Laden, and escaping with his body – announcing to the world that the most wanted terrorist had been hiding in a military cantonment in Pakistan.

The written agreement opened by expressing the desire to "strengthen democracy and good governance in the country" and for the "benefit of the citizens of Pakistan to solve the problems and difficulties faced by them".

The realisation that the raid on the OBL compound was taking place just as politicians were wrangling over power-sharing while the defenders remained unaware was deeply unsettling, evoking feelings of embarrassment, despair, and fear.

Chapter 3

The power-sharing MOU

The Memorandum of Understanding on power-sharing opened with an expression of "desire to strengthen democracy and good governance" and to "solve the problems and difficulties faced by the people".

Below is the text of the MOU signed that night but not made public. It is reproduced here in its original form.

"This Memorandum of Understanding is made on this 2nd day of May, 2011 by and between Pakistan People's Party Parliamentarians (PPPP) and Pakistan Muslim League Quaid-e-Azam (PML-Q).

WHEREAS the PPPP and PML-Q desire to strengthen democracy and good governance in the country.

AND WHEREAS PPPP and PML-Q desire that Pakistan's political culture of transfer of power must be based on fair and transparent election.

AND WHEREAS PPPP and PML-Q have decided to work together for the benefit of the citizens of Pakistan in order to solve the problems and difficulties faced by them.

AND WHEREAS PPPP and PML-Q have thus agreed to form alliance/ coalition government in the Centre headed by the Prime Minister of PPPP.

NOW THEREFORE PPPP and PML-Q enter into this Memorandum of Understanding on the following mutual covenants and undertakings set forth hereinafter:-

1. PPPP and PML-Q covenant that either of them will not enter into any political talk or understanding with PML-N without taking each other into confidence.

2. PPPP covenants to offer six Federal Ministries whose Federal Ministers shall make oath as envisaged by the Constitution of Islamic Republic of Pakistan, 1973 to the parliamentarians nominated by PML-Q. The Federal Secretaries of the said ministries will also be appointed as requested by the PML-Q in accordance with the prevailing rules and laws.

3. PML-Q covenants to nominate five parliamentarians who shall be appointed Minister of States in the Ministries to be decided with the mutual consent by PPPP and PML-Q

and shall make oath as envisaged by the Constitution of Islamic Republic of Pakistan, 1973.

4. PML-Q covenants to nominate two persons who shall be appointed Advisors to the Prime Minister with the status of the Federal Minister.

5. PPPP and PML-Q covenant that out of the six Federal Ministers having made oath on the nomination made by PML-Q one of them will designated as Senior Federal Minister along with Makhdoom Amin Fahim. He will be entitled to the use of helicopter and aircraft earmarked for the use of Prime Minister of Islamic Republic of Pakistan subject to availability and the rules/laws in this regard. The Senior Federal Minister will also be entitled to maintain an office in Lahore preferably in State Guest House, Lahore, subject to rules and laws in this regard.

6. PPPP and PML-Q covenant that in the next election of National Assembly, four Provincial Assemblies and Local Government, seat adjustments with regard to the candidates contesting these elections will be made between PPPP and PML-Q. Both the parties PPPP and PML-Q undertake to fully support each others' nominated candidates in the next elections as mentioned hereinabove.

7. PML-Q candidates, if any, will be considered in the next election of the Senate of Pakistan by PPPP subject to PML-Q candidates having majority of votes for getting elected on the seats they are contesting.

8. PPPP and PML-Q covenant that post of Deputy Prime Minister of Pakistan will be created, if possible, after making necessary amendments in the Constitution of Islamic Republic of Pakistan 1973, to accommodate PML-Q.

9. PPP undertakes that the development funds of the same amount will be disbursed to the Member of National Assembly (MNA) of PML-Q as are being disbursed to the MNA of PPPP.

10. PML-Q undertakes to fully support the coalition government headed by Prime Minister of PPPP on all the policies and decisions taken by President and Prime Minister

of Pakistan, failing whereof this Memorandum of Understanding is liable to termination at the option of PPPP.

11. PPPP and PML-Q undertake to cooperate with each other in Provinces and Provincial Assemblies on the terms and conditions to be mutually agreed upon.

12. PPPP and PML-Q undertake to co-operate with each other for the creation of new provinces specially South of Punjab (Seraiki) and Hazara province subject to Constitution and approval by Awami National Party (ANP) inclusive of making necessary amendments in 'the Constitution of Islamic Republic of Pakistan, 1973'.

13. A Committee comprising of Mr Yousaf Raza Gilani, Prime Minister of Pakistan and Chaudhry Shujaat Hussain, former Prime Minister of Pakistan, is hereby formed for giving effect to the covenants and undertakings contained in this Memorandum of Understanding to oversee the working of alliance/coalition and remove difficulties, wherever and whenever, they would occur in the smooth functioning of the alliance/coalition.

14. Any difference or dispute arising between alliance/coalition partners viz PPPP and PML-Q will be settled by the said committee.

15. However, in case of difference between the two members of the said committee, the matter will be referred to Mr Asif Ali Zardari, President of Pakistan, to resolve the difference or dispute, whose decision shall be final and binding on both PPPP and PML-Q.

16. NOW IN WITHNESS WHEREOF Makhdoom Amin Fahim President and Raja Parvez Ashraf Secretary General respectively of PPPP and Chaudhry Shujaat Hussain President and Chaudhry Parvez Elahi, Secretary General respectively of PML-Q have set and subscribed their respective hands on the Memorandum of Understanding, having authority and power to do so, on the date and year aforementioned at Islamabad."

After the meeting ended, Chaudhry Parvez Elahi handed me a draft of some points he wanted included in the press release. Among other things, it stated that higher education and curriculum were federal subjects and would remain with the federal government.

I said, "Chaudhry Saab, how can we include it in the press release? These were not even discussed."

"*Kee faraq painda ae, paa dewo*" (What difference does it make? Just include it), he replied.

Chapter 4

Early hours of the crisis

The Army Chief was already on his way to the Presidency. The Prime Minister, foreign secretary, and DG ISI (Director General, Inter-Services Intelligence) also arrived. The huddle took place on the residence side of the presidential complex. Foreign Minister Hina Rabbani Khar came a little later, having just returned from a foreign visit.

The meeting in the conference room lasted for over ninety minutes.

The dimly lit conference room, opening into the lobby, was heavy with tension.

I was in the lobby when the President and the Army Chief emerged together from the meeting, pacing towards the lift.

It wasn't easy to read Zardari's face. The space in the lobby seemed unreal. Every minute felt like hours. It was challenging to readily believe every word spoken in this zone of time and space.

Unreadable though his face may have been, Zardari's mind must have been racing with questions and thoughts, but he did not show it.

As Kayani left, the President took me aside and, looking over his shoulder, asked: "What do you think?"

"Complicit or sheer incompetence, nothing else," I said almost spontaneously.

I added, "An inquiry must be ordered immediately. Some action must be seen to have been taken against the army and ISI chiefs."

I thought of the inquiries ordered by civil governments into Ojhri and Kargil in the past, which resulted in the sacking of the civilian governments instead of uncovering the truth and punishing the guilty.

It was as if I spoke only to myself. It was a monologue. Zardari listened but did not utter a word. It was impossible to discern his thoughts in those moments.

Zardari often used to say, *"Deewaron ke bhi kaan hotai hain."* (the walls also have ears.) He always kept his cards close to his chest.

"We will talk about it later," he said and turned back, leaving me alone.

As he walked away, he paused to look at a picture on the wall. It was as if he wanted to reassure those around him not to worry and that everything was under control. Through body language and gestures, he seemed to project a sense of calm and display a measure of confidence. It was difficult to say whether he was pretending.

President Obama had already called President Zardari soon after the raid. In his memoirs, Obama wrote that once the U.S. had killed bin Laden, he called several world leaders to break the news. He also phoned the then-President of Pakistan, Asif Ali Zardari, who "showed genuine emotion, recalling how his wife, Benazir Bhutto, had been killed by extremists with reported ties to Al Qaeda," Obama said.

"I expected my most difficult call to be with Pakistan's beleaguered President, Asif Ali Zardari, who would surely face a backlash at home over our violation of Pakistani sovereignty," Obama wrote. "When I reached him, however, he expressed congratulations and support. "Whatever the fallout," he said, "it's very good news."

By 9 A.M. Pakistan time, President Obama had addressed his nation. The world had come to know that the most wanted terrorist had been taken out in Pakistan, where he had been sheltering for almost a decade.

National and international media were getting restless for an official reaction, but in utter confusion and disbelief, no state organ was ready to say a word. The Presidency, the Prime Minister's House, the foreign office, the ministry of information, and the ISPR (Inter-Services Public Relations)—none had anything authoritative to say.

Shock, confusion, and paralysis reigned.

It took more than 14 hours to formulate an official response.

Pakistan was caught in a most embarrassing situation. It could neither claim credit for the operation nor admit to a dismal intelligence failure and lack of army preparedness. It was a clear case of complicity or incompetence. Caught between a rock and a hard place, it took long to formulate a response.

If the army leadership indeed had any prior knowledge, they

would have at least been ready with a statement for immediate release. It would not have taken them so long to prepare an official press release. The confusion, indecision, and groping in the dark were obvious.

When the official response was finally prepared, it stated, "We have had extremely effective intelligence-sharing arrangements with several intelligence agencies, including that of the U.S." It claimed to have had "extremely effective intelligence-sharing" in the past but could not go beyond that.

Osama had been hiding in a military cantonment for years. Now, the U.S. had taken him out as completely and as secretly as he had been sheltered without informing Pakistan. The official press release's claim that intelligence-sharing with the U.S. had made it possible looked hollow and unconvincing. The web of lies and deceit had been exposed and failed to arouse any conviction.

Obama spoke to his people early because he was prepared to say what had to be said. There was no confusion and no procrastination. His initial comments were as swift and decisive as the operation by Navy SEALs, meticulously planned and successfully executed within 40 minutes.

The contrasting initial responses of Washington and Islamabad during the early hours – indeed throughout the first day on 2 May – of the crisis said it all.

The intelligence and military leadership had been boxed into a situation of "complicity or incompetence". Some retired generals later tried to spin the narrative, suggesting that the army's top leadership knew of the raid. They were not ready to swallow the spectacular humiliation. They tried unsuccessfully to claim that the top army leadership had even cooperated in its execution. It was hard for them to admit that the institution they had served for so long was caught unaware. The image of invincibility had come crashing down before their eyes.

The apologists mistakenly thought that people readily believed them. Later, the U.S. also publicly stated at the highest level and in bilateral talks that it had kept the operation secret from Pakistani authorities. The spurious claims initially made by the apologists that the army leadership knew were exposed.

Chapter 5

Defending the indefensible – the Washington Post article

By the end of the first day of the raid on 2 May, it appeared that a decision had been taken to vigorously defend the ISI and military leadership against allegations of complicity or failure.

The first indication came when the lobbyist placed an article by President Zardari in the *Washington Post.* The article, titled "Pakistan Did Its Part", stated:

"Although the events of Sunday were not a joint operation, a decade of cooperation and partnership between the United States and Pakistan led up to the elimination of Osama bin Laden as a continuing threat to the civilised world. And we in Pakistan take some satisfaction that our early assistance in identifying an Al Qaeda courier ultimately led to this day."

It also claimed, "The war on terrorism is as much Pakistan's war as it is America's."

The operation to eliminate Osama bin Laden was America's success, not Pakistan's. The claim made in the article that Pakistan made it possible was farfetched and aroused disbelief. To draw "satisfaction" from, and even claim credit for, a brazen military operation on its soil by the U.S. without its knowledge did not reflect well on its author. Moreover, this narrative diverged significantly from that of the PPP under Benazir Bhutto, who had said that General Musharraf was "running with the hare and hunting with the hound" in the war on terror and that the security apparatus had "run amok." The article appeared to defend what was indefensible. I believed Zardari was ill-served.

I was unaware of the decision to publish the article and was surprised. I sent an e-mail to the lobbyist:

"I wish there had been some consultation before placing an article in the name of President Zardari and that too in a U.S. paper on a subject as sensitive as OBL operation. We had avoided direct comments by President thus far. A decision had been taken in consultation with the President that only Foreign Office will issue formal statement and the President will not be exposed to media unless absolutely necessary. I have serious reservations about it. By placing such an article the President seems to be pandering unconvincingly to U.S. public opinion at enormous cost to domestic public opinion. I fail to understand the need for the article at this time. Regards FB."

The lobbyist did not respond.

The next day, the article was discussed during a media briefing session with the President. When I said it was ill-timed and ill-served the President, he remained silent. He looked towards Farah Ispahani, a competent media professional in the President's media team and wife of Pakistan's ambassador to the U.S., Hussain Haqqani. I presumed the lobbyist might have placed the article in consultation with Ambassador Haqqani.

The President did not want to discuss it further. I guessed that someone had recommended it to him. He may have authorised it in principle but did not review its contents. He trusted his advisors and was ready to accept the blame if the advice was wrong.

The President often talked of finding an opportunity in every crisis and the need to turn it to one's advantage. This morning, however, he admitted that nothing in the OBL raid could be termed an opportunity or turned to advantage.

The OBL operation had provided an opportunity for ISI and the military leadership to be held accountable. It also presented a chance for introspection and self-assessment by the military leadership. However, no one was prepared to even discuss these possibilities.

Ambassador Haqqani in Washington had, in reply to a question, said that it was "normal to hold an inquiry into such incidents." This statement was not repeated by any state official in Islamabad, and Haqqani also did not reiterate it. There was no word in the *Washington Post* article about introspection, let alone accountability of the state's intelligence apparatus.

Indeed, on 5 May, the foreign secretary addressed a press conference and declared that no inquiry was being held into the OBL incident. "A review of workings after such incidents is normal," he said, but categorically stated that there would be no inquiry.

Not only was any inquiry ruled out, but gloss was also put

on the failure of intelligence agencies by claiming that such failures were not unusual. On a visit to Paris, Prime Minister Yousaf Raza Gilani said that Pakistan's intelligence agencies were not alone in failing in their missions. He remarked that such failures of intelligence agencies had been observed throughout the world.

The *Washington Post* article, the foreign office statement, and the Prime Minister's statements effectively exonerated those responsible for the OBL fiasco.

In contrast, the corps commanders' meeting in Rawalpindi declared that an inquiry would be held. The Army Chief cancelled his planned visit to Brussels to emphasise the seriousness of the commanders' declaration.

The commanders wanted to be portrayed in a positive light. The civilian leadership, on the other hand, looked rather pale in comparison.

Simultaneously, mysterious demonstrations began to be held in Islamabad and other cities in support of the army and intelligence leadership. One incident of the show of public support was quite telling.

Ten days after the OBL fiasco, the President visited Moscow. I had already arrived there with the advance party.

While I was waiting at the Moscow airport to receive President Zardari, Political Secretary Fouzia Habib rang from Islamabad. She had been approached by an official who advised her to direct party workers to participate in a public rally the next day in support of the army and intelligence agency. He told her that the rally had been organised by some political parties, traders, and civil society members.

As an experienced and highly responsible political worker, she sought the President's permission before asking the local party chapter to participate in the demonstration. The President was already airborne, and she could not reach him, so she called me for advice.

I told her the PPP would look bad if its workers participated in such a mysterious rally. Those who had organised the rally should have gathered the people themselves and not asked the

PPP to organise it.

When I asked who had made the request, she said: "*Bas ye na poochain telephone par.*" (Don't ask about this on the phone.) She also said that the caller was not a political worker from any political party.

The PPP did not participate in the rally. It was a flop.

When I talked to her about it back in Islamabad, Fouzia Habib said that she did not personally know the caller. "No, I didn't know him. I don't even remember his name," she said.

When I asked if he had introduced himself with some title or rank, she confirmed that he had claimed to be a uniformed officer. She further said, "He may have been an impersonator who, thinking that being the daughter of a former army officer, I would be more amenable to a request from him."

Every effort was made to defend the indefensible.

Chapter 6

Opportunity for intelligence overhaul lost

Two weeks after the OBL raid, the Tehrik-i-Taliban Pakistan (TTP) and Al Qaeda launched a deadly attack on PNS Mehran Airbase in Karachi, the headquarters of the Pakistan Navy's Air Arm and a highly protected military installation near the Air Force's Faisal Air Base. This was no ordinary attack; two P3-C Orion surveillance aircraft were also destroyed.

The assault demonstrated the militants' capability to strike at the heart of a military establishment. The attackers had not only infiltrated the base but also held off military personnel for nearly 17 hours. The unsettling thought that terrorists could strike anytime, anywhere, loomed large. Fears were expressed that the attack could only have happened with inside help. Some likened it to a "blueprint for an attack on a nuclear facility."

This incident dealt another blow to the state's intelligence apparatus, still reeling from the OBL fiasco.

I had an opportunity to discuss the matter in detail with the President. Regarding preparations to repel similar attacks, the President said, "It was not just lack of it [preparations]; there was no preparation at all."

He added, "I keep my four guns well protected, but they had left precious aircraft and equipment unprotected."

The OBL and PNS Mehran fiascos presented an opportunity for intelligence overhaul.

The President acknowledged that he wanted an inquiry commission, but not with a view to punish anyone. "Its aim should be to plug loopholes in the security arrangements and not to punish anyone," he said, rejecting suggestions of accountability.

Zardari mentioned he had read the 9/11 report and the report on the 2008 Mumbai attack. He noted that investigations in both cases focused on improving procedures and systems, not on punishing individuals.

"Download these reports from the internet and read them," he urged me.

I looked up the reports online.

The U.S. 9/11 Commission's report resulted in a major reform of the U.S. intelligence apparatus. A new office, the Office of the Director of National Intelligence (ODNI), was created, bringing all intelligence agencies under one umbrella.

In the Mumbai attacks, where the operational control of terrorists was in the hands of people from abroad, the National Security Guards (NSG) commandos killed all the attackers. The incident also resulted in the creation of a major maritime defence and surveillance architecture to prevent a repeat of 26/11. Several suspects inside India were arrested and faced trials.

There was a qualitative difference between the 9/11 and Mumbai attacks on the one hand and the OBL operation on the other. In the former cases, the attackers were non-state actors operating from foreign lands. In the case of OBL, a wanted terrorist was hiding in Pakistan and was taken out by state actors from a foreign land amid suspicions that elements within the Pakistani state had sheltered him. There was a strong case not only for intelligence overhaul but also for accountability. However, nothing happened. Indeed, a Private Member's Bill to bring the intelligence agencies under the ambit of legislation was not allowed to be moved.

During Benazir's first government, a commission set up under Air Chief Marshal Zulfikar Ali Khan had recommended an intelligence overhaul, but its recommendations were never implemented. Like 9/11 in the U.S., the OBL raid in Abbottabad provided ample justification, indeed the need, for overhauling the ISI and bringing it under some legislation. But it was not done. The opportunity was lost.

Zardari thought that an inquiry would drag the army leadership through the mud when the country was in a state of war against militants, and it would be unwise and counterproductive.

"Let bygones be bygones," he seemed to say, endorsing Chaudhry Shujaat Hussain's philosophy of "*Matti pao.*" (Forget it).

Zardari also mentioned that an important country had

expressly advised him not to take punitive action against the army generals. He did not name the country.

I remembered that the President had paid a two-day visit to Kuwait and met the Emir. As the hour-long delegation-level formal meeting was coming to an end, the Emir asked Zardari about the OBL raid.

The President asked the delegation members to leave so he could meet with the Emir one-on-one. No one knew what transpired in that meeting. Was Kuwait the foreign country that had advised against punishing the generals?

Thus, there would be no investigations, accountability, or restructuring of the intelligence apparatus in the wake of the OBL fiasco. The civilian leadership had cold feet and did not want it. The military leadership did not want it to protect their pride. It was claimed that some foreign governments also did not want it.

The opportunity for intelligence overhaul was lost.

Chapter 7

Tough diplomacy post-OBL

Two weeks after the OBL raid, Senator John Kerry, Chairman of the Senate Foreign Relations Committee, arrived in Islamabad from Kabul on 15 May to engage in some "tough-talking". Before leaving Kabul, he told reporters that the discovery of OBL in a military cantonment close to Islamabad had raised "some very serious issues". Calling it a "critical moment", he also warned of "consequences that can be profound".

Kerry had set the tone for tough diplomacy before arriving in Islamabad.

The foreign office faced a challenging and complex task of cleaning up a mess that was not its creation. On the one hand, it had to defend the indefensible decision that no inquiry would be held and no heads would roll; on the other, it had to convince that there was no complicity in hiding OBL. It was a tall order, as Kerry had said, "There is some evidence of Pakistan government knowledge of some of these activities in ways that are very disturbing."

"I will demand answers from Pakistani leaders on Osama bin Laden," he had declared. The foreign office had to formulate these answers and confront Kerry, who was coming with "evidence" and warnings that Washington would consider "all options", the foreign office was expected to produce miracles.

Upon arrival, Kerry first met with the Army Chief. The next day, he met with the Prime Minister before going to the Presidency for a joint meeting with the President, the Prime Minister, and the Army Chief.

Kerry wanted no media coverage and only a small call group for the meeting. For him, it was not business as usual.

The joint meeting lasted 150 minutes, causing another high-level foreign delegation to wait for their scheduled call with the President. Ambassador Haqqani had arrived from Washington for the meeting.

Before the meeting started, Haqqani confided to me that the security establishment had been caught on the wrong foot. He explained that instead of pointing fingers directly at some individuals or an institution, the U.S. preferred using the euphemism of "government".

He added that the Americans even knew the contractor who had built the OBL hideout in Abbottabad and several other "safe houses". Furthermore, he mentioned that a trove of pictures was available to the U.S. Administration.

As everyone settled down, Kerry looked around and said that someone had suggested to him that the press conference at the end of the meeting should call for the need to repair damaged ties and avoid isolation. Without mentioning who had advised him, he stated, "No. Repairing damaged ties and avoiding isolation requires concrete measures and evidence."

CIA chief Leon Panetta had publicly stated that the U.S. did not inform Pakistan about OBL's location due to a lack of trust and past experiences of terrorists being tipped off after information was shared with Islamabad. He found it "difficult to believe" that nobody in Pakistan was aware of Osama bin Laden's Abbottabad compound.

General Kayani was miffed about this. He wanted to dilute Panetta's poignant remarks by mentioning in the joint statement that the U.S. trusted Pakistani authorities. Towards the close of the meeting, Kayani slipped a handwritten note to Haqqani.

Haqqani proposed that the joint statement could also say that the OBL raid was kept secret for reasons of "operational security" and "not for lack of trust".

Kerry was willing to say that the OBL raid had been kept secret even from key members of the Obama administration, the military, and congressional leaders. However, he was reluctant to declare that there was no "lack of trust" in the Pakistani leadership, whether civilian or military.

Foreign Secretary Salman Bashir proposed the formulation: "He (Kerry) opened the door for rebuilding the essential trust between our two countries." Kerry said he would prefer to use the words "press the 'reset button'".

Kerry again rejected the suggestion that the sentence "it was hoped that the process of opening the door for trust will result in building mutual trust," he added.

Chapter 8

No guarantees of the safety of nukes

The *Sunday Express* had published a report stating that the U.S. was ready to deploy troops if Pakistani nuclear weapons came under threat. According to the plan, President Barack Obama would order troops to parachute in to protect key nuclear missile sites without President Zardari's consent, the paper claimed.

The Pentagon had refused to deny the existence of such a plan. A U.S. government spokesman only stated, "We are confident that Pakistan has taken appropriate steps towards securing its nuclear arsenal," provoking a strong reaction from Islamabad.

Earlier, in a meeting with the Prime Minister, Kerry had said that he was prepared to "give a guarantee in his blood" that the U.S. had no designs against Pakistan's nuclear and strategic assets. However, this statement was not included in the official press release of the meeting, which instead stated that the Prime Minister "underlined the imperative of mutual trust, mutual interest and respect for Pakistan's sovereignty."

In a preparatory session before meeting Kerry, Foreign Secretary Salman Bashir proposed that Kerry's assurances about the safety of nuclear assets, made during his meeting with the Prime Minister, should also be included in the press statement.

Bashir also proposed that the joint statement mention that any future operation against high-value targets in Pakistan would be carried out after mutual consultation. Kerry listened but did not respond to these suggestions.

The President raised the issue of nuclear safety with Kerry, expressing a desire to allay fears and suspicions that the U.S. wanted to neutralise Pakistan's nuclear capability. Kerry was not forthcoming but said he would consider how to formulate this in the joint statement.

When the draft of the joint statement was prepared, Kerry reviewed it several times, comparing it with notes from his pocket.

Kerry objected to the phrase "clear affirmation by Senator Kerry, on behalf of the U.S. Administration, that the U.S. policy has no designs against Pakistan's nuclear and strategic assets." He explained, "How can I commit on behalf of the U.S. Administration, which I am not representing at the moment? I am a Senator and not representing the Administration."

He was also uncomfortable with the phrase "guarantees in blood". Although he had actually used those words, he felt it would not be well-received by people back in the U.S. He was prepared to affirm such a guarantee personally but not use the phrase "guarantees in blood" regarding any designs against Pakistan's nuclear programme.

The joint press statement issued by the foreign office welcomed Kerry's remarks that "he was prepared to personally affirm such a guarantee." There was no mention that the U.S. guaranteed it. Instead, it stated, "Pakistan's leadership made clear that Pakistan's sovereignty and national interests must be respected and accommodated by the U.S."

After tough negotiations and refusing to guarantee the safety of nuclear weapons, Kerry added a sentence to the draft saying that senior U.S. officials would visit Pakistan to discuss the way forward. He then offered a visit "in the near future" by U.S. Secretary of State Hillary Clinton, stating that the senior U.S. officials visiting Pakistan would also undertake preparatory work for her visit.

Kerry seemed to think that Clinton's proposed visit was a significant incentive. After briefly pausing, he said, "There should be a quid pro quo to it." He explained that people in the U.S. would ask what he had got in return from Pakistan.

Senator Kerry then wrote his proposed quid pro quo to be included in the joint statement: "Pakistan agreed to take several immediate steps to demonstrate its serious commitment for renewing the full cooperative effort in counter-terrorism with the United States." President Zardari interjected, saying this formulation would be viewed negatively in Pakistan. "Words have energy in them, and if the energy is negative, it can be counterproductive," he explained. General Kayani seconded Zardari's concerns.

Kerry then proposed a revised formulation: "In furtherance

of its existing commitment to fight terrorism, Pakistan agreed to take several immediate steps to underscore its seriousness in renewing the full cooperative effort with the United States." He agreed to delete the words "in counter-terrorism" as it implied that Pakistan was not cooperating in counter-terrorism efforts. This revised formulation was readily agreed upon.

The joint statement was initially titled "Joint U.S.-Pakistan press statement". However, Kerry insisted it is titled merely "Joint statement on the visit of John Kerry", emphasising that he was not representing the government and implying that the commitments made in the statement were not binding on the U.S. government.

Chapter 9

Fixing bolts and nuts

A few days after Kerry left, the Special Representative on Afghanistan and Pakistan, Ambassador Marc Grossman, arrived in Islamabad for what was described as "fixing bolts and nuts". He met with President Zardari, accompanied by Ambassador Munter and CIA Deputy Director Mike Morell, who had earlier also met with the Army Chief and DG ISI.

Zardari began the meeting with a pointed observation: "The U.S. Administration has not supported democratic institutions in Pakistan, while dictators like Musharraf have been shown greater consideration. What have you given to us?" he asked bluntly.

He continued, "Musharraf did not take anyone into confidence and failed to take resolute actions against militants. My government, on the other hand, cleared Swat and South Waziristan and gave political ownership to the fight against militancy. For us, it is a fight to the finish for our survival."

The President then explained his strategic calculus in combating militants:

"The Khyber Pakhtunkhwa province has suffered hugely from militancy and extremism," he said. "The PPP could have formed its government in the province, but instead, I invited the Pakhtun nationalists to form the government. It is the Pakhtun belt that has suffered the most at the hands of militants, and a strengthened Pakhtun nationalism was needed to take on the militants' ideology."

Zardari elaborated on his approach: "For this reason, I gave political recognition to the cultural identity of the people and introduced the area to the world as 'Pakhtunkhwa' in my first address to the UN General Assembly and later embodied it in the Constitution as well."

The U.S. delegation listened attentively as the President relished explaining his political strategy.

The militants in Swat, under the banner of Tehreek-e-Nafaz-e-Shariat-e-Mohammadi (TNSM), had been demanding enforcement of Islamic Shariah Law in the province. The ANP-led Pakhtun nationalist government wanted to accept these demands. The U.S. was concerned that Pakistan was giving in to hardliners' pressure.

With this context in mind, Zardari continued: "I first asked the Awami National Party to negotiate with Sufi Muhammad, the militants' leader in Swat. When the truce agreement was sent to me, I did not sign it and instead referred it to Parliament. The Parliament passed a resolution recommending that it be approved. I gained time, knowing that Sufi Muhammad would not deliver on his bargain. This created an enabling environment for action against him when the time came."

Grossman appreciated the President's strategy in dealing with the religious militants in Swat. He then broached the subject of the India-centric religious outfit Lashkar-e Taiba (LeT), saying that it should also be neutralised and "not allowed to strike inside India."

The President responded, "We will do our best not to let LeT strike anywhere, not only in India."

Grossman attempted to delve deeper into the LeT issue, but the President avoided further discussion.

Morell interjected, mentioning that he had discussed the Lashkar-e-Taiba threat with Pakistani officials. As he began summarising these talks, the President advised him not to share details of his meetings.

It became apparent that the "nuts and bolts" Grossman had come to fix related more to India-specific militant outfits like LeT than to the militants inside Pakistan. Notably, he offered no assurance that there would be no repeat of unilateral operations like the one targeting Osama bin Laden in the future.

President Asif Ali Zardari shaking hands with U.S.
President George W. Bush in New York, on 23 September 2008.

President Asif Ali Zardari shaking hands with French
President Nicholas Sarkozy in New York, on 23 September 2008.

President Asif Ali Zardari's meeting with Turkish President Abdullah Gul in New York, on 23 September 2008.

Former U.S. Secretary of State Madeleine Albright called on President Asif Ali Zardari in New York, on 24 September 2008.

President Asif Ali Zardari shaking hands with Jia Qingling, Chairman, Chinese People's Political Consultative Conference Beijing, China, on 16 October 2008.

President Asif Ali Zardari meets Afghanistan's Foreign Minister Abdullah Abdullah who called on him at the Aiwan-e Sadr in Islamabad, on 28 October 2008.

President Asif Ali Zardari being received by King Abdullah of Saudi Arabia on his arrival at the Presidential Palace in Riyadh, on 4 November 2008.

President Asif Ali Zardari holding talks with Khadim al-Haramain al-Sharifain King Abdul Aziz of Saudi Arabia and President of Afghanistan Hamid Karzai in New York, on 13 November 2008.

President Asif Ali Zardari talking to British Prime Minister Gordon Brown who called on him at the Aiwan-e Sadr in Islamabad, on 14 December 2008.

President Asif Ali Zardari conferring the Award of Hilal-i-Pakistan on Senator Joseph Biden during an Investiture Ceremony held at the Aiwan-e Sadr in Islamabad, on 9 January 2009.

President Asif Ali Zardari in a meeting with the Supreme Leader of Iran Ayatollah Seyyed Ali Khamenei in Tehran, on 10 March 2009. Iranian President Mahmoud Ahmadinejad was also present on the occasion.

A group photograph of President Asif Ali Zardari, Turkish President Abdullah Gul, Turkish Prime Minister Tayyip Erdogan and President of Afghanistan Hamid Karzai at Ankara, on 1 April 2009.

President Asif Ali Zardari and Prime Minister Yousaf Raza Gilani in a meeting with Richard Holbrooke, U.S. Special Envoy for Afghanistan and Pakistan, who called on them at the Aiwan-e Sadr, on 6 April 2009. Admiral Mike Mullen and Foreign Minister Shah Mahmood Qureshi are also present.

President Asif Ali Zardari with his daughter Aseefa Bhutto Zardari at a dinner hosted by the Libyan President Muammar Gaddafi, on 30 April 2009 in Tripoli.

President Asif Ali Zardari having a one-on-one meeting with the President of USA Barack Obama at the White House, on 6 May 2009.

President Asif Ali Zardari with Secretary United Nations Ban Ki-Moon in New York, on 12 May 2009.

Presidents of Pakistan, Tajikistan, Russia and Afghanistan join hands in solidarity after the Quadrilateral Summit in Dushanbe, Tajikistan, on 30 July 2009.

President Asif Ali Zardari with German Chancellor Angela Merkel, prior to a breakfast meeting between them in Brussels, on 19 June 2009.

President Asif Ali Zardari called on the Belgian King Albert-II at the Royal Palace in Brussels, on 17 June 2009.

President Asif Ali Zardari shaking hands with the Chinese President Hu Jintao in Yekaterinburg, Russia, on the sidelines of the SCO Summit, on 15 June 2009.

President Asif Ali Zardari with Secretary United Nations
Ban Ki-Moon in New York, on 12 May 2009.

President Asif Ali Zardari and former President of the USA Bill Clinton, shaking hands before a meeting in New York, on 21 September 2009.

President Asif Ali Zardari and Iranian President Mahmoud Ahmadinejad exchanging views in New York, on 25 September 2009.

Secretary of State Hillary Clinton called on
President Asif Ali Zardari in New York, on 24 September 2009.

President Asif Ali Zardari in a meeting with Mirwaiz Umar Farooq, Chairman of the All-Parties Hurriyat Conference, in New York, on 27 September 2009.

President Asif Ali Zardari reviewing the Guard of Honour with the Prime Minister of Italy Silvio Berlusconi in Rome, on 30 September 2009.

President Asif Ali Zardari with his Afghan counterpart Hamid Karzai inspecting the Guard of Honour accorded to him on his arrival at the Presidential Palace in Kabul, on 18 November 2009.

President Asif Ali Zardari in a meeting with the President of Syria Bashar al-Assad at the Al-Shaab Palace in Syria, on 8 January 2010.

President Asif Ali Zardari greets the Palestinian President Mahmoud Abbas on his arrival at the Presidency in Islamabad for a meeting , on 12 February 2010.

President Asif Ali Zardari and U.S. Secretary of State Hillary Clinton at the Aiwan-e Sadr, on 18 July 2010. His daughters, Bakhtawar and Aseefa, are also present.

President Asif Ali Zardari and British Prime Minister David Cameron outside the Chequers in the UK, after a meeting, on 6 August 2010.

President Asif Ali Zardari and Turkish Prime Minister Recep Tayyip Erdogan shaking hands before their meeting at the Aiwan-e Sadr in Islamabad, on 13 October 2010.

President Asif Ali Zardari shaking hands with British Prime Minister David Cameron at the Aiwan-e Sadr, on 5 April 2011.

President Asif Ali Zardari with the Chinese President Hu Jintao inspecting the Guard of Honour upon his arrival at the Great Hall of the People in Beijing, China, on 7 June 2012.

Chapter 10

Hillary Clinton arrives—warns of no future for Pakistan

John Kerry had offered the visit to Pakistan by Secretary of State Hillary Clinton to resume the strategic dialogue if "Pakistan was prepared to make amends and move forward in a constructive manner."

She arrived on 27 May and met the President, Prime Minister, and Army Chief together in the Presidency.

The President personally received her on the ground floor and escorted her in the lift after someone persuaded him at the last minute to breach protocol and receive her on the ground floor.

Foreign Secretary Salman Bashir cryptically remarked that leaders were prone to change their minds about protocol details on the advice of anyone who whispered last into their ear. Who was the last person who had whispered into Zardari's ear? No one knew.

There was some commotion on the fourth floor as if some celestial visitor had descended from the sky above.

The one-on-one meeting in the President's office continued for over an hour. The Prime Minister, Army Chief, and note-taker were not present. No one knew what was discussed.

A U.S. embassy official later told me that the Secretary of State was there to ask how Osama bin Laden had remained hidden in a military cantonment for years.

The delegation-level meeting was scheduled to have eight members from each side besides the President and Hillary. At the last moment, she asked to restrict it to only four and, undiplomatically, requested that Pakistan also cut its delegation.

Hillary then requested a separate meeting with the Army Chief and DG ISI in the Presidency. Both were already in the delegation-level talks, but she wanted to also meet them separately.

After the army and ISI chiefs were informed of separate meetings with her, she cancelled them as abruptly and unceremoniously as she had earlier requested them.

At the delegation-level talks, Hillary appeared frigid and stone-faced. The photographer had to be called in again to take another set of pictures when everyone pretended to be relaxed and smiling.

Mincing no words, Hillary said, "There are serious questions that we need to address together." She wanted "a clear understanding of what we should do together." The meeting did not last very long. She seemed to have come to deliver a message.

No joint statement was issued at the end of the meeting. The foreign office only issued the remarks of the presidential spokesperson talking to the media that "a candid, constructive and positive exchange of views" had taken place in the meeting "on a host of issues and covered the full spectrum of Pakistan-U.S. relations and issues of regional stability and security including countering terrorism and peace in Afghanistan."

The *New York Times*, reporting on the visit and quoting an unnamed senior official travelling with her, said that she demanded specific operations against some individuals whose names might never be made public. It did not say whether the individuals against whom action had been demanded were within the state institutions.

Later in the evening, Hillary addressed a press conference at the U.S. embassy, along with the top U.S. military commander, Admiral Mike Mullen.

"There can be no peace, stability, no democracy, no future for Pakistan unless the violent extremists are removed," she warned.

She also said that she had received assurances of "some very specific actions" that Pakistan would take but did not give any detail except that Pakistan would provide access to a CIA team to bin Laden's compound in Abbottabad to search for new clues.

The Pakistani government had all along maintained that there was no official complicity in the OBL hideout. Hillary, however, did not believe it.

She disclosed: "Our counterparts in the (Pakistani) government were very forthcoming in saying that somebody, somewhere, was providing some kind of support, and they are carrying out an investigation and we have certainly offered to share whatever information we come across."

The chief concern of Pakistan had been the threat of unilateral U.S. action against militants, as in the case of OBL. It wanted assurances that it would not be used as a precedent for unilateral strikes in the future. It was one time too many. But from Kerry to Grossman and Hillary, no one was ready to give this assurance.

A day after Hillary departed, reports said that a CIA team visited the army-controlled Abbottabad compound. Nobody was allowed to pass near the surrounding area and the streets leading to the compound.

The CIA team also met with Osama's widows in the compound, who had been in the custody of Pakistani investigation agencies since the killing of the Al Qaeda chief.

Was it part of the investigation that Hillary had talked about in her press conference a day before?

Chapter 11

Finding scapegoats

A Commission headed by retired Supreme Court Judge Javed Iqbal was appointed to probe the raid on the Osama bin Laden (OBL) compound.

As a judge, Iqbal had readily accepted General Musharraf's offer to replace Chief Justice Iftikhar Chaudhry when the latter was "suspended". He also served as Chairman of the Commission on Enforced Disappearances to investigate disappearances blamed on intelligence agencies. As Chairman for over a decade, he did not prosecute a single state official even though those involved had been exposed both in the Supreme Court and Parliament. He was known for washing the dirty linen of the establishment.

Other members of the Abbottabad Inquiry Commission were Abbas Khan, a former IGP (inspector general of police); Ashraf Jehangir Qazi, a former diplomat; and retired Lt General Nadeem Ahmad. The Commission submitted its report to the Prime Minister in early 2013.

The report's findings have not been made public, but parts of it, which were leaked to foreign media, claimed that the ISI and military leadership had been criticised in the report.

Javed Iqbal presented his report to Prime Minister Raja Pervaiz Ashraf. He later recalled to me that while presenting it, Justice Javed remarked,

"Sir, *humare laeq koi khidmat ho tau bataain.*" (Sir, if there is anything I can do, please ask.) Later, Raja remarked to me that he did not personally know Javed Iqbal and was disappointed in him.

Later, in July 2013, Ashraf Jehangir Qazi, a member of the Commission and a highly respected former diplomat, informed the Senate Committee on Defence that there were differences among members over fixing the responsibility.

He said the report leaked to the media had subsequently been watered down by the chairman to "reconcile" the differences. Ashraf Jehangir Qazi wrote a 40-page note of dissent to the watered-down version, to which Chairman Justice Iqbal added his own observations again.

An organised campaign was also launched to find scapegoats.

Soon after the OBL raid, a doctor, Shakil Afridi, was arrested for running a vaccination campaign in Abbottabad, allegedly to help the CIA trace OBL's hideout. He was tried not for helping CIA trace OBL but for providing medical aid to militants of a banned outfit "Lashkar-e-Islam" in his clinic.

Dr Shakil was sentenced to 25 years in jail under the century-old Frontier Crimes Regulation (FCR). In 2012, Zardari repealed the British-era regulation, but Dr Shakil has remained in prison.

Media hype was also created against Ambassador Haqqani, accusing him of issuing visas to some shadowy American nationals at the instance of President Zardari. The Zardari-Haqqani combine had allegedly conspired to help blow the cover on OBL through them. It was claimed that Haqqani had breached national security by wrongfully issuing over seven hundred visas to U.S. nationals on the orders of Zardari, bypassing the foreign office and the security agencies.

On the surface, Haqqani was targeted, but the actual target on the radar was President Zardari.

Ambassador Haqqani hit back. He held a press conference and made public the complete data on the number of visas the embassy had issued, and the procedure followed.

"The embassy has not issued any visa without proper authorisation," he claimed and challenged that a single instance of visa issuance without authorisation be made public. There was a deafening silence to the challenge thrown by him.

Later, he also provided a comparative statement showing the issuance of visas over the years since 2007 when a military general was in power.

It was only after Haqqani's forceful rebuttals and Gilani's asking on the floor of the National Assembly, "Who gave Osama a visa?" that the campaign to blame the President lost steam.

A bogey called "Memogate" was crafted to blame President Zardari and Ambassador Haqqani for conspiring with the U.S. Administration against the Pakistan army. Nothing came out of it, but it painted President Zardari black and drove him to the edge.

Civilians were blamed for the misdeeds and failures of uniformed personnel, and the real issue was trivialised.

It had also been done before.

In 2006, General Musharraf acknowledged in his memoir that nuclear materials had been clandestinely shipped from Pakistan to Iran, North Korea, and Libya for atomic bomb-making. Even though the military had taken over the complete command, control, safety, and security of nuclear materials, he blamed a lone civilian. The head of the programme, Dr A.Q. Khan, a civilian, was made into a scapegoat and forced to fall on his sword.

Once again, the civilian President and ambassador were painted dark and made into scapegoats.

Even if no punitive actions were taken, the national humiliation could have been mitigated to some extent by holding the intelligence agencies accountable and reforming the intelligence network.

Unfortunately, no one in the state apparatus was prepared to do it. A few months later, a private member bill was presented in the Senate to determine ISI's mandate and functions. Zardari said it was not the right time and asked that the Bill be withdrawn.

The hunt for scapegoats went on while the ISI continued to operate without its mandate determined by law, without oversight, and any accountability.

Section Six

THE RAYMOND DAVIS AFFAIR

Chapter 1

The Raymond Davis affair

On 27 January 2011, Raymond Davis, a U.S. embassy official, killed two Pakistanis in Lahore, claiming that the men he had shot dead were chasing him with the aim of robbing him. Within minutes of the shooting, four CIA agents in an SUV, rushing to his rescue, also crushed a bystander to death. The incident hit the headlines.

Initially, the U.S. embassy stated that Raymond was a diplomat working in Islamabad's technical and administration wing. Later, they claimed that Raymond was actually based at the American consulate in Lahore and demanded diplomatic immunity for him.

The U.S. demand for diplomatic immunity created an uproar in the media, which claimed that Raymond was not a diplomat according to established conventions. His background as a former U.S. Army soldier and private security contractor raised suspicions that he was a U.S. spy on some special secret mission.

Desperate over reports that her husband's killer might escape justice, Shumaila Kanwal, the wife of one of the men killed by Raymond, committed suicide. In her dying statement, she said, "I want blood for blood. I want the killer to be shot in the same way as he shot my husband."

While the foreign office examined the record to determine whether Raymond Davis had diplomatic status, the Lahore High Court took notice and called for records from the foreign office.

As the wrangling over his status continued, criticism was directed at President Zardari. It was alleged that spies like Raymond Davis secretly entered Pakistan because Ambassador Hussain Haqqani had issued visas to shady American nationals, bypassing the intelligence agencies with Zardari's connivance. The President was also accused of planning to let Raymond Davis go under the cover of diplomatic immunity.

The situation worsened for Zardari when Foreign Minister Shah Mahmood Qureshi claimed that the President wanted Raymond recognised as a diplomat, but he (Qureshi) refused.

As a senior Party member, Shah Mahmood had been part of all party meetings in the Presidency. Neither the President nor anyone in the Party had ever indicated that Raymond should be given diplomatic immunity and set free. There was consensus in these meetings that payment of blood money under the qisas and diyat law to the heirs of the victims, not diplomatic immunity, was the only way out for Raymond. Shah Mahmood attended these meetings and endorsed these observations.

While the Lahore High Court had called for the record and Qureshi had given it a spin, Prime Minister Gilani had another story to tell.

In a Party meeting, he disclosed that an additional secretary of the foreign office had come to him earlier in the day with a summary and wanted him to sign it. The summary had been brought directly to him and not routed through his principal secretary as the procedure required. When asked, the officer told him it was a summary of the foreign office's views on Raymond Davis' diplomatic status and was "very sensitive and secret".

"What is the foreign office view?" the Prime Minister had asked him.

The officer handed him the summary without saying anything. Gilani read it.

It stated that limited, but not full, diplomatic immunity was available to Raymond Davis and that he could be released on the basis of limited diplomatic immunity.

Gilani was surprised that the foreign office wanted him to sign it. He pointed out that the Prime Minister does not keep the foreign office records. The Lahore High Court had already asked for the record, and the foreign office should have sent it to the court.

Handing back the summary, Gilani told the officer that it did not require his signature.

Those attending the Party meeting said that Raymond should not be given diplomatic immunity regardless of the foreign office bureaucracy's views on limited immunity. They agreed that he could earn his freedom only by paying blood money to the heirs of the victims under Islamic law. The President concurred.

Qureshi, however, continued to double-speak mercilessly,

suggesting that Zardari planned to set Raymond free. In reply to a media question, he said, "I will not permit it." He claimed to have told both President Asif Ali Zardari and Prime Minister Gilani that Raymond was not a diplomat and not entitled to diplomatic immunity.

Finally, Raymond was released on 16 March 2011 after the heirs of the two victims accepted blood money, not because he was deemed a diplomat with immunity from prosecution.

Chapter 2

Why Qureshi turned against Zardari

Qureshi's gunning for Zardari was hardly based on any principles. In early February, the President had decided to reshuffle the cabinet and asked all ministers, state ministers, and special assistants—over 60 in total—to resign, paving the way for a new cabinet.

Zardari had decided to move Qureshi to the ministry of water and power, replacing him with the no less competent, dynamic, and articulate Hina Rabbani Khar. Qureshi, however, was intent on retaining the portfolio of foreign minister.

Qureshi claimed he was being shifted from the foreign ministry because of his disagreement over the Raymond Davis matter. Zardari countered that the cabinet was oversized and needed to be reduced as required by the 18th Constitutional Amendment passed a year earlier. The President maintained that Qureshi was being shifted to the equally important ministry of water and power, not removed entirely.

I had heard the President casually remark at times about Shah Mahmood Qureshi in unflattering terms. Zardari thought Qureshi had become too ambitious and projected himself as the sole architect of foreign policy. "He hijacked ideas about the economy, trade, and water issues with India and flaunted them as his own without acknowledging the Party," Zardari told me. "I had even confronted Qureshi with clippings of his speeches and statements."

Prime Minister Gilani told me that the President had long wanted to replace Shah Mahmood Qureshi, who was from Gilani's home district of Multan. Qureshi would see changing his portfolio as a hostile act by the Prime Minister, so Gilani had been urging Zardari not to change his portfolio.

Now that a major reshuffle had been decided, Zardari wanted to change the portfolios of all ministers, not just Qureshi's. However, Shah Mahmood Qureshi resented this decision.

On the day of the oath-taking ceremony, Qureshi called on the Prime Minister again, attempting to retain his portfolio as top diplomat. Gilani told him it was the President's decision and advised him to see Zardari.

Qureshi claimed he had been trying to meet the President

but had not been able to secure an appointment. Gilani then rang up the President in Qureshi's presence, requesting he meet Qureshi. The President agreed.

The oath-taking was only a few hours away in the evening. Qureshi was invited to see the President during the day. He did not come to the meeting. The President waited. Qureshi's mobile phone was switched off. He was unreachable.

Where did he go from the PM's House after Gilani had fixed the appointment for him with the President? No one knew. Only Shah Mahmood Qureshi could tell where he had gone from the PM's House.

On 11 February 2011, chairs were laid in front of the presidential dais in the Darbar Hall for the new cabinet to be administered oaths by Zardari. Guests started arriving for the ceremony at the Presidency. The protocol office had the list of the new ministers-designate to be seated around the special table for oath-taking. It included Shah Mahmood Qureshi.

The countdown for the oath-taking ceremony had already started. I went to see the President. "Qureshi hasn't come yet," I said.

The President chuckled and said he knew where Qureshi had gone without explicitly saying where. I also did not ask what he thought Qureshi might have done after leaving the PM's House, ostensibly to meet the President.

Qureshi's phone remained turned off. It became clear that he would not come to meet the President or to take the oath.

What to do with the empty chair in the Darbar Hall reserved for Qureshi?

If one chair remained unoccupied, it would mean a minister-designate had failed to turn up for oath-taking. Why? Who was he? Everyone would notice it. Media persons would ask questions. No chair should be left unoccupied. One chair must be pulled out.

But the guests were already seated. If just one chair were removed at the last minute, it would attract media attention, and even more questions would be asked.

It was decided that all the chairs should be removed and

brought back to the hall except for one. There would be no empty chair, and nobody would notice.

All chairs were pulled back and, within minutes, brought back into the Darbar Hall, one less.

A journalist, however, still noticed it. He was suspicious.

"Why remove the chairs and soon replace them?" he pointedly asked me.

When told that the chairs were not of good quality and the protocol officials had decided to replace them, he said,

"*Nahi, kuch to hai jis ki parda daari hai.*" (No, there is something that is being kept secret.) He did not find the explanation satisfactory but did not press further.

Ministers in the new, reshuffled cabinet took their oaths. Qureshi was not among them.

The next day, Shah Mahmood Qureshi, who had not taken the oath, claimed that Secretary of State Clinton had "forced" him to confirm diplomatic immunity for Raymond Davis, but he had declined.

Making an issue out of the Raymond Davis case, he turned against Zardari for withdrawing the foreign ministry portfolio from him.

Qureshi was now openly gunning for Zardari.

"I know the guts of Shah Mahmood. He can't do it on his own. He is playing into the hands of somebody," Zardari said to me.

Chapter 3

Kerry comes to secure Raymond Davis' release

It had been decided that Raymond would not be set free because of the diplomatic status claimed by the U.S. Embassy. He could only be freed under Shariat Law after paying blood money to the victims' heirs. This would take time, while the U.S. was impatient to secure his release.

John Kerry, Chairman of the U.S. Foreign Relations Committee, came to Islamabad on 16 February 2011 and called on President Zardari. Before arriving at the Presidency, Kerry disregarded diplomatic norms by meeting the estranged Shah Mahmood Qureshi, even though the latter had left the cabinet and had been publicly criticising Zardari.

Kerry, accompanied by U.S. Ambassador Cameron Munter, waited for the President in the committee room. Officials of the foreign office were also present. Kerry appeared relaxed, but Munter was deeply distressed. Anxiety and tension were writ large on his face; wearing a drawn expression, he seemed pulled down.

Zardari entered the committee room with a smile, warmly greeting Kerry. Turning towards the Ambassador and noticing his stress, he said, "Cheer up, things will be OK," patting him on the arm. Ambassador Munter smiled as if under compulsion.

As they settled, Kerry said, "I have come to Islamabad not to speak but to listen. How can we get Davis out?" He asked without mincing words.

Zardari began by referring to media reports of Kerry's meeting with Shah Mahmood Qureshi. He said, "Kerry's meeting with Qureshi has provided the latter with even more ammunition to politicise the Raymond Davis case further and project himself as a hero."

Kerry acknowledged this, saying, "We realise that Qureshi is playing it up, trying to convert it into a political opportunity for himself." He quickly added, "We will talk about it later in private."

Kerry had come to hear about Raymond, not about Qureshi. He wasn't apologetic about breaching diplomatic norms in meeting Shah Mahmood Qureshi. His desperation to seek

Raymond Davis' immediate release overrode conventional protocol.

Ignoring Kerry's reluctance to discuss Qureshi, Zardari continued, "Shah Mahmood will not get much political mileage, and it will be short-lived. For three days, Shah Mahmood remained quiet and didn't say anything. But today, as we are meeting, he has come out more openly in criticising me publicly. We have survived such gimmicks before; I will survive this one too."

Refocusing the conversation, Kerry asked, "OK, Mr President, how do you see it and what can be done?" He reiterated that he had come to hear about Raymond Davis and not to talk.

"OK, we will talk about it in my office," Zardari said, rising from his seat and asking Kerry to follow him. Kerry and Ambassador Munter complied. Munter still looked worried; Zardari's words of comfort were inadequate to cheer him up.

From Munter's body language, it appeared that a deep-seated fear lurked in his mind. It would have been a disaster if Raymond had not been released immediately and investigators had begun questioning him. Munter didn't talk much, but his body language spoke more clearly and loudly than his speech. The exact nature of his fear was difficult to discern.

In his office, the President called Farooq Naek to brief John Kerry and Ambassador Munter on the legal aspects of what could possibly be done. Zardari told Kerry that diplomatic immunity for Raymond Davis was not an option, "but there are ways." For once, Munter smiled.

Zardari said that the spontaneous reaction by the U.S. Consul General in Lahore claiming diplomatic immunity for Raymond was not right. Kerry agreed, saying, "Yes, it was a mistake. But I couldn't say publicly that the Consul General had blundered."

Zardari explained that even if the government allowed diplomatic immunity, it would be struck down in a judicial review, making matters even worse. He then showed Kerry some pictures of religious parties demanding criminal prosecution of Raymond for murder. Leaning towards Kerry, he said, "I do not want the mullahs to take it to the streets."

"It has to be an out-of-the-box solution," Zardari stated.

"What is the out-of-the-box solution?" Kerry asked.

"We have to think about paying good compensation to the families of victims under Islamic law," the President replied.

Munter's face lit up.

"But it is not automatic," the President cautioned. "The processes involved will take some time."

Munter slumped again. He was in a hurry to secure Davis' release.

Chapter 4

Why was Munter so desperate?

Washington was desperate to secure Raymond Davis' early release from Pakistan. Washington postponed the scheduled dialogue between the U.S., Pakistan, and Afghanistan and the official bilateral strategic dialogue to pressure the Pakistani government. Reports suggested that the U.S. had threatened to withdraw the US$1.5 billion aid package promised for the war on terror and cut off some military aid.

The U.S. was determined to get Raymond Davis out of Pakistan safely and swiftly, regardless of the cost. Neither Kerry nor Munter nor any other U.S. interlocutor was willing to entertain concepts like "due process", "taking some time", or "it is not automatic". They all demanded Davis' immediate release.

Even after his release, following the payment of US$2.4 million in compensation to the victims' families, U.S. fears persisted. Ambassador Munter flew with Davis to Kabul on the same plane. In his book, Davis later revealed that Munter accompanied him to ensure "the Pakistanis would not dare mess around by denying it clearance to take off."

This desperation and impatience for immediate release puzzled President Zardari. At the heart of this anxiety lay Raymond Davis' CIA background. Before joining the Agency, he had worked for XE Services (previously known as Blackwater), a private security contracting firm. CNN reported at the time that Davis had been providing security to CIA officers in Pakistan.

In December 2010, a curious incident occurred. A resident of North Waziristan, who had lost several family members in U.S. drone strikes, filed a police complaint. Remarkably, he named Jonathan Bank, the CIA station chief in Islamabad, for the murders of his family members. It was baffling that a private citizen knew the name of the CIA station head in Islamabad and included it in his complaint.

With his cover blown, Jonathan Bank immediately left Pakistan. Until his replacement arrived, Raymond Davis reportedly worked as the CIA's acting station chief. If he indeed acted in this capacity, his shooting skills and suspicious activities make it highly probable that he played a central role in the secret operation to capture Osama bin Laden (OBL) later that year in May.

The planning for the raid on the Abbottabad compound must have been at an advanced stage when Raymond shot dead two Pakistanis. Had he remained in jail in Pakistan and been investigated for the murders, crucial information might have been revealed to the investigators. The stakes for the U.S. were immense.

Raymond Davis himself later provided some insight into the situation. In his memoirs, *The Contractor: How I Landed in a Pakistani Prison & Ignited a Diplomatic Crisis*, he stated, “The reason for the U.S. government to get me out sooner rather than later was growing increasingly urgent, and the reason was even more secretive than the efforts to get him out.”

Davis claimed that the U.S. Administration wanted to extract him from Pakistan because it had plans to capture Osama bin Laden. However, he did not explicitly state that he was part of the U.S. plan to raid OBL’s hideout in Abbottabad a few months later. It’s worth noting that the CIA had heavily redacted his book before publication, and one may never know whether Raymond mentioned anything about this in the original draft of his manuscript.

“They needed to get me out of the country first, and they needed to do it fast before bin Laden could slip away once again,” he writes. Davis knew about bin Laden and the plans to capture him, information that could have been revealed during his prosecution and trial had he remained in jail.

The clock was ticking for the planners of the OBL operation. Raymond Davis needed to be freed and returned to the U.S. before the operation was launched. The U.S. Administration’s impatience was not irrational; their desperation to quickly evacuate Davis appears directly linked to the impending OBL operation.

It seems Ambassador Munter knew too much about Raymond Davis and struggled to maintain his composure during those tense days.

Chapter 5

ISI on Raymond Davis contingency plans

In a private conversation, Zardari said that ISI and the army also wanted Raymond released, but everyone wanted to avoid being blamed for it. He, however, did not care.

Zardari may have been right.

Describing the roles of different characters involved in securing his release, Raymond Davis wrote in his memoirs: "No two characters in this unfolding drama worked farther below the waterline than ... Panetta (Director CIA) and ... Pasha (Gen Pasha DG ISI)."

He acknowledged that "ISI ... orchestrated my exit. Several guards led me out of the courtroom through a back entrance. ... One of the men opened the door, stepped out into a courtyard, and scanned the horizon ... once he'd cleared the area, I was waved through the door and directed to the SUV idling in the courtyard."

Later, recalling the Raymond Davis trial in a Lahore court, the *New York Times* Magazine on 9 April 2013 wrote:

"General Pasha sat in the back of the courtroom, his cell phone out. He began sending out a stream of nervous text messages to Ambassador Munter, updating him about the court proceedings." The article continued, "Then Pasha sent another text message to Munter: The matter was settled. Davis was a free man. In a Lahore courtroom, the laws of God had trumped the laws of man."

Raymond Davis also claimed that his release was finally facilitated after a secret meeting in Oman between CIA chief Leon Panetta and ISI chief Ahmad Shuja Pasha.

Government spokesmen were quick to reject it, calling it a "pack of lies" maligning Pakistan's military. Allegations about the extent of Pasha's role were denied.

While the ISI was more than active in securing Raymond's release, it suited the intelligence agency if the media painted Zardari black.

This was not surprising. After all, not long ago, the ISI, along with the Army Chief, had petitioned the Supreme Court that the Memogate scandal was a reality in a stinging public indictment of their supreme commander.

The Contingency Plan

As the procedures for Raymond's release under Shariat Law took time, some religious extremists opposed his release on any grounds and wanted him hanged. If they created chaos and the opposition played politics, it would worsen things.

Zardari called a meeting of the Party's core committee to discuss the situation. Briefing them, Zardari said that the U.S. Congress, dominated by the Republicans, was poised to cut off aid to Pakistan. The IMF and other international financial institutions would also be asked to impose even harsher conditions. There was a need to think of alternatives, he said.

He disclosed that he had been talking with the rulers of Abu Dhabi about "Contingency Plans".

Zardari explained that a few days ago, he had visited the UAE on an unannounced one-day trip and sought payment of 850 million dollars owed to it in the PTCL (Pakistan Telecommunications Company Limited) privatisation deal. He hoped the money would come soon and the country's urgent needs would be met even if aid was cut off or harsher conditions were imposed by international lenders.

He also said he had offered the UAE the chance to securitise Pakistan's foreign remittances and advance payments against them.

Zardari mentioned that he had sent a message to former Prime Minister Nawaz Sharif through some businessmen, urging him to stay away from any agitation by the extremists.

He had asked a delegation of the Business Council for Economic Reforms to convey his message to Nawaz Sharif, he said, and then rattled off the gist of his message:

"The war on terror is not going to end overnight. It will stay with us for a long time. I have come to the Presidency by votes and not with the help of Obama. I will not create anarchy in the country by giving in to U.S. pressure (to release Raymond by giving him diplomatic immunity). Let them (the U.S.) withdraw from Pakistan if they decide. In that case, everyone will suffer. I will not bow to U.S. pressure. It is their election politics also.

The Republicans have taken control. They can impose sanctions. Iran had oil and survived pressures, but we have nothing. We will not be able to stand. Those two boys (those who chased Raymond Davis) were criminals; everyone knows. We can't buy isolation."

He had asked the businessmen to convey this to Nawaz Sharif.

Zardari then asked Prime Minister Gilani to brief all coalition partners and the Army Chief and take them into confidence about the need for contingency plans.

Section Seven

THE FATEFUL MEMOGATE

Chapter 1

What was Memogate?

The Memogate scandal, which rocked the Presidency and drove Zardari to the brink, originated from an article titled "Time to Take on Pakistan's Jihadist Spies" published in the *Financial Times* of London on 10 October 2011. The author, Mansoor Ijaz, a Pakistani-American, made several explosive claims.

According to Ijaz, on 9 May 2011, just a week after Osama bin Laden's hideout in Abbottabad was stormed, a senior Pakistani diplomat contacted him with an urgent request. The diplomat allegedly stated that President Zardari wanted to convey a message to White House National Security officials, bypassing Pakistan's military and intelligence channels.

Ijaz's article claimed that President Zardari, fearing a military coup in the wake of the OBL raid, sought U.S. intervention to warn General Kayani against any misadventure. In return, Zardari allegedly offered to bring in a new national security team and shut down the ISI cell purportedly supporting the Taliban and Haqqani network.

The article further stated that Zardari preferred Admiral Mike Mullen, Chairman of the U.S. Joint Chiefs of Staff, as the conduit for conveying his urgent, confidential message to the Obama Administration. Mullen was described as "a time-tested friend of Pakistan" who could effectively communicate the message to both President Barack Obama and General Kayani.

According to Ijaz, a memo was prepared and delivered to Admiral Mullen on 10 May at 1400 hours. The article claimed that a meeting between Mullen and the Pakistani national security officials took place the next day at the White House. However, it appeared that Pakistan's military and intelligence chiefs neither heeded the warning nor acted on the admiral's advice.

The article also advocated for the U.S. government to devise precise policies to address "the cancer that ISI and its rogue wings have become on the Pakistani state." The alleged memo was rooted in the fear that army leaders, feeling humiliated by the OBL operation, might seek scapegoats in the civilian government or even attempt to overthrow it.

Initially, there was no immediate reaction from the Pakistani government. However, two days later, the issue was raised at a meeting of the Party core committee in the Presidency. Prime Minister Gilani provided a brief summary of the article and its author, Mansoor Ijaz. He noted that although not explicitly named in the article, fingers would likely point to Pakistan's ambassador in Washington, Hussain Haqqani, as the "senior Pakistani diplomat" who had contacted Mansoor Ijaz. Gilani also anticipated that the opposition would seize upon this issue.

During the meeting, several PPP members criticised Ambassador Haqqani and demanded explanations. President Zardari, however, strongly defended Haqqani, emphasising the difficult circumstances under which he was serving as Pakistan's ambassador to Washington. Zardari stated, "We have no friends left in the U.S. Haqqani is working in a very difficult environment as no one is prepared to even talk to us. You people don't know."

Zardari praised Haqqani's performance, noting his past assistance to "Shaheed Bibi" (referring to Benazir Bhutto) in Washington and his valuable contacts. The President questioned who else could handle the challenging role of explaining Pakistan's position after the raid on Osama's hideout. He also expressed doubt about the authenticity of the transcripts attributed to Haqqani.

The meeting concluded with a decision to recall Haqqani to Islamabad for a personal explanation, though Zardari insisted this be done without publicly embarrassing the ambassador or appearing to withdraw government trust. A press release stated that Haqqani was being called to "brief the country's leadership on a host of issues impacting on Pak-U.S. relations and the recent developments."

The recall of Haqqani to Islamabad marked the first formal reaction to the *Financial Times* article, which was rapidly becoming known as "Memogate". The story quickly dominated headlines, with many speculating that Haqqani might not return to Pakistan.

As the controversy grew, opposition leader Chaudhry Nisar

Ali Khan held a news conference on 20 October, raising questions and demanding investigations. It later emerged that on 22 October, ISI chief Lt General Pasha secretly met with Mansoor Ijaz, unbeknownst to Zardari and the government.

The political landscape shifted further when Imran Khan held a massive rally at Minar-e-Pakistan in Lahore on 30 October. Khan claimed that Haqqani had indeed asked Mansoor Ijaz to deliver the memo. Imran's growing popularity, allegedly supported tacitly by the establishment, threatened Nawaz Sharif's power base in Punjab.

In response, Nawaz Sharif decided to target his political rival, Zardari. Despite the memo's focus on the fallout from OBL's discovery in Abbottabad, Nawaz chose not to question how bin Laden had lived in the cantonment for a decade or how American helicopters had flown hundreds of miles over Pakistani territory undetected. Instead, he declared his belief that the memo was written by Haqqani under Zardari's direction.

When asked if he wanted Haqqani sacked, Nawaz said, "This issue won't get resolved by somebody's resignation. It constitutes a treason charge." Notably, neither Nawaz, other political parties, nor the media raised the fundamental question of who had sheltered Osama for so long.

The media and opposition intensified their focus on the scandal, with the PML-N organising demonstrations. Nawaz Sharif stated that he "easily" believed the memo was written by Haqqani under Zardari's directions. The *Financial Times* article had provided him with a significant political opportunity.

Chapter 2

The war is on me, not Haqqani

The memo unleashed a political storm. While accusing Haqqani of writing the memo, the opposition actually targeted Zardari as the mastermind. Zardari was aware of this. He wanted the Party leaders to defend Haqqani, but they were reluctant. Zardari alone was defending Haqqani.

The PPP leaders' reluctance to wholeheartedly defend Haqqani made Zardari vulnerable. At a party meeting, Zardari said he had been watching television talk shows and noticed that the Party leaders did not defend him. Praising Haqqani, he said that if he (Haqqani) had skeletons in the cupboard, he would have made excuses and not returned to Pakistan when asked.

Zardari was rather blunt in expressing his anguish. He pointed towards Raza Rabbani (a senior Party leader from Sindh and a senator who later went on to become chairman of the Senate) and said, "In the Parliamentary Committee on National Security, Rabbani, you did not want to describe Haqqani as 'honourable'. You could have simply stated that the fact that Haqqani returned to Pakistan showed his innocence. These things are not taught but should come to mind automatically."

Rabbani replied, "I defended Haqqani by describing his decision to return as a 'significant development.'"

Zardari countered, "Returning to Pakistan was an 'honourable' act, not merely a 'significant decision.'"

Zardari went on to explain Haqqani's background and contributions. He said that Haqqani lived and worked in the U.S. and had learnt the intricacies of the American system. Shaheed Benazir faced isolation during her exile and wanted Haqqani "delivered to her". Zardari revealed that Haqqani was passing through a rough patch of life at the time, embroiled in some personal issues. Zardari had leaned on a media baron to help Haqqani in this matter, though he did not name the media baron nor elaborate on the "personal issues" Haqqani faced.

He also recounted that after the dismissal of Shaheed Bibi's government by President Leghari, Haqqani stood firmly by her while many others switched loyalties and abandoned her.

Zardari named some of these individuals. He mentioned that Haqqani had been tortured in jail and was now implicated in the Memogate scandal, only to make him turn approver against Zardari.

The President said that he expected party leaders to reciprocate the honour shown to them by following the Party line (to defend Haqqani) in return. Looking at Rabbani again, he said he expected him to have described Haqqani as "honourable".

Rabbani replied, "Sir, I am sorry if you feel unhappy with it. Old habits die hard."

"Will you do it now?" the President asked.

"Sir, do not ask me to use the word honourable," Rabbani responded.

"He (Rabbani) is like a fighter bomber," Zardari remarked.

"Sir, I am merely a Cessna and not a jet fighter," Rabbani quipped.

Commending Ambassador Haqqani, the President said he had earned a professorship in a U.S. University on his own merit. Once again, he said that Haqqani served as Benazir's bridge with senior state department staffers during her exile in the U.S. when it was so difficult to open doors for her.

President Zardari also mentioned Mansoor Ijaz and recounted an incident involving Benazir Bhutto's meeting with him in Washington. He noted that Farhatullah Babar had advised Benazir against having an exclusive one-on-one meeting with Mansoor, suggesting instead a brief interaction followed by the inclusion of other journalists. Zardari emphasised that this advice must have been based on sound reasons, given Benazir's trust in Babar's judgment.

The President then returned to the subject of Haqqani's return to Pakistan. He said that it would have been embarrassing for him if Haqqani had not returned. Fingers would have been pointed at him, and he would have been held guilty. Zardari revealed that the Americans had warned Haqqani of potential harm if he returned to Pakistan. He also mentioned that the military had told him Haqqani would not return.

"I told them that if he returned, it would be my win, and if he didn't, it would be their win," Zardari said, relishing that he was proven right and the Hawks wrong.

The President said that when they "destroyed" Haqqani, he posted Sherry Rehman to replace him. "War is not on Haqqani; war is on me," he reiterated.

During the meeting, there was also some discussion on the promised inquiry into the Memogate scandal. The President said that the inquiry would be conducted at the highest level by the Parliamentary Committee on National Security.

Zardari also sought to garner support for Haqqani from other political parties. He noted that serious and pertinent questions could be legitimately raised for a forceful defence of Haqqani. For instance:

1. The DG ISI had secretly visited London and met Mansoor, ISI's enemy. Did he have authorisation from a competent authority for the visit, and if not, what were the motives? It was strange that no one seemed to ask such questions.

2. A civilian ambassador was being hounded and chased without evidence. Still, no one had been questioned over who sheltered Osama, the raid on the Abbottabad compound, the Mehran base attack, and the attack on the GHQ.

When the narrator wanted to say something, the President stopped him, saying, "You are my spokesperson, and whatever you say will be seen as the President saying it."

The President later called the coalition partners separately for a meeting. The first to meet him was Asfandyar Wali of ANP (Awami National Party). After the meeting, Asfandyar addressed a press conference and strongly defended Haqqani.

Chapter 3

Services chiefs angry

On 14 November, the President hosted a banquet for the visiting Turkmen President. The three service chiefs had also been invited. However, neither any service chief nor their deputies attended.

The service chiefs' absence from the President's banquet was highly unusual. There was no official explanation for their abstention, but official records confirmed that invitations had been sent to all of them.

Captain (PN) Amir, the deputy military secretary, disclosed that Brigadier Adnan, the military secretary, had informed him that the Army Chief would be away from Islamabad on a planned visit and should, therefore, not be invited to the dinner. As the invitations had already been sent, he requested that it be withdrawn. This order to withdraw the invitation already issued to the Army Chief was baffling. The military secretary could not have made such a request without the express directions of the Army Chief himself.

The Presidency staff found themselves in a catch-22 situation. If the protocol officer had obeyed the orders and withdrawn the invitation, it would have inevitably reached the media, creating another storm. Indeed, it likely would have been deliberately leaked to paint the Presidency in a negative light.

The invitation issued to the Army Chief was not withdrawn.

Everyone noticed the service chiefs' absence from the state banquet, leading to speculations about why they had "boycotted" the event.

It appeared they were angry with the President over the Mullen memo. They did not want to be seen with Zardari in a relaxed and joyous setting. The message they wished to send was clear: this was not business as usual. It was the first public sign of tension over the Memogate affair between the service chiefs and their supreme commander, Asif Ali Zardari.

The following day, on 15 November, the Army Chief called on the President for a one-on-one meeting. It was their first meeting in the past fortnight and the first since the Mullen memo controversy erupted. The meeting lasted over 90 minutes.

The photographs taken as the two settled into their seats were nothing short of a public relations disaster.

The pictures almost announced that the room was filled with an invisible energy of tension, unease, and an awkward sense of discomfort between the Army Chief and the supreme commander. The President was looking disapprovingly at the Army Chief, who was holding a general's cane in his hand.

Almost all the pictures the photographer snapped in the short time showed the two looking in different directions. It resembled an interaction between a deaf and a mute person. Some showed the Army Chief pointing his cane menacingly at the President. One picture captured the President almost frowning.

Selecting a suitable picture for release to the media proved challenging. I was reminded of a similar situation I had encountered long ago when Benazir Bhutto called on President Farooq Leghari days before her second government was dismissed in 1996. Those pictures of the meeting were also a PR disaster.

I sent her a slip saying, "Bibi, please allow the photographer in again; the pictures are a disaster." She instantly called the photographer. In the subsequently snapped picture, she was smiling, albeit under compulsion, undoubtedly.

However, today, the photographer could not re-enter the meeting room.

The pictures and footage of the Zardari-Kayani meeting spoke volumes. Except for one photograph and a short piece of footage, all others were destroyed.

The following morning, on 16 November, Zardari discussed the meeting during the media briefing session. He revealed that he had first asked the Army Chief about the service chiefs' absence from the banquet. The Army Chief had told him they did not come because they had not been invited.

"I immediately called the MS (military secretary) to explain.

He (the MS) said that since the chairman, joint chiefs, and the air chief were both out of the country, he thought it best not to invite any service chief."

The President said he also told the Army Chief that a deputy should have attended if a service chief was not in the country. He did not disclose the Army Chief's response to this observation.

Recounting the conversation, the President laughed, as if mocking the excuse offered, and said: "I know that in the absence of the chief, the next in line is deputed to attend. But I don't care. We are here not because of them, but they are here and are safe because of us. It is we who have taken the world community off their back. Let them handle the world if they think they can. Let Imran Khan or somebody else come and protect them from the world."

While uttering, "But I don't care," the President also gestured in disgust. At one point, he even grimaced.

The service chiefs were angry, and the supreme commander was fuming at them.

Chapter 4

The Army Chief had his halfway

A day after the President-COAS meeting, the President invited the Prime Minister and Army Chief together to a dinner meeting on 16 November. To keep it off the media radar, it was listed as a "private dinner" in the official calendar of presidential engagements.

However, the official photographers in the Presidency were already aware of the meeting. It was their duty to stay informed about any suddenly scheduled presidential engagements. I was surprised to learn that the ADC had asked the cameramen to stay away, as there would be no coverage of the event.

I rang up the ADC to emphasise the need for photo coverage. He informed me that the military secretary had instructed against any photo coverage of the dinner meeting. This puzzled me.

The military secretary was acting under the Army Chief's orders, and there was no way to convince him of the importance of photo coverage.

I texted the President: "Sir, The meeting tonight should be covered on camera. TV channels have already run the story about it. There is no point in denying it. Indeed, we cannot and should not deny it. The absence of footage will only send negative signals. It will be interpreted that cameras were disallowed due to tension in the meeting."

The President agreed and texted back, "OK-A."

The media team, which had already been sent back, was summoned to do their job and cover the meeting.

Just as the meeting began, the military secretary and ADC went inside to seek instructions about media coverage again. They returned, saying there would be no photo coverage or press conference about the meeting. The Army Chief wanted to keep it secret and did not like the optics that suggested the ice had broken and it was business as usual. He may have thought that coverage of the meeting would not align with his angry posturing.

The Army Chief had decided that no press release about the meeting was to be issued.

I sent a message again stating that the decision to keep the meeting secret was that of the GHQ, not the Presidency. As the media already knew about it, they would report the meeting, quoting unnamed sources. Subsequent media handling would, therefore, have to be done by the ISPR, not the Presidency. I added that the Presidency would be unable to do the whitewashing, and pointed media questions would have to be directed to ISPR.

The ADC called to say that the military secretary had again discussed it with both the Prime Minister and the Army Chief, who now agreed to issue a brief press statement about the meeting.

A bare-bones press statement without photographs and TV footage stated:

"Islamabad, November 16, 2011: Prime Minister Syed Yousaf Raza Gilani called on President Asif Ali Zardari at the Aiwan-e-Sadr tonight. Chief of Army Staff General Ashfaq Parvez Kayani was also present during the meeting. The current security situation in the country was discussed during the meeting. The President also hosted dinner for them."

I liked to think the Army Chief had his way, but only halfway.

Chapter 5

Haqqani asked to resign

The President's daily official engagements, including the time, duration, venue, and list of participants are typically printed in detail. However, the entry on the official calendar for 22 November 2011 was strikingly unusual and immediately piqued curiosity.

It simply stated: "Meeting at 3:15 P.M." without any further details. This brevity was extraordinary.

The meeting was held in the Prime Minister's House, which had not announced it. Attendees included Chief of Army Staff General Ashfaq Kayani and his trusted ISI Chief, Lt General Shuja Pasha. It was uncommon for the President to visit the PM's House for a meeting.

Later that evening, the Prime Minister's Office issued a press release.

"The Prime Minister has directed to conduct a detailed investigation at an appropriate level and in the meanwhile has asked Pakistan Ambassador to the USA Mr Hussain Haqqani to submit his resignation so that the investigation can be carried out properly."

"All concerned would be afforded sufficient and fair opportunity to present their views and the investigation shall be carried out fairly, objectively and without bias."

"As a result of controversy generated by the alleged memo which had been drafted, formulated and further admitted to have been received by Authority in USA, it has become necessary in national interest to formally arrive at the actual and true facts."

Foreign Minister Hina Rabbani Khar, who met me shortly after the meeting, was unaware of the decision to dismiss Haqqani and conduct an inquiry.

Haqqani had already submitted his account of events. While he did not deny communicating with Mansoor Ijaz, he emphatically denied the existence of any memo. He insisted that he had neither authored nor dictated its contents to anyone.

The request for Haqqani's resignation implied that powerful elements hostile to both Haqqani and President Zardari found his statement unsatisfactory. Given the President's strong support for Haqqani and the secrecy surrounding the meeting, it appeared that the army leadership had forced the decision to demand his resignation.

The President displayed no emotions but must have been aware of the implications. It meant one less strong voice in support of civilian supremacy. As Haqqani was the President's choice for ambassador, forcing his resignation was embarrassing for Zardari.

Upon learning of these developments, I attempted to send out a press release about Haqqani's resignation and the impending inquiry. However, I discovered that my Gmail account had just been hacked.

For the few hours that my account remained compromised, the hackers had already sent out fake messages. One such message claimed that in a private communication with a friend, I had acknowledged that the memo sent to Mike Mullen was genuine. Another falsely stated that I had told a friend the memo was indeed written at Zardari's behest. The FIA was unable to trace the hackers.

I found Haqqani, casually dressed and looking tired, sitting in the ADC's office. I took him aside to another room.

He disagreed with suggestions that the U.S. Administration was involved in conspiring against Zardari. "The U.S. Administration is least bothered," he said.

Stepping closer, he whispered, "Tell the boss that now that I have resigned, I should be allowed to leave Pakistan."

He added, "*Mujhai media mai hero bananai ka koi faaeda nahin hoga.*" ([I have already been asked to resign], it would serve no purpose to make a hero of me in the media.)

During a media briefing two days later, I conveyed this message to the President, but he did not respond.

As Haqqani's chapter closed, the appointment of Sherry Rehman as the new ambassador to the U.S. was announced.

Zardari had refused to appoint a bureaucrat or retired army officer to the post, insisting on having his own nominee in Washington. The press release stated that the President congratulated Sherry Rehman and instructed her to focus on "strengthening democracy and democratic institutions and trade, commercial and investment ties."

The emphasis on "strengthening democracy and democratic institutions" was deliberate and at the President's own insistence. The ongoing war of nerves intensified.

Chapter 6

Zardari haters go to court

Haqqani's resignation did not satisfy Zardari's detractors. Instead, they were encouraged to intensify their pressure.

Nawaz Sharif had already threatened legal action. On 23 November, immediately following Haqqani's resignation, Nawaz filed a petition in the Supreme Court requesting it to help unravel a "dreadful conspiracy" to demonise Pakistan's armed forces. Wearing a black coat, Nawaz Sharif personally appeared before the court, a petition in hand, painting Zardari and Haqqani as anti-Pakistan conspirators.

Naming Asif Ali Zardari, former Ambassador Husain Haqqani, American citizen Mansoor Ijaz, Chief of the Army Staff General Ashfaq Parvez Kayani, ISI chief Lt. General Ahmed Shuja Pasha, and foreign and interior secretaries as respondents, he demanded the court summon them to explain the "detestable, despicable and treacherous memorandum."

Saying that a war had been waged against Pakistan, Nawaz Sharif prayed the court: "The ones responsible or involved in initiating the process leading to the secret memorandum, authoring the same; providing any assistance whatsoever in the process and the ones blessing or approving the act, be graciously identified by the Supreme Court."

The petition stated: "The culprits exhibiting grave disloyalty to the state and the people of Pakistan and who are found guilty of the crimes should be brought to book." It argued that the memo's contents were designed solely to demoralise and intimidate the armed forces.

Asserting that the memo "threatened the very foundation of Pakistan", the petition contended that those "who initiated the memo, those who rendered any help or assistance in the matter, and those who blessed or approved of it are culpable for acts of high treason against the state and the Constitution."

On the same day, JUI leader Hafiz Hussain Ahmed suggested that Haqqani could be persuaded to become an approver against Zardari.

He claimed that Haqqani had completed a hat-trick of blunders that posed serious threats to Pakistan's interests and yet had escaped consequences each time. According to Ahmed, the three blunders were:

1. The government's attempt to bring the ISI under civil control in July 2008.
2. The anti; establishment clauses in the Kerry-Lugar Bill.
3. Placing an article in the *Washington Post* under President Zardari's name soon after the raid on Osama bin Laden's compound, in which the President seemed to laud the raid.

Seven years later, in March 2018, Nawaz Sharif expressed regret for his decision, but it was too late.

A private citizen, an advocate, also filed a similar plea calling for placing Husain Haqqani's name on the exit control list for committing "high treason".

In an article in *The Nation* on 25 November, leading Supreme Court lawyer Akram Shaikh stated, "It has not been denied by a stalwart jurist in the PPP that the President or anyone committing an offence of a heinous nature is not immune from accountability and could be tried like President Bill Clinton or President Nixon. Chaudhry Aitzaz Ahsan, member of CEC (Central Executive Committee) and a longstanding member of the Party, has publicly said before the electronic media that President Zardari could be investigated, though he could not be prosecuted for the offence as of now."

On 28 November, the Prime Minister formally asked the Parliamentary Committee on National Security to probe the incident. However, the Chaudhry Court, which had been sitting for over a decade on a petition by Air Marshal (Retired) Asghar Khan against an ISI chief for funding anti-PPP parties in the 1988 elections, instantly took up the petitions. The Court promptly issued notices to the respondents and Nawaz Sharif, fixing the petition for hearing from 1 December. Meanwhile, the Inquiry Commission on the Abbottabad operation also summoned Haqqani and Khawaja Asif to appear before it on 14 December.

There were some ironies in this situation:

1. In September 1999, Shehbaz Sharif, the Chief Minister of Punjab, rushed to the U.S. urging Mr Inderfurth, the assistant

secretary of state for South Asia, to issue a public warning to the military against any attempt to overthrow the Sharif government. Now, the PML-N accused Zardari of seeking U.S. assistance to forestall a possible coup against the civilian government.

2. The writer of the article, Mansoor Ijaz, harboured a strong dislike for the ISI and believed it was a sponsor of state terrorism. His article in the *Financial Times*, titled "Time to Take on Pakistan's Jihadist Spies", accused the "S-Wing" of ISI of providing the Haqqani network (Pakistan-based armed group of Afghan Taliban) with military and logistical support to challenge U.S. forces in Afghanistan. It pleaded with the Obama administration to designate this particular wing of the ISI as a "foreign governmental organization" sponsoring terrorism.

In his reply to the court, the DG ISI stated that he had met Mansoor Ijaz and found that the evidence regarding the memo was overwhelming. Kayani had expressed his desire for the players in the Memogate scandal to be brought to book.

Zardari did not submit a reply. When Chief Justice Chaudhry warned that this could lead the court to make adverse presumptions, Zardari remained unmoved.

Zardari's critics had united in a ruthless campaign against him. He saw no point in responding to their allegations in court. The battle lines were drawn—his detractors in court, Zardari outside it.

Chapter 7

The 2011 Memogate timeline

10 October: The *Financial Times* London publishes an article by Mansoor Ijaz claiming that on 9 May, a senior Pakistani diplomat requested him to deliver a secret memo to U.S. Admiral Mike Mullen from President Zardari. The memo allegedly sought U.S. intervention in case of a military coup following the U.S. raid on Osama bin Laden's hideout in Abbottabad a week earlier, on 2 May. In exchange, the U.S. was offered a revamp of Pakistan's national security and intelligence architecture and the closure of a special intelligence unit within the ISI with ties to the Taliban. The memo was reportedly delivered to Mike Mullen on 10 May.

22 October: Lt General Shuja Pasha, Director General of the ISI, flies secretly to London to meet Mansoor Ijaz.

14 November: The three service chiefs boycott the President's official dinner for the visiting Turkmen President as a mark of displeasure over the Memogate controversy.

16 November: Prime Minister Yousaf Raza Gilani, General Kayani, and President Zardari meet at the Presidency in Islamabad to discuss the secret memo controversy.

19 November: Haqqani is asked to return to Islamabad.

21 November: The Pentagon confirms that former U.S. National Security Adviser James Jones passed the memo to Admiral Mullen, but the admiral "did not find the contents credible at all."

22 November: President Zardari meets Prime Minister Yousaf Raza Gilani at the latter's house. The meeting is kept secret and described simply as a "Meeting" in the President's official calendar for that day without disclosing its location or attendees. General Kayani and the Director General of ISI, Lt General Pasha, also attended.

22 November: The Prime Minister's House announces that Haqqani has been asked to resign and states that investigations into the memo will be held at an appropriate level.

23 November: Nawaz Sharif files a petition in the Supreme Court requesting it to unravel the "dreadful conspiracy to demonise the armed forces of Pakistan."

23 November: Sherry Rehman is appointed Pakistan's

ambassador to the U.S.

28 November: The Prime Minister formally announces that the Parliamentary Committee on National Security will probe the Memogate controversy.

28 November: The Supreme Court admits the petition filed by the PML-N and issues notices to respondents named in it for a hearing on 1 December.

Chapter 8

The unsigned memo to Mike Mullen

The Memo that pushed Zardari with his back to the wall and the country into a tailspin, was not signed by anyone. Mansoor Ijaz claimed that he had drafted the memo for delivery to the White House on the instructions of a senior Pakistani diplomat (implying Ambassador Haqqani), a charge the ambassador had vehemently denied and which was never proved.

However, a memo had been drafted and, though unsigned, was delivered to the Chairman of Joint Chiefs of Staff, Admiral Mullen, through James Jones, a former National Security Advisor, on 10 May 2011. Jones was the National Security Advisor for Obama's Administration from January 2009 to October 2010.

James subsequently confirmed to the media that he received the memo from Pakistani businessman Mansoor Ijaz for delivery to Mullen. He stated that he was not in the government when he acted as an intermediary. James also confirmed his role as an intermediary to the *Financial Times*, which had published Mansoor Ijaz's article.

Later, the Pentagon said that former Chairman of the Joint Chiefs Admiral Mike Mullen knew James Jones, who had brought the controversial Memo to him.

"Mr Mullen knew the intermediary, but the letter was not signed, and he did not find the contents credible at all," a Pentagon spokesman, Captain John Kirby, said in a briefing in November 2011.

Kirby was also Mullen's spokesperson when the latter served as Chairman of the Joint Chiefs of Staff. "Nothing in it indicated it was from President Zardari," John Kirby had reportedly said.

The following is the full text of the unsigned memo delivered to Admiral Mullen:

"CONFIDENTIAL MEMORANDUM

Briefing for

Admiral Mike Mullen, Chairman, Joint Chiefs of Staff

During the past 72 hours since a meeting was held between the President, the Prime Minister and the Chief of Army Staff, there has been a significant deterioration in Pakistan's political atmosphere.

Increasingly desperate efforts by the various agencies and factions within the government to find a home – ISI and/or Army, or the civilian government – for assigning blame over the OBL (Osama Bin Laden) raid now dominate the tug-of-war between military and civilian sectors. Subsequent tit-for-tat reactions, including the outing of the CIA station chief's name in Islamabad by ISI officials, demonstrate a dangerous devolution of the ground situation in Islamabad where no central control appears to be in place.

Civilians cannot withstand much more of the hard pressure being delivered from the Army to succumb to wholesale changes. If civilians are forced from power, Pakistan becomes a sanctuary for OBL's legacy and potentially the platform for the far more rapid spread of al Qaeda's brand of fanaticism and terror. A unique window of opportunity exists for the civilians to gain the upper hand over the army and intelligence directorates due to their complicity in the OBL matter.

Request your direct intervention in conveying a strong, urgent and direct message to Gen Kayani that delivers Washington's demand for him and Gen Pasha to end their brinkmanship aimed at bringing down the civilian apparatus – that this is a 1971 moment in Pakistan's history. Should you be willing to do so, Washington's political/military backing would result in a revamp of the civilian government that, while weak at the top echelon in terms of strategic direction and implementation (even though mandated by domestic political forces), in a wholesale manner replaces the national security adviser and other national security officials with trusted advisers that include ex-military and civilian leaders favourably viewed by Washington, each of whom have long and historical ties to the U.S. military, political and intelligence communities. Names will be provided to you in a face-to-face meeting with the person delivering this message.

In the event Washington's direct intervention behind the scenes can be secured through your personal communication with Kayani (he will likely listen only to you at this moment) to stand down the Pakistani military-intelligence establishment, the new national security team is prepared, with full backing of the civilian apparatus, to do the following:

1. President of Pakistan will order an independent inquiry into the allegations that Pakistan harboured and offered assistance to OBL and other senior Qaeda operatives. The White House can suggest names of independent investigators to populate the panel, along the lines of the bipartisan 9-11 Commission, for example.

2. The inquiry will be accountable and independent, and result in findings of tangible value to the U.S. government and the American people that identify with exacting detail those elements responsible for harbouring and aiding OBL inside and close to the inner ring of influence in Pakistan's Government (civilian, intelligence directorates and military). It is certain that the OBL Commission will result in immediate termination of active service officers in the appropriate government offices and agencies found responsible for complicity in assisting OBL.

3. The new national security team will implement a policy of either handing over those left in the leadership of Al Qaeda or other affiliated terrorist groups who are still on Pakistani soil, including Ayman Al Zawahiri, Mullah Omar and Sirajuddin Haqqani, or giving U.S. military forces a "green light" to conduct the necessary operations to capture or kill them on Pakistani soil. This "carte blanche" guarantee is not without political risks but should demonstrate the new group's commitment to rooting out bad elements on our soil. This commitment has the backing of the top echelon on the civilian side of our house, and we will ensure necessary collateral support.

4. One of the great fears of the military-intelligence establishment is that with your stealth capabilities to enter and exit Pakistani airspace at will, Pakistan's nuclear assets are now legitimate targets. The new national security team is prepared, with full backing of the Pakistani government – initially civilian but eventually all three power centers – to develop an acceptable framework of discipline for the nuclear program. This effort was begun under the previous military regime, with acceptable results. We are prepared to reactivate those ideas and build on them in a way that brings Pakistan's nuclear assets under a more verifiable, transparent regime.

5 The new national security team will eliminate Section S of the ISI charged with maintaining relations to the Taliban, Haqqani

network, etc. This will dramatically improve relations with Afghanistan.

6. We are prepared to cooperate fully under the new national security team's guidance with the Indian government on bringing all perpetrators of Pakistani origin to account for the 2008 Mumbai attacks, whether outside government or inside any part of the government, including its intelligence agencies. This includes handing over those against whom sufficient evidence exists of guilt to the Indian security services.

Pakistan faces a decision point of unprecedented importance. We, who believe in democratic governance and building a much better structural relationship in the region with India AND Afghanistan, seek U.S. assistance to help us pigeon-hole the forces lined up against your interests and ours, including containment of certain elements inside our country that require appropriate re-sets and re-tasking in terms of direction and extent of responsibility after the OBL affair.

We submit this memorandum for your consideration collectively as the members of the new national security team who will be inducted by the President of Pakistan with your support in this undertaking."

Chapter 9

Heat turned on Zardari

The Supreme Court had initiated its own investigations into Memogate, disregarding the fact that the Parliamentary Committee on National Security had already taken up the matter. Nawaz Sharif demanded that Haqqani be placed on the no-fly list, declaring his actions as treason against the state and calling for him to be tried under Article 6 of the Constitution. Pasha and Kayani had stated that the evidence was overwhelming and sought to bring the players to book. Zardari's close advisors were growing increasingly concerned.

At the media briefing session, Zardari put up a brave face: "Let them try me under Article 6. Javed Hashmi (a former PML-N leader) was tried, but he didn't make an opportunity of it. I will turn it into an opportunity," he declared.

He then questioned, "Why did Pasha (DG ISI) go to London secretly to meet Mansoor without the government's permission?" implying a conspiracy against him.

Noticing the worried expressions of those gathered around him, he said, "You all seem demoralised for nothing. I want you to cheer up. Fight back."

When someone remarked that they weren't demoralised, Zardari responded, "If someone told me he was not demoralised, I know if he is speaking the truth or not. I can read the energy around the face of a demoralised person."

He then discussed various topics, hopping from one subject to another. No one interrupted him as he spoke.

"Walk in the thought of the leader," he said to me. "Trust the leader."

I felt uncomfortable, reminded of a similar situation three years ago in November 2008, when he had asked me to "Trust your leader" as he offered India a unilateral "No-First-Use" of nuclear weapons policy.

Zardari continued, "When I married Shaheed Bibi, no one imagined that one day she would become the Prime Minister." His voice carried a deep sense of both satisfaction and determination.

Emphasising his resilience in facing challenges, he declared,

"I have walked from the gallows to the Presidency."

He then adopted a more humble tone, "Humility is my best weapon. I have to be forgiving in this position and also because Allah has been so kind to me. Moula Ali says that Allah forgives you, and so you must also forgive others. I cannot afford to be arrogant."

Regarding the possibility of foreign powers working against him, Zardari disagreed, stating that the U.S. Administration did not want action against the ISI after the raid on the OBL compound.

"This is a bigger mischief," he said. "Perhaps some people want a fight between the civil and the military."

Turning philosophical, he remarked that national institutions, once destroyed, cannot be easily rebuilt. "Look at Afghanistan and Iraq," he said. "I can't allow this (destruction of state institutions)."

The thought of a possible military coup seemed to lurk at the back of his mind as he said, "So what if they come and take over. Let them come. Let them handle it if they can."

"*Wo aaingai aur kahaingai hamain dhakka dia gia hai*" (they will come and say that they have been forced into it), he added. "Let them," he repeated, "I will not be the loser."

"I will not lose, they will lose," he asserted.

This brought to mind an article published in a U.S. newspaper on 24 November. Commenting on Haqqani's resignation, the article stated, "Mr Haqqani's exit should make clear that Pakistan's generals have no intention of accepting the democratic principle of civilian supremacy." The article added, "Ironically, the worst effects will be felt by Pakistan's army and its powerful spy wing, the ISI—even though they may not realise it yet."

The media briefing session with the President extended well beyond its usual duration.

It was evident that the heat had been turned on him.

Chapter 10

The President stressed

The first sign of stress taking its toll on President Zardari came during a meeting with the Sri Lankan delegation at the Presidency on the afternoon of 29 November 2011, hours after the Chaudhry Court announced it would hear petitions in the Memogate case on 1 December.

That afternoon, the chief of the defence staff of Sri Lanka, the high commissioner of Sri Lanka in Islamabad, and some senior officials called on the President. General Khalid Shamim Wyne, chairman of the joint chiefs of staff committee, was also present.

Exuding a mix of confidence, frustration, and emotion, the President dominated the conversation during the 35-minute meeting. He began speaking even before the dignitary could make customary remarks to thank him and convey greetings from the Sri Lankan leaders.

Zardari did not discuss Pak-Sri Lanka relations. Instead, he spoke about the Salalah incident three days prior, in which U.S.-led NATO forces attacked a border check post in Mohmand Agency, killing over two dozen Pakistani soldiers.

"It will not be a trial of Asif Zardari; it will be a trial of the U.S.," he said emotionally.

"I want to convey a message," he continued without indicating to whom it was directed.

"We are a strong nation of 200 million people. We know how to fight."

"Our soldiers fight very bravely. They take risks, even unnecessary risks. They blew up enemy tanks by going under them."

The President then criticised the U.S. and the West for their approach in Afghanistan: "They have blundered by not addressing the core issue of drug trade financing by the militants. They think they are smarter, but they should not assume that the other fellow is stupid."

Regarding the fight against militants, he asserted: "We will select the targets ourselves and also our own timing. We cannot take on every group at one time. We will not be dictated to by others."

He then spoke of the U.S. raid on Osama bin Laden's

compound a few months earlier:

"We did not make Osama; they made him. If my boys knew where Osama was, they would have also known that they were under surveillance and would have covered their tracks."

Zardari claimed to have told the CIA chief that if he had been informed about bin Laden's hideout, he could have sorted it out. However, he said the CIA chief maintained he hadn't heard even a "squeak" about bin Laden's whereabouts.

The President then spoke of his personal courage: "I am the supreme commander and will pay the price. I will go to Guantanamo Bay (high-security prisons in Cuba controlled by the U.S.) if needed. I will fight military dictators but not the institution."

He emphasised his role as an elected President who had transferred powers to Parliament: "I gave up the command of the National Command Authority. The whole nation, from top to bottom, knows it."

As Zardari's speech became less coherent, he jumped from one subject to another. His emotions were evident as he tapped his knee, words gushing out. It was clear that something was troubling him deeply; a storm seemed to be building up in his mind.

Salman Faruqui looked towards the ADC, silently indicating that the meeting should end. The ADC understood and stood at attention, signalling to all that the meeting time was over. Throughout the entire meeting, the Sri Lankan dignitary did not have a chance to utter even a single word.

The following day, 30 November, the President met with a Korean business delegation visiting Pakistan. Once again, Zardari's conversation was random and incoherent.

He began by talking about himself: "I don't care about my life. Life and death are in the hands of Allah. I stood my ground and faced three hostile governments. They could not break me." He did not specify whom he meant by "they".

Zardari insisted he was not vengeful: "In prison, Nawaz Sharif asked for forgiveness, and I forgave him."

He expressed readiness for a long-drawn battle: "Mine is not a tenured job. We are in the business of politics and will remain in it."

"We are a seven-thousand-year-old civilisation. What will this democracy of 200 years (referring to the USA) teach us?"

Perhaps to reassure himself, he addressed the Koreans: "Nothing will happen; don't worry. Let us grow up; move on. I see tense faces." He then advised them, "Relax, relax."

The President's incoherence was more pronounced than when he met the Sri Lankan air chief the previous day.

All other engagements for the day were cancelled. The President needed rest.

A President may seem to be at the top, but the top can also be lonely. A stressed Zardari was lonely at the top.

Chapter 11

Haqqani confides

During the Memogate crisis, I had a lengthy conversation with Ambassador Haqqani. He viewed Memogate as a conspiracy against President Zardari and lamented that the President went to great lengths to appease the generals. Haqqani shared his thoughts candidly:

"The Osama bin Laden (OBL) raid presented a perfect opportunity to dismiss both the Army Chief and the Director General of Inter-Services Intelligence (DG ISI)," Haqqani explained. "The case against the Army Chief was clear: he was unaware of what was happening under his nose. As for the DG ISI, he was either complicit or incompetent. The first 48 hours were crucial. Any action taken then would have been manageable."

Haqqani continued, "If timely action had been taken, there would have been no Memogate. But Zardari had cold feet. He feared being ousted from power."

As pressure on Haqqani increased, many suspected he might turn against the President. "Even Zardari asked if I would become another Masood Mahmood," Haqqani revealed, referring to a former paramilitary federal security force chief who had turned approver against Zulfikar Ali Bhutto in the late 1970s. "The President had become somewhat paranoid."

Haqqani took pride in recounting how Benazir Bhutto had trusted him to engage with Army Chief General Jahangir Karamat and the ISI chief. He also spoke of his role in softening the stance of U.S. Vice President Dick Cheney's staff towards Bhutto, creating space for dialogue. "Bibi acknowledged my contributions," he said. "She even told her American interlocutors that she trusted me." Haqqani claimed that his groundwork in Washington had made possible the direct talks between Musharraf and Bhutto in Abu Dhabi.

Emphasising that a policy of appeasement was misguided, Haqqani drew a parallel with Aung San Suu Kyi, Myanmar's democratic leader. "Suu Kyi pandered to the army for over a decade, accepting all their demands, but was ultimately rebuffed by ambitious generals," he noted. "She earned a bad name and did not serve democracy when she defended human rights violations by the military junta in her country."

Haqqani pointed out that Benazir Bhutto had adopted a hard line on Kashmir and supported the Taliban during her second term at the establishment's insistence. "Yet she was not allowed to complete her term," he said. "FB, you once quoted her saying about the generals, "*inn ke mun ko khoon lag gia hai*" (they have tasted blood)," he reminded me.

He cautioned that even low-level functionaries in the ISI sometimes pursue their own agendas, and political leaders take them too seriously. To illustrate this point, Haqqani shared an anecdote about "Brigadier Samosa", a retired military officer who had set up a private business supplying samosas in Islamabad. "Everyone in town sought to appease him," Haqqani explained. "A well-known 5-star hotel purchased samosas from his bakery in large quantities. When storage space ran out, the samosas were distributed among the elite in gift packs, benefiting both parties."

Haqqani then recalled a conversation with former air chief, Air Marshal (retired) Asghar Khan. "Asghar Khan confessed to me that he had been misled into believing that agitation against Bhutto would not result in martial law," Haqqani said. "Lt General Chishti had told him that after the 1971 debacle, the army was not in a position to impose martial law. Thus misled, Asghar Khan continued agitating for Bhutto's removal, inadvertently paving the way for the 1977 martial law. Asghar Khan told me he felt cheated."

Haqqani concluded our conversation with a warning: "Beware of calculated deception plans."

Chapter 12

Suicide attack on Zardari

The Memogate scandal, which turned into a political and security crisis, seemed like a suicide attack on Zardari by the Army Chief and DG ISI, aided by the opposition leader at the time and CJP (Chief Justice of Pakistan) Iftikhar Chaudhry. It consumed Zardari worse than any other personal or political crisis he had thus far endured. While it is indeed remarkable that he survived it, to claim that he was unscathed would be wrong and not borne out by facts. He was badly bruised.

The army and ISI chiefs claimed that the memo to Mike Mullen was not fake. They asserted it existed and that Zardari wanted to use the U.S. against the army and ISI in the aftermath of the raid on the Osama bin Laden (OBL) compound. They blamed Haqqani as the conduit for the memo but actually aimed at Zardari as the mastermind.

In TV talk shows, Zardari was painted as an evil incarnate who conspired against the military leadership and the ISI. References were made to the Kerry-Lugar Bill that linked U.S. aid to Pakistan with democracy in the country and blamed it on Zardari-Haqqani. Doomsday predictions were made that Ambassador Haqqani would turn into an approver. References were made to his alleged admission in the past of having links as a student with the ISI chief Akhtar Abdul Rehman. Suggestions were made that some civilians who were aware may have blown the OBL cover. Who else among the civilians would know more about the cover than President Asif Ali Zardari?

The President, indeed, was under siege. Accused of treason, he stood at the centre of the storm.

Embattled and defiant, Zardari decided to go down fighting. To send a message of defiance, he announced he would address a joint session of Parliament and make some hard-hitting statements by directly addressing the nation. He was ready to fight to the finish.

The announcement to address Parliament created an uproar. He was accused of pitting Parliament against the judiciary and the army. Zardari did not care.

"President and supreme commander of the armed forces Asif Ali Zardari has decided to address joint session of the

Parliament after Muharram and called upon the government to take appropriate steps in this regard," said a brief press release issued by the Presidency.

Never before had the title "supreme commander of the armed forces" been used for President Zardari in official press releases. But today, Zardari asked that the press release clearly state that the "supreme commander of the armed forces" had decided to address Parliament. The decision about the time and date of the address was left to the government to allow him to choose the timing.

The press release also referred to iconic pro-democracy leader Aung San Suu Kyi of Myanmar for "standing up to mountains of hardship for the cause."

The President approved the draft press release before it was issued. The die was cast. Enough was enough.

He invited a small group of advisors to his residence for discussions to prepare the draft of the address to Parliament. Nearly half a dozen advisors came for the preparatory meeting.

Zardari began speaking to prepare the pitch for his speech points. I pulled out my pen and notebook.

Soon, it became clear that he was laying bare his distressed mind and soul more than indicating points for a formal speech. It was yet another monologue, as in meetings with the Sri Lankan dignitaries and Korean business delegation the previous week. He alone spoke uninterruptedly, words coming out of his mouth like a torrent.

He spoke for nearly two hours. Words and sentences gushed out of his lips like a heavy downpour. Sometimes he was highly sublime, at other times too mundane and abrasive. That he was deeply distressed was not in doubt.

Aware that the President had been stressed this past week, his personal physician, Dr Asim, barged into the meeting uninvited. He did not want the President to remain engaged in a brainstorming session for too long. Dr Asim was casually dressed, as if straight from the bedroom.

Seeing him, the President clapped as if to draw attention to an unwelcome intrusion and firmly asked Dr Asim not to disturb him. Dr Asim retreated.

As emotions turned into anger, Zardari resumed: "I am the supreme commander. I can destroy my enemies. If anyone thinks that I will surrender, he is mistaken. I am not going to run away."

He also threatened: "I know many things. Kayani is under me; I am not under them. Nobody should think that manipulations against me will succeed."

"I will defeat all manipulators," he declared.

Without naming anyone, he said, "They are playing with me, but I will play with them."

He seemed to indict Kayani and Pasha.

Then he softened somewhat: "But I will not talk. I have to protect the country. I will."

I scribbled in shorthand as he spoke. I did this not to prepare his speech but for the sake of history and to record how intrigues at the highest state levels had pushed the civilian President to the brink.

"I am radiating energy, Farhatullah, that you don't understand," he said, looking at me as he noticed me scribbling.

He once again clapped his hands and said, "Laughter is the best medicine. It releases frustration." Then he laughed out loud, asking us to laugh with him. Obligingly, everyone giggled. Once or twice, he clapped, which exaggerated the laughter.

It brought to mind Henry Kissinger's memoirs of President Nixon when he was mired in Watergate and deeply distressed. One night, the President telephoned Kissinger and called him to the White House during the crisis. When Kissinger came, Nixon told him, "Henry, you are not a very orthodox Jew, and I am not an orthodox Quaker, but we need to pray" and went down on his knees. Obligingly, Kissinger knelt, too.

Zardari, mired in Memogate, asked his advisors to laugh with him as he laid bare his soul, and everyone did.

Suddenly, looking at me, he said, "Do you know why I did not send you to the Senate? [in the last Senate election in 2009.] You are a credible face of the Party, and when you speak, people trust you. You speak for me. I asked you to work with me even though when you worked with Bibi, you did not think highly of me. You also thought I was corrupt."

When I tried to say something, he stopped me.

Turning sublime and philosophical, he started talking about how, with a trained mind, focused thoughts, and an outpouring of love, one can even control the universe. Love embraces everything. He seemed to be reading from Rumi's treatise on love.

He hopped from one subject to another as everyone listened.

Next, he spoke about the power of words. Positive words inspire, while negative words cause stress and anxiety and can be demoralising. "Watch your words," he asked everyone.

He alternated between the sublime and the mundane as he said again: "No one should think of intrigues against me. I will defeat them."

Exhausted, he asked for tea for everyone.

After over two hours of monologue, the President called off the meeting and asked to reassemble later that night.

The "briefing session" was postponed until after dinner.

The aborted midday preparatory meeting resumed after dinner.

Once again, the President began by lamenting how he had been demonised and wronged in life. Some unforgettable and telling words and sentences stuck in the mind:

"I worshipped Bibi, not merely loved her. She was far beyond even the feelings of love. I have lost her. She sacrificed her life."

"What else is there for me to give?"

"I was accused of every crime on earth. I was accused of murder, of killing my own brother-in-law. I was accused of drug smuggling, of tying a bomb to the leg to extort money."

"Is there anything of which I have not been accused?"

"I endured all this. I have been wronged."

Baring his anguished soul, his words came out from the depths of his heart, creating a tapestry of admiration and respect that was difficult to explain. His words pierced the heart as he spoke and were profoundly moving.

His voice became louder, and his speech incoherent. The next moment, it faltered, and his body shook. Then he began to stutter.

He struggled for the words to come out of his lips.

Words that had flowed like a torrent before were now coming out with difficulty and haltingly. Each word was a struggle to come out of his mouth.

Then the stutter vanished, and he turned pale. His head swung to the right as he slipped on the sofa.

A bottle of water was rushed, but it was hard to make him drink. He lay on the sofa, his feet dangling. He was helped to lie on the carpet on the floor. Someone rushed out to call for medical help.

Before the physician arrived, a trained valet barged into the room and administered some emergency tablets on his own. He knew what to do almost by reflex action if something went wrong. He removed Zardari's socks, which were moist with sweat.

Artificial resuscitation was also tried, but only briefly. It was not needed.

The military secretary also rushed in. Everyone left the room. Minister of State Kamal Majidullah and I, however, stayed behind.

Doctors called in emergency had arrived. A stretcher was brought in to take the President to his bedroom. The shades of night had fallen. It was 10.30 P.M.

As he was being shifted to the bedroom, I looked at him more closely again, fighting back the thought that it might be the last time.

This was not the fate he deserved. It was hard to look at him. He was going down fighting. If it was his last battle, it was also his best.

Shakespeare wrote: "He was a man, take him for all in all, I shall not look upon his like again."

Chapter 13

Distrusting military facilities

The small group of advisors huddled together in the adjoining room. What next?

Preparatory sessions for the President's address to Parliament were no longer a priority. Dr Asim, the personal physician and petroleum minister, had left for Baku a few hours earlier but was now recalled to Islamabad. Bilawal Bhutto Zardari was also informed.

The doctors would make the necessary decisions about medical procedures, but only Bilawal could authorise them. It was imperative that he be with his father. The Prime Minister was also informed of the situation.

A scheduled meeting of the President, Prime Minister, and Army Chief for the next day was cancelled.

The President needed to be persuaded to go to Karachi for rest. Some close members would stay overnight in case he needed company and support.

Considering the President's sensitivities, it was suggested that Haqqani travel with him if the former agreed to go to Karachi. The President had already told his DMS (deputy military secretary) that Haqqani should always accompany him during his travels.

The President's address to Parliament had become inconsequential. Work on the draft preparation was put off.

Secretary General Salman Faruqui would carry out the presidential secretariat's usual business in accordance with the standard operating procedures (SOP), as had happened during President Ayub Khan's illness in the 1960s when his principal secretary (Syed Fida Hassan) performed the day-to-day work.

It was night-time, and the President was in his bedroom. Doctors advised that he should be taken to the Armed Forces Institute of Cardiology (AFIC) or CMH (Combined Military Hospital) for an MRI and other tests. The President, who had regained his composure, declined.

In the morning, two doctors examined him in his bedroom and again tried to persuade him to go to the CMH. He refused.

Reputed cardiologist Dr Major General Azhar Kayani (no relation to Army Chief General Kayani) came to examine him. When he came out, he reached out to Army Chief General Ashfaq

Kayani and spoke with him.

After speaking with the Army Chief, Dr Kayani once again went to the President's room but soon came out. He may have tried to persuade him again to go to the CMH, and the President may have refused yet again. No one could tell.

After Dr Kayani had left, Zardari called for the real estate tycoon Malik Riaz to come. He came to see the President in his bedroom.

Malik Riaz told us that he, too, had advised the President against going to any military facility for tests and check-ups and that the President had agreed.

The President's personal physician, Dr Asim, called from Baku, saying that he was on his way back to Islamabad. "Babar Saab, under no circumstance should the President be taken to the CMH." he said emphatically. He did not say why. He suggested the President be shifted to his private hospital in Karachi if needed.

The day passed. Later in the evening, the Army Chief called and wanted to talk to the President. When Secretary General Salman Faruqui told the Army Chief that the President needed rest, General Kayani did not insist and hung up.

No visitors were allowed to see him, and no calls were connected to him. All attempts to persuade him to go to the CMH failed.

Late at night, the Army Chief called again and wanted to talk to the President.

Although doctors had advised that no calls should be put through to him, the ADC on duty connected the call to the President.

The phone call lasted for over 140 minutes. Given the President's state of mind, he must have done most of the talking while the Army Chief only listened. Anxious staffers in the Presidency watched the lights on the switchboard to see if the call had ended.

Some staffers anxiously paced up and down.

The long call from the Army Chief made many feel uncomfortable. The President was not in the right frame of mind. He may not have been very coherent, and he needed rest. One wished that the Army Chief had terminated the call himself rather than engaging the President in conversation for nearly two and a half hours.

Some apprehended that the recording of an incoherent monologue might later be used to declare the President incapable of holding office on medical grounds. Whether right or wrong, the distrust was palpable.

As soon as the Army Chief's phone call ended, the doctors again went inside and tried to persuade him. Malik Riaz also followed them.

Once again, the President firmly told the doctors that he would not move to the CMH.

Past midnight, around 1:30 A.M., the Army Chief again called Salman Faruqui, saying that he had already made security and other arrangements at the Armed Forces Institute of Cardiology (AFIC). The President could be taken there if the need arose. He also said he would be available and could be contacted on the phone anytime. He did not insist on talking with the President over the phone.

The President was sedated and went to sleep.

I had been asked to call Senate Chairman Farooq Naek in Karachi to ask him to return to Islamabad immediately. It was around 4 A.M. He did not know why and asked for the reason. He was told, "It is absolutely urgent and important that you are available in Islamabad early today."

Under the Constitution, the Senate chairman acts as the President during the President's absence or illness. Quick to realise the implications, Farooq Naek said he would take the first available flight to Islamabad.

As during the day, all attempts made at night to take him to the CMH failed. The night passed.

Yesterday, the Army Chief and the DG ISI distrusted him in the Memogate case. Today, Zardari was no less distrustful.

The civil-military disconnect was dramatised.

It is hard to say whether the Army Chief ever considered why the President was so distrustful or why there was such a gulf. It would be strange if he did not.

Chapter 14

Tests only in Dubai

Early morning on 6 December, Bilawal Bhutto Zardari, accompanied by his aunt Azra Fazal Pecheho, arrived from Karachi and went straight to see his father in the bedroom. When he came out, Bilawal declared that he would take his father only to Dubai and nowhere else. The doctors strongly advised against air travel to Dubai.

The medical team again insisted that the President be shifted to the CMH for tests, particularly MRI scans. However, the President, Bilawal, and his family disagreed. Personal physician Dr Asim had already sent a message that under no circumstances should the President be shifted except to his private hospital in Karachi. Zardari then put the discussion to rest by saying that he would follow the advice of his son Bilawal and no one else.

Preparations for taking the President to Dubai commenced.

The lounge was abuzz with rumours, gossip, hopes and fears, and occasionally some serious talk. Conspiracy theories floated around in whispers. "Haqqani will soon throw in the towel and become an approver," the conspiracy theorists said.

As the day warmed up, the Prime Minister also arrived. A helicopter had landed in the compound to take the President to the Islamabad airport, where an air ambulance was waiting to take him to Dubai in the evening.

Senate Chairman Farooq Naek also arrived from Karachi.

Once again, the President emphasised that Ambassador Haqqani must accompany him to Dubai. He did not want to leave Haqqani behind at any cost.

Zardari then called in Senate Chairman Farooq Naek, who was to act as President in his absence.

The photographer was turned back, as taking pictures was not advisable. The President's mood and body language did not permit it. It was also an internal meeting, and there was no need for photo coverage. Farooq Naek had been a trusted Zardari lieutenant, but today, the President did not easily trust anyone.

Zardari's personal physician Dr Asim (who had returned from Baku, cutting short his visit) was pacing up and down, waiting to see the President. When Naek came out, Dr Asim went in but quickly came back disappointed. He said he had failed to persuade the President not to insist on taking Haqqani along.

No one could say whether it was for Haqqani's security or something else. However, it delayed the helicopter's departure for the airport.

Haqqani was worried. He was on a no-fly list under court orders, and leaving the country would create huge problems for both him and the President.

The Prime Minister warned that if Haqqani travelled out of the country, shrieking newspaper headlines the next day would read, "Zardari, Haqqani flee the country". This would provoke strong reactions from the judiciary, political parties, and the army and be impossible to control.

"If Haqqani left the country, the government would not survive for a day," he warned without mincing words.

He also advised against the President's medical tests in Pakistan. He said the reports would be exploited in the media and the court to disqualify the President on medical grounds. The President should, therefore, go to Dubai for tests, but without Haqqani.

It was a case of Hobson's choice.

Someone even suggested sedating the President and escorting him to the helicopter without Haqqani. No serious thought, however, was given to this idea.

The President insisted on taking Haqqani along, but everyone opposed it. Gilani had said that Haqqani leaving the country with the President would be the end of his government. The situation was becoming increasingly complicated. Hour after hour, the helicopter's departure for the airport was delayed because the President could not be persuaded to drop Haqqani from the entourage to Dubai.

Some journalists got wind of what was going on. Soon, TV channels were abuzz with stories that all was not well in the Presidency.

The optics inside the Presidency needed to be corrected for the media's consumption. Prime Minister Gilani played a deft hand.

He said that he would make a formal call on the President. The photo coverage of the meeting would convey the optics of business as usual, suggesting there was nothing abnormal in the Presidency.

When told that a positive photo-op was unlikely given the President's mood, he said, "Let us see how it goes."

When Gilani met him, the President did not smile—his usual broad grin was missing. He looked uneasy, tense, and even angry. Gilani strained to wear a smile, hoping to make Zardari smile, but failed.

Gilani then addressed the President in the Seraiki language.

"Would you smile, Sir, to tell the people *"Ke tusi apnai Prime Minister si khush ho."* (That you are happy with your Prime Minister.)

He pulled it off.

Involuntarily, the President smiled. His face lit up, wearing the trademark broad grin. Cameras clicked.

Photos and video footage of the meeting dispelled negative media reports that all was not well in the Presidency.

Chapter 15

Zardari refuses to go sans Haqqani

As the departure for Dubai was delayed due to Zardari's insistence on taking Haqqani with him, the Army Chief called Yousaf Raza Gilani. "Time is running out, and a decision on medical tests needs to be taken urgently," he told the Prime Minister.

"Travelling to Dubai will take time," he said, suggesting that tests be carried out locally and urgently, as further delay could have serious consequences for the President's health.

The Prime Minister knew that Haqqani going with the President to Dubai was inviting a political disaster. Kayani emphasised that delaying medical procedures endangered the President's life, stressing the need for medical tests within the country.

Gilani once again went to the President and assured him that Haqqani would be safe and well-protected in Islamabad, even when he was away in Dubai. "There's no need to take him along to Dubai," he suggested to Zardari.

The President declined. He had said he was ready to go to Dubai as Bilawal had advised, but Haqqani had to accompany him.

Malik Riaz was standing nearby within hearing distance. He knew more than anyone that any aircraft with both Zardari and Haqqani on board would not be allowed to leave Pakistan's airspace. "It will be turned back," he told me without mincing words.

He then tried to persuade the President to go to Karachi instead of Dubai. He was certain that the aircraft would be turned back only if it crossed Pakistani airspace and not if it went only to Karachi.

Malik Riaz did not tell the President that his aircraft would be turned back and not allowed to leave Pakistan's airspace with Haqqani on board. However, he tried to persuade him to go to Karachi instead of Dubai. Zardari was uncomfortable and looked at Malik Riaz as if saying, "*Et tu, Brute*?" and declined to go to Karachi instead of Dubai.

Bilawal was watching with a brave face.

Leaping forward, he said authoritatively, "Let's go, Baba. Your health is most important." He was confident that his father would not refuse him.

We retreated further, allowing them to talk between themselves. They talked for a while. I did not overhear what Bilawal said to his father, but Zardari's body language suggested that he agreed to whatever Bilawal had told him. Zardari turned back to his living room.

Someone whispered that Bilawal had threatened to resign as Party Chairman if his father declined.

It is highly unlikely that Bilawal would have threatened his father with consequences. Although he resented some of his father's political decisions, he never disagreed that far.

A little later, the President emerged from his living room, ready to leave for the airport by helicopter. I thought Bilawal had been successful in persuading him to travel to Dubai without Haqqani. As usual, a goat was sacrificed before he stepped out.

Haqqani was standing nearby in the lobby. Zardari asked him if he was ready with his passport and bag, to which he again said "yes."

Just as the President was walking towards the lift, he spotted his friend Anver Majid, the Sindhi business tycoon who had also arrived from Karachi.

The President greeted him with folded hands raised to shoulder level. Then he almost leapt towards him and gestured to touch Majid's knees in the traditional mark of respect among Sindhis.

Blushing, Anver Majid retreated a step as he held the President's hand.

The conspiracy theorists said, without evidence, that Haqqani actually wanted to accompany the President to Dubai to escape and had readied his passport and bag.

Along with the President, we moved towards the waiting cars and the helipad, which is not far away in the presidential complex.

Two helicopters, with engines roaring, were already there, ready to take off at short notice.

While walking with him toward the lift, the President said to me without any provocation:

"If (Army Chief) Kayani had listened to me last night, things would have been different and much better. If they want to impose martial law, let them do so now and not wait. I will see how they will do it." I wondered why he said this.

Apparently, during the 140-minute phone conversation, the President and the Army Chief disagreed over some issues, but he did not elaborate.

Haqqani and his wife also came down to take a car for the helipad.

As he emerged from the lift, the President again asked for Haqqani and his wife.

On seeing them, he said: "*Shabash beta, betho, jaldi karo.*" (Well done, son. Sit, hurry up.)

The few people around the President at the time milled together like family members. Grief and a sense of emergency had brought them closer together.

The President then looked around and said, "I made you ministers and all; listen to me," as he walked towards the waiting car. It was not clear whom he was addressing. What was clear was that he was stressed.

Chapter 16

To the helipad with a loaded gun and Haqqani

Two helicopters were waiting at the helipad in the Presidency to take the President and his staff to the airport. I was already at the helipad.

President Zardari was adamant about taking Ambassador Haqqani along to Dubai despite the fact that Haqqani was not supposed to leave the country.

The President boarded helicopter #1 with Ambassador Haqqani by his side.

The rotors roared menacingly for nearly half an hour, but the helicopter did not take off.

The pilots made excuses for the delay. The President grew restless as one deadline after another passed and the helicopter remained grounded.

When Zardari enquired about the delay, he was told that permission to land in Dubai was still awaited.

After long, agonising moments in the suspense-filled air, it was announced that the helicopter was ready to take off for the Islamabad airport. It remained unclear whether the President would then proceed to Dubai by air ambulance or to Karachi by another flight. The possibility that Zardari might create a scene at the Islamabad airport, insisting on taking Haqqani to Dubai, was unsettling.

I entered the helicopter to see the President one last time before his departure. Haqqani and the President's personal staff were already seated, wearing seatbelts.

An aide rushed in to inform the President that Dubai had still not granted permission to land, and it had been decided to go to Karachi instead.

The President refused to go to Karachi, insisting on travelling to Dubai with Haqqani.

"I will wait for 30 hours for the permission, but I'm not going to Karachi," he declared.

Suddenly, the engines stopped roaring, and the power went off. Something had gone wrong. The President had refused to go to Karachi and wouldn't budge, even as the engines had stopped.

I soon learned that permission from Dubai authorities to land was not the real issue.

Business tycoon Malik Riaz approached me. Naming a senior Islamabad-based officer of an intelligence agency, he said, "I have just received a call on my mobile from him. He said authoritatively that any helicopter or aircraft with Haqqani on board will not be allowed to leave Pakistani airspace."

It sounded ominous.

If the flight carrying the President and Haqqani was actually forced to land anywhere in the country, it would explode into a huge scandal. The media would shriek that the army had foiled Zardari's bid to flee the country along with Haqqani. That would be disastrous. I remembered the Prime Minister's warning.

Rehman Malik was also nearby. He made a call from his mobile phone.

Malik instructed the person he had called to treat his previous instructions for the special plane to land in Dubai as cancelled. He asked his staff to convey these instructions in writing to all concerned parties.

Rehman Malik explained to me that he did this to prevent agencies from intercepting the aircraft and forcing it to land back in Islamabad, which would have caused the President huge embarrassment.

Time seemed to have come to a standstill. Every minute felt like an endless age as a high drama unfolded.

The President had boarded helicopter #1 with Haqqani, believing he was going to Dubai, not Karachi. He was also carrying a loaded gun.

Rehman Malik claimed that Dubai had cancelled permission for the air ambulance to land.

Dr Asim refused to board the helicopter with the President and backed out.

"He (the President) is highly agitated. I know he's carrying a gun. I also know that he will fight to the last. He can do anything. He has already instructed his son Bilawal to stay behind in Islamabad at the Prime Minister's House. He is capable of doing anything and even going too far," Dr Asim said.

Dr Asim feared that Zardari might start shooting randomly inside the plane if it landed in Karachi instead of Dubai. "He will feel cheated and will react violently," Dr Asim explained. "I will not travel in this helicopter."

Malik Riaz again warned that under no circumstances would Haqqani be allowed to leave Pakistani airspace, citing the officer who had informed him.

On the way to the helipad, a well-informed staffer confided that the President had remarked he would go to the bitter end, no matter what the consequences.

The Memogate affair had pushed the President to the brink.

The Prime Minister was apprised of the situation. On his father's advice, Bilawal was already safely ensconced in the Prime Minister's House. Together, Gilani and Bilawal came to the helipad. Gilani was driving the car. It was around 4:30 P.M.

Rehman Malik briefed Gilani before he went to see the President seated in helicopter #1.

The Prime Minister then drove to the steps of the helicopter and went inside to speak with the President.

In the few minutes he was inside the helicopter, he somehow managed to charm the President. No one knew exactly how he did it, but the President agreed to return to the President's House and not insist on going to Dubai or anywhere else.

Gilani later said that he had told the President, "Since Dubai hasn't given permission to land, you have to return to the house. You're not going to Karachi. Haqqani will go with you wherever you go, but now you're not going anywhere, so let's go back."

Everyone breathed a sigh of relief and returned from the helipad to the President's House.

It was almost 5 P.M. The President went to his bedroom.

Chapter 17

Order of the Supreme Commander

Zardari felt reassured after Gilani told him that he could travel anywhere with Haqqani. His temper cooled down. The President might still have refused if anyone else had similarly assured him. But he readily believed Gilani.

The anxious Presidency staff had climbed the balcony, watching with bated breath from a safe distance as the high drama unfolded at the helipad.

As tempers cooled, it breathed new life into the "more loyal than the king" types. One of them suggested that Secretary General Salman Faruqui send a letter to the defence secretary stating that the President had allowed Haqqani to travel with him on his personal guarantee that Haqqani would return to Pakistan.

The President had not actually asked for this.

A go-getter type federal minister insisted that the letter be sent out soon.

Salman Faruqui said that the President had not asked for it and that using the President's name without authorisation would be wrong.

The minister tried to convince Faruqui that in an emergency like this, the President's secretary general could make appropriate decisions on his behalf. He argued that as the President was not in the right frame of mind, it became Faruqui's moral and official responsibility to take personal charge.

Faruqui knew it would be a fatal mistake. It would be too costly politically, not only for him but also for the President.

He said bluntly that carrying out his orders in the President's current frame of mind would still be unwise, even if the President had asked. He added that everyone knew that the President was incapable of making sound decisions in this state.

He added that he was morally bound to keep the President out of harm's way at all times and to ensure that due diligence and principles of propriety were applied to orders purportedly made by the President.

He flatly refused to misuse the President's name and forcefully reasoned with the minister why it was important that nothing illegal or wrong was done.

He refused to be provoked or flattered when the minister

taunted, "Your loyalty is under test."

Calmly, Faruqui gave a brief lecture on what "true loyalty" meant.

"Sir, the President believes in the 'out-of-the-box solution', and this indeed is an 'out-of-the-box solution,'" the minister pleaded. Faruqui was unmoved.

"What is the out-of-the-box solution? How will you do it?" Faruqui asked.

"Sir, the order will be issued under your signatures on behalf of the President as 'Supreme Commander of the Armed Forces.' Copies of the 'Order' will be sent to the three services chiefs, the Chief Justice of Pakistan, and everyone along the chain of command involved in its implementation," the minister said rather audaciously.

"What will the order say?" Faruqui asked.

"It will simply say 'The Supreme Commander of the Armed Forces has decided to take Haqqani to Dubai on his personal guarantee,'" the minister responded.

"What next?" Faruqui asked.

"Copies of the 'Order' will be sent to all departments requiring them to facilitate implementation of the 'Supreme Commander's Order.'"

"Nothing doing," Faruqui gave a shut-up call.

The smart alec, however, did not give up.

Salman Faruqui was on the residence side of the President's House at the time.

Someone was sent up to Faruqui's office to get blank letterheads. Initially, Faruqui's staff refused but relented later and gave the blank letterhead.

The "Order" was typed on it and brought to Salman Faruqui to sign.

"Sir, your loyalty is under test," said the person again while placing it before Faruqui for his signature.

Faruqui was flabbergasted.

"Am I mad?" he asked. "Is this the way you want to help the President?"

Faruqui said that as his secretary general, it was his duty to protect the President instead of pushing him into harm's way. He flatly refused.

The loyalists instantly denounced him for "disloyalty" and taunted him for ditching the President in his time of need.

Faruqui retorted, "You do not even know what loyalty is."

Tenaciously, he refused to be blackmailed into signing the order.

The unrelenting federal minister proposed that Faruqui sign the order only for showing to the President to make him feel comfortable. It would not actually be sent out to the government departments.

He said that he would manage to convey instructions to the relevant departments of the government without actually forwarding them a copy of the order. Faruqui would have none of it.

Addressing him by his name, Faruqui asked the minister, "How can you do that?"

"Sir, we have been doing it. I know how to do it. You do not worry. Trust me. We will protect the President as well as not do anything wrong," the go-getter minister insisted.

The sure-footed Faruqui, however, did not relent. Nothing persuaded him into doing something which he believed was palpably wrong.

Addressing the minister again by name, he said, "Saab, this may be your way of doing things, but I cannot do it."

Malik Riaz also interceded and asked Faruqui to help the President at this time of critical need, almost giving a lecture on the virtue of loyalty to the boss.

Faruqui was not at all impressed. He refused.

He went up to Prime Minister Gilani, who was also around watching it all from a distance, hoping he would come to his rescue.

"*Mujhe iss main na daalain*" (Don't put me into this), a circumspect Gilani said when he was asked by the loyalists to persuade Faruqui to sign the "order".

He was caught between the devil and the deep sea. He did not want to appear disloyal to the President but also did not want to endorse anything that was wrong and illegal.

As the drama of the order on behalf of the supreme commander of the armed forces was being played out, Bilawal went up to see his father in the bedroom. While Bilawal was with his father, the President called Haqqani.

"One of the two, you or your wife, should go with me to Dubai," he told him. Haqqani readily agreed.

Zardari no longer insisted that only Haqqani must accompany him to Dubai.

He had come around to accepting that Haqqani could not leave the country because of a court restriction. It would be OK if his wife travelled to Dubai with him instead.

Zardari had already said that he would do only what his son Bilawal advised him to do.

"I have been held hostage," Haqqani's wife, Farah, remarked to me. To her credit, however, she did not refuse to travel with the President to Dubai. Separate logistics were made for her stay in Dubai.

The helicopters had already flown out of the presidential complex a day before. Zardari travelled to Islamabad airport by motorcade on his way to Dubai. He was accompanied by Haqqani's wife, Farah, and his sisters.

Zardari had finally agreed to leave for Dubai without Haqqani, who stayed behind in the Prime Minister's House in Islamabad.

Chapter 18

Faruqui sacked, but not really

The loyalists complained to the President about Faruqui's "disloyalty". They seemed able to convince him that Faruqui was indeed disloyal and must be shown the door.

A few days after the President had left for Dubai, the cabinet secretary phoned Faruqui: "Sir, where would you like to be posted?"

Faruqui did not want any posting. He offered to resign, preferring to be relieved of his job entirely. He wanted to talk with the President in Dubai but could not reach him. Determined to clarify his position, Faruqui decided to see the President in Dubai personally.

Zardari had landed in a hospital in Dubai, and consequently, Senate Chairman Farooq Naek became the Acting President of Pakistan.

Faruqui spoke with Farooq Naek who, being a pacifist, also wanted to help diffuse the tensions. Together, they devised a plan.

Acting President Farooq Naek formally asked Faruqui to go to Dubai to discuss some "important official matters" with President Zardari. They finalised a list of "important" matters for Faruqui to discuss with President Zardari in Dubai and seek his instructions.

This strategy served a dual purpose:

1. It conveyed that Acting President Naek did not take important decisions himself but referred them to President Zardari.
2. It opened a window for Faruqui to meet Zardari, who had previously declined to even speak with him to clarify his position.

For both Farooq Naek and Faruqui, it was a win-win situation.

Armed with directions from Acting President Farooq Naek, Faruqui was seated in the aircraft en route to Dubai. Moments before take-off, the captain approached him, saying he had been ordered to offload him. Faruqui was surprised but kept his composure, wondering who could have issued such an order.

Instead of disembarking, Faruqui requested a few moments from the captain to sort out the situation. He called the Acting President from the aircraft and, after explaining that he had been ordered to disembark, handed the phone to the captain.

"I am Farooq Naek, Acting President. I have asked and authorised Faruqui to go to Dubai to discuss some issues with President Zardari," he told the captain. He also assured the captain that Faruqui was not on any no-fly list. Out of abundant caution, Naek thought Prime Minister Gilani might have placed Faruqui on a no-fly list. If so, Naek promised the captain he would also speak with Gilani. The plane took off for Dubai with Faruqui on board.

Zardari had just been discharged from the American Hospital and was resting at home in Dubai. A few days later, when visitors were allowed to see him, Faruqui, carrying a few files, called on Zardari. He did not need to discuss official matters; his primary goal was to clarify his position.

Zardari was waiting to receive him. Faruqui explained why he had not signed the "Order" he had been asked to do in the name of loyalty. He outlined the potential consequences:

"Within minutes of the 'Order of Supreme Commander of the Armed Forces' being signed, it would have hit the headlines. The first reaction would have been from Iftikhar Chaudhry (CJP) in the shape of a suo moto notice. The control tower would have turned back the plane carrying the President and Haqqani under orders of the GHQ. It would have snowballed into a huge scandal within no time, and impeachment proceedings against the President would have been initiated," he explained.

The President listened attentively. By now, he had recovered from the trauma he had experienced in Pakistan. He did not dwell on the incident and asked Faruqui to return to Islamabad, assuring him that he still trusted him.

Faruqui returned to Islamabad on the next flight. He had been sacked, but not really.

President Asif Ali Zardari receiving the Guard of Honour after taking Oath at the Aiwan-e Sadr, on 9 September 2008.

President Asif Ali Zardari shakes hands with the leader of the MQM, Altaf Hussain, in London, on 16 September 2008.

President Asif Ali Zardari being briefed at the Strategic Planning Division, on 9 October 2008.

President Asif Ali Zardari addressing a representative meeting comprising members of the Provincial Cabinet, MPAs, political party leaders and notables from Balochistan in Islamabad, on 29 November 2008.

President Asif Ali Zardari talks to Prince Karim Aga Khan,
who called on him in Islamabad, on 1 December 2008.

President Asif Ali Zardari talking to delegation members of APCNA, who called on him at the Aiwan-e Sadr, on 22 December 2008.

President Asif Ali Zardari addressing the participants of a seminar on the mainstreaming of FATA at the Aiwan-e Sadr, on 24 January 2009.

President Asif Ali Zardari in a meeting with the leader of the MQM, Altaf Hussain, who called on the President in London, on 3 May 2009.

President Asif Ali Zardari in a meeting with the Chief Justice of Pakistan Iftikhar Mohd. Chaudhry, who called on the President in Islamabad, on 5 June 2009.

President Asif Ali Zardari administering Oath to Justice Agha Rafiq Ahmed Khan as Chief Justice Federal Shariat Court, at a ceremony held at the Presidency in Islamabad, on 5 June 2009.

President Asif Ali Zardari conferring the Hilal-i-Shujaat on veteran politician and former Provincial Minister from the Frontier, Muhammad Afzal Lala, at a special Investiture Ceremony held at the Aiwan-e Sadr, on 10 June 2009.

Group editor, *Daily Jang*, Mehmood Sham presenting his book titled *Pakistan Par Qurban* to President Asif Ali Zardari at the Aiwan-e Sadr in Islamabad, on 25 June 2009.

President Asif Ali Zardari laying a floral wreath at the Memorial of National Unity of Tajikistan in Dushanbe, on 29 July 2009.

Spokesperson to the President, former Senator Farhatullah Babar, briefing the media after President Asif Ali Zardari's and British PM Gordon Brown's meeting, at 10 Downing Street, on 28 August 2009.

President Asif Ali Zardari signing the Gilgit-Baltistan (Empowerment of Self-governance) Order 2009, at the Presidency, on 7 September 2009.

The Archbishop of Canterbury, Dr Rowan Williams, called on President Asif Ali Zardari in London, on 18 September 2009.

President Asif Ali Zardari signing the NCA Ordinance transferring powers of Chairman NCA to the Prime Minister, at the Presidency, on 27 November 2009.

President Asif Ali Zardari in a meeting with the elders from Balochistan at the Aiwan-e Sadr, on 21 December 2009.

President Asif Ali Zardari conferring the Award of Hilal-e-Imtiaz on Asma Jahangir at a ceremony held at the Aiwan-e Sadr in connection with the Pakistan Day, on 23 March 2010.

President Asif Ali Zardari shaking hands with Maulana Abdul Sattar Edhi at the Bilawal House in Karachi, on 22 July 2010.

President Asif Ali Zardari recording his condolence message for the late Ambassador Richard Holbrooke at the U.S. Embassy in Islamabad, on 15 December 2010.

President Asif Ali Zardari exchanging views with Prime Minister Yousaf Raza Gilani at the Aiwan-e Sadr, on 15 May 2011. The Chief of Army Staff General Ashfaq Parvez Kayani is also present.

President Asif Ali Zardari during a press-talk after his meeting with the Kazakh President at Ak Orda (Presidential Palace) in Astana Kazakhstan, on 14 June 2011. MOS for Foreign Affairs, Hina Rabbani Khar, was also present.

President Asif Ali Zardari and Prime Minister Yousaf Raza Gilani chaired a meeting of coalition partners at the Aiwan-e Sadr, on 28 July 2011.

Prime Minister Yousaf Raza Gilani called on President Asif Ali Zardari at the Aiwan-e Sadr, on 26 November 2011. Foreign Minister Hina Rabbani Khar was also present.

President Asif Ali Zardari on his arrival at the Gayari Sector in Siachen, on 18 April 2012. Interior Minister Senator Rehman Malik and the Army Chief General Ashfaq Parvez Kayani are also present.

President Asif Ali Zardari signing the Investigation for Fair Trial Bill 2013 into law, in a ceremony held at the Aiwan-e Sadr, on 20 February 2013.

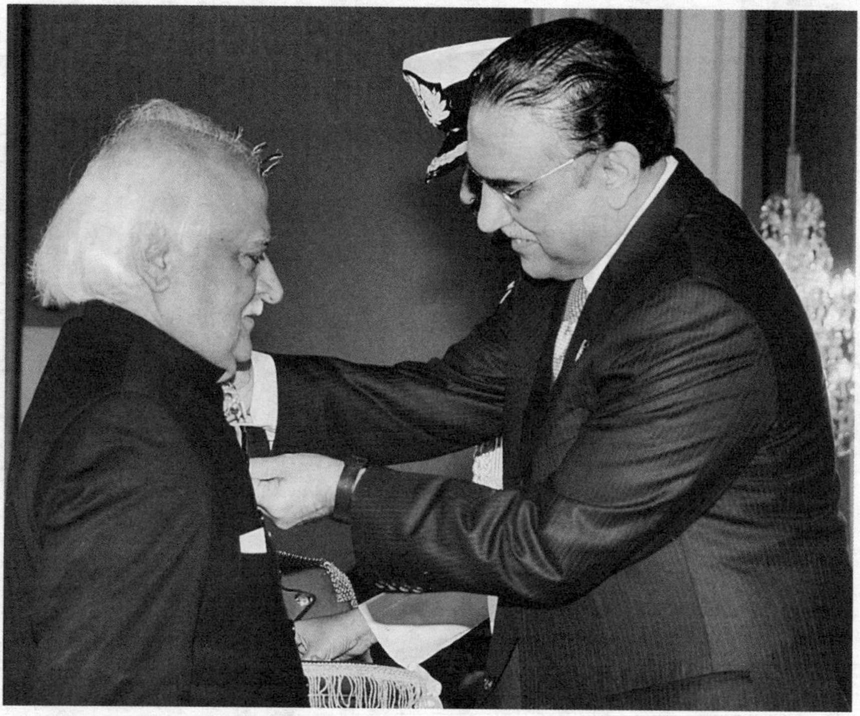

President Asif Ali Zardari conferring the Hilal-i-Imtiaz upon Anwar Maqsood at the Investiture Ceremony held at the Aiwan-e Sadr in Islamabad, on 23 March 2013.

Section Eight

SOME EPISODES

Chapter 1

How security trumped FATA reforms

The heavy military presence in the ex-FATA (Federally Administered Tribal Areas) bordering Afghanistan, later merged into the Khyber Pakhtunkhwa province, and its resistance to political reforms in the area has been no secret. One of the most significant initiatives of the Zardari Presidency was to undertake reforms in these areas before their formal merger into the province in 2018. However, this initiative was scuttled by the security establishment in a most brazen manner, just as Zardari was set to announce it.

FATA had always been remotely controlled by the President in Islamabad and, acting on his behalf, by the provincial governor of Khyber Pakhtunkhwa in Peshawar. The very name "federally administered" speaks volumes about its actual status: an area remotely controlled by the power centre in Islamabad. Its land, deemed a "strategic area", received primacy in security calculations, but its people were treated as cannon fodder in the strategic games played out.

Central control and the draconian century-old Frontier Crimes Regulation (FCR) have been instruments of the civil-military bureaucratic complex since the colonial era to control these areas. Religious political parties, fearing democratic challenges to their narrative, have also been wary of meaningful social and political reforms in these regions.

Towards the end of 2008, a Jirga of elders from all tribal agencies had been discussing for weeks a "minimum reforms agenda" under the auspices of a think tank, the Shaheed Bhutto Foundation (SBF), which worked for the promotion of democracy and human rights. During their deliberations, the tribal elders, nearly two hundred in number, also called on the President. They unanimously demanded reforms, prompting Zardari to announce his intention to undertake reforms in consultation with all stakeholders.

Apart from meeting the long-standing demand of its people, there was another reason to undertake political reforms in the tribal areas. A massive democratic reform agenda, in the form of the 18th Constitutional Amendment, had already been set in motion. Political reforms in tribal areas would lend further momentum to this democratic reform process.

Over the next few months, a reform package for tribal areas was finalised based on consultations held on different platforms involving tribesmen, political parties, and stakeholders.

Under the reform package, political parties were allowed for the first time to open offices and engage in political activities such as public meetings in the tribal areas. Previously, this had not been permitted, ostensibly to respect tribal customs and due to fears that political differences taken into the public domain would exacerbate tribal feuds. Allowing political activities also meant the end of the monopoly of a single narrative promoted by mosque and pulpit, dealing a blow to the mosque-military alliance. This was a far-reaching change.

Fundamental changes were also made to the FCR. Previously, under this regulation, anyone could be sent to jail for three years without trial, and the jail term could be extended indefinitely. Under its territorial responsibility clause, women and children were also jailed. The reform package changed all of this.

Arbitrary arrest powers in the hands of the administration were curtailed, and the accused were given, for the first time, the right to bail. Women and children below 16 years of age could no longer be arrested under the reformed FCR.

The reforms called for setting up an Appellate Authority for appeals against arbitrary orders of the political agents and a FATA Tribunal, with powers of a High Court under Article 199 of the Constitution, for reviewing orders of the Appellate Authority.

A new section was added to the Land Acquisition Act, providing compensation at prevailing market value for the government's acquisition of property.

For the first time, the auditor general of Pakistan was to audit the political agent's funds, and rules were to be framed for the previously unregulated Agency Welfare Fund.

It was decided that President Zardari would announce the reform package in his Independence Day speech at midnight on 14 August 2009.

As midnight approached, all preparations were made for the historic announcement, and a galaxy of guests were invited to witness the event.

Zardari rehearsed his speech several times.

However, just as he had completed several rounds of speech rehearsal and guests had started trickling into the Presidency, the military conveyed that the President should not announce the reform package.

Zardari's reform package for the tribal areas was stillborn. Security concerns had trumped it.

Chapter 2

How Zardari was stopped

Preparations for the President's speech on the eve of Independence Day 2009 to announce reforms were in full swing. Guest lists had been finalised, and invitations were sent out. However, unbeknownst to the Presidency, the defence secretary wrote a letter to the Prime Minister's principal secretary arguing against allowing political activities in the tribal areas.

The letter stated that extending the Political Parties Order 2002 to tribal areas could provide "militants and religious extremists" with "additional space, cover and influence under political-religious garb." It further claimed this would hamper "ongoing military operations against militants" and recommended that "The extension of Political Parties Order 2002 to FATA may be pended for the time being." The letter emphatically concluded, "In no case should political activities be allowed in FATA."

It was unprecedented for the defence secretary to write such a letter after the decision had been taken and was about to be announced. Questions arose: Could he have written such a letter without orders from a higher authority? Who had directed him? Even the defence minister was unaware that his secretary had written such a letter to the Prime Minister's House.

At around 9 P.M. that night, the President called me to his office. Zardari informed me that he had been advised to postpone the announcement of the reforms. Aware that all arrangements had been made for the announcement in just a few hours, he was seeking a way out.

"Sir, it is impossible to go back. It will be a huge embarrassment," I protested.

"Let us not make it an issue. Some way must be found," he replied.

When I tried to argue further, he cut me off. "*Samjho Farhatullah*" (Understand it, Farhatullah), he said, asking me to give it some thought and return to him later.

The President was not prepared to discuss it any further. He had clearly decided to act on the advice given to him.

Meanwhile, guests were streaming into the Presidency, their numbers swelling. They eagerly anticipated hearing about the important reform package directly from the President later that night. The atmosphere in the Darbar Hall was charged with anticipation as attendees felt they were about to witness history in the making. A press release of the President's speech had been finalised earlier in the day, ready for release as "embargoed till 12 PM midnight".

I returned to my office, deeply disappointed.

After a while, the President summoned me again. As I entered his office, he declared, even before I could speak:

"*Haan tau mai ilaan nahi kroonga.*" (I will not make an announcement.) His tone was decisive.

He revealed that the advice to postpone the announcement had been conveyed to him through his military secretary, clearly originating from the GHQ (General Headquarters of the Army).

As I began, "Sir, a way has been found, and you will not make the announcement tonight," he visibly relaxed and asked me to sit, eager to hear more.

He nodded approvingly when I explained, "We will set aside the prepared draft of the speech containing details of the reforms package. You will only announce that we have decided to undertake significant reforms."

"What are the reforms, people will ask?" he interjected.

I reassured him, "There will be no formal speech by you, you will not announce details of the reforms package, and there will be no question-and-answer session at the end of the speech." I further explained that this approach would comply with the advice that the President should not announce the reform package.

The President appeared relieved but asked about potential media questions the following day.

I assured him that the spokesperson's office would handle media inquiries without directly involving the President. The President would neither make the detailed announcement nor discuss the reforms with the media.

Visibly relaxed, he asked, "So, what will I do then?"

"Sir, you will take to the rostrum, welcome all the guests, and emphasise the need for reforms in general terms. Also, thank all political parties and stakeholders that have been engaged in reform discussions," I advised.

"But this will be too short and abrupt," he remarked.

"Yes, it will be. To make it appear longer, you may begin by mentioning one by one the names of some high-profile political and tribal leaders present, acknowledging their contributions and paying tribute to them. You will have a list of their names beforehand. This way, the address will not seem too brief," I suggested.

"And what about the reforms?" he asked, emphasising, "*Mai reforms announce nahi karoonga.*" (I will not announce the reforms package).

"No Sir, you will not," I reassured him. "The President will only say: 'We have decided to introduce far-reaching political, judicial and administrative reforms in the tribal areas' without giving any details. We will manage the rest."

He then inquired about how this would be managed and what his spokesperson would do.

I explained, "Sir, the President has agreed not to announce the reforms package tonight and merely state that reforms will be carried out. Why would they object to that? *Unn ki khwahish ki takmeel ho gai hai.*" (Their desire has been fulfilled.)

When I suggested that micromanagement be left to the spokesperson, the President smiled.

Ultimately, the President had been prevented from announcing the reform package for the tribal areas, and he complied with this directive.

Chapter 3

Reforms announced, but not by Zardari

Five minutes before midnight the buglers in the Presidency trumpeted their bugles announcing that the President was marching towards the Darbar Hall. The chatter in the hall suddenly came to an end and all gaze turned toward the main door to witness the President arriving in to the hall. The audience was excited about the anticipated announcement by the President of high stake political reforms in the tribal areas that had eluded them for over a century.

Just as the trumpets fell silent the panels of the high door slowly opened as if automatically. They had actually been flung open by immaculately dressed, turbaned presidential body guards holding long ceremonial spears in hand.

A hush fell as the President entered the Darbar Hall accompanied by his ADC and escorted straight to the dais to address the galaxy of guests. A thunderous applause greeted him as he bowed to greet the hundreds of guests anxiously waiting to witness the President addressing the nation and laying bare the reforms package. I was one of the very few who knew at the time that the President will not make a speech and there will be no announcement by him of the reforms package. it was highly embarrassing that the army had trumped Zardari and did not allow him to announce the reforms. Zardari never talked about his disappointment at the time or even later. But it was not difficult to imagine what must have also churned in his mind at the time.

As had already been decided the formal text of his prepared speech had not been placed on the rostrum, only a paper containing the names of some political elders attending the ceremony that night.

The President started speaking as an eager audience listened in hushed audience. It was hardly a speech and he did not look into the eyes of the silence. In what seemed more of a monologue he welcomed the guests, mentioning a few of them by name also and expressed delight that they had come from far-off places to the Presidency for the event.

Zardari talked about the association of PPP with the tribal people and the courage, resilience and patriotism of the tribal people. He also recalled his meeting with the tribal elders who had come to the Presidency and held a grand jirga demanding reforms. Then almost abruptly he declared that it had been decided that far-reaching political reforms in the tribal areas will be undertaken. But he did not disclose what the reforms were and when these would be implemented and exited from the hall rather hurriedly. Contrary to the customary practice he did not tarry to meet and talk with the guests on such occasions.

The guests were stunned. Disbelief and disappointment were palpable among them. They had come to see and hear the President in person making a "historic" address to the nation instead of watching it on television screens. But it had turned out to be no more than a whimper.

A number of disappointed tribal elders and political leaders approached me and asked why the President had not announced the reforms and wondered if he had backtracked. All I could tell them was to deny any backtracking. A few grinned when I told them that details of the reforms will become known through the media.

I had prepared an elaborate press release giving full details of the reforms package and had already issued it to the media before the President's address. It was "embargoed" and not to be published and broadcast before midnight soon after the presidential address. As the President had not announced any reforms the press statement giving complete details had been issued in the name of the spokesperson. A vague formulation in it also suggested that the reforms would soon be implemented without giving a firm date.

The press release hit the newspaper headlines the next day. The reform package may have been attributed to the spokesperson, not the President, but it gave all the details that had been under discussion with representative jirgas of tribal people as well as all stakeholders and had been in the works for a long time.

The announcement was not well-received in quarters opposing the reforms and they frowned upon it. But the

President had a safe cushion: the spokesperson had said it, not the President. One liked to believe that there was enough room for plausible deniability.

It may have provided some face-saving for the President, but those who had stopped him from making the announcement had their way. All talk of the reform package suddenly ended. For the next two years, reforms in the tribal areas did not figure prominently in the civilian corridors of power.

Two years later, in March 2011, representatives of all major political parties called on the President, urging the implementation of reforms. They pointedly asked why the President did not walk his talk of reforms and why he did not actually announce the reforms package on the eve of Independence Day in 2009, despite promising it.

The President looked at me. Smiling he told them,

"*Har cheez ka waqt hota hai.*" (There is a time for everything.)

On 2 May that year, the U.S. Navy Seals took out Osama bin Laden, who had been hiding in the military cantonment in Abbottabad. Some people thought the civilian government would be made a scapegoat, but the military leadership had also been under great pressure. Perhaps the time had come to announce the reform package.

On the eve of Independence Day that year, Zardari signed two orders implementing a series of reforms in the tribal areas, disregarding all opposition.

A year later, on the eve of the 66th Independence Day in 2012, he also announced the introduction of local governments in tribal areas to bring its people further into the mainstream. It is hard to say whether the army did not object to these reforms or Zardari went ahead despite the army's reservations.

Chapter 4

The army's creeping control of FATA

Zardari's Presidency ended in 2013. Two years prior, in 2011, he had announced details of the reform package in the tribal areas. The 18th Constitutional Amendment, guaranteeing devolution and provincial autonomy, had already been passed in 2010. However, the military was not prepared to relinquish total control of FATA.

In 2016, the PML-N government formed another committee under Foreign Affairs Advisor Sartaj Aziz to implement and further advance the process of reforms in the tribal regions. Aziz also sought the views of the security establishment.

The new reform package, drawing heavily from the inputs of the security establishment, envisaged an ambitious ten-year development plan worth 900 billion rupees and the creation of a new post of chief executive of FATA. This position would have wide-ranging financial and administrative powers to implement large infrastructure projects.

The reforms package stipulated that the post of chief executive was to be filled by a BS 22 or equivalent grade officer. Although not explicitly stated, it was anticipated that the equivalent of BS 22 in the army—a serving three-star general—would be appointed to the post.

The nomenclature of "Chief Executive" also evoked memories of General Musharraf. When he staged his coup in 1999, he first assumed control under the innocuous-sounding title of "Chief Executive". After the title gained currency in public discourse as equivalent to the head of state, he removed President Rafiq Tarar and himself assumed the office of President.

The new reforms package had paved the way for a three-star general in uniform to become chief executive of FATA, potentially displacing all civilian authority—including the provincial governor—in the affairs of the tribal areas and introducing a new power dynamic.

The very nomenclature "Chief Executive, FATA" seemed to formalise the military's control of the tribal areas.

Both the chairman of the Reforms Committee, Sartaj Aziz, and the governor of Khyber Pakhtunkhwa, Iqbal Jhagra, did not favour the move but appeared helpless before the security establishment whose brainchild it was.

The knowledge that both Sartaj Aziz and Jhagra did not favour it was very encouraging. It afforded an opportunity to oppose it in Parliament. The proposal to create the post of chief executive officer for FATA was opposed inside and outside Parliament.

Those opposing it argued that an immediate outcome of posting a 3-star general would be that contracts worth billions would be awarded to army-run enterprises FWO (Frontier Works Organization) and NLC (National Logistics Cell) without bids, displacing civilians. The already uneven economic playing field would be further tilted in favour of the military, adversely impacting overall national economic development.

The power to initiate social and political reforms and economic development would further shift from civilian to military control.

The army-run FWO is already the country's biggest contractor, the Fauj Foundation (FF) the largest industrial and commercial conglomerate, and the over a dozen Defence Housing Authorities (DHAs) the largest real estate developers. Further tilting the balance in favour of MILBUS (Military Business) would not be advisable in the interest of the national economy. Besides, the region would be further militarised, and FATA would remain a black hole.

Relishing the opposition to creating the post of chief executive for FATA, Sartaj Aziz chuckled.

The new post was not created due to stiff opposition. Subsequently, the nomenclature was changed to chief operating officer (COO), but it, too, was strongly opposed.

Despite thwarting this move, the civilian authorities have continued to be marginalised in the administration of the tribal areas. Even civilian contractors have been systematically displaced to award contracts to military-run organisations like FWO.

During a meeting of a Senate Committee, it was learnt that an Army's Engineers Division, based in Peshawar, had sent out a letter instructing the political agents that no contract be given to civilian contractors who are reported by the intelligence agencies to be engaged in "criminal and anti-state activities".

In the absence of any formalised procedures for declaration by intelligence agencies of civilians involved in "anti-state activities", who could challenge the opinion of unbridled intelligence agencies?

On the pretext of "source reports", civilians were already denied contracts. With a uniformed officer as a chief operating officer, the region would be effectively militarised, and civilians would be pushed out of all contracting and economic activities.

Due to vigorous opposition in Parliament, the post of chief executive officer for FATA was not created, and no uniformed officer was appointed to it. However, the military's efforts to wrest control of FATA were not abandoned. The military's creeping control of the ex-FATA region has continued.

Chapter 5

Strategic land

The military has viewed the tribal region purely from a security perspective. Its land was considered "strategic", but not its people. Meaningful social and political reforms were not expected to be undertaken.

Zardari's first attempt at reforms in 2009 had been thwarted. He was not allowed to announce the reforms on Independence Day that year. The proposed modest reforms had to wait another two years before the President formally signed the legal instruments to effect them. Implementing the reforms was bound to face resistance from different power centres from the beginning.

So, when the area was merged into the Khyber Pakhtunkhwa Province in 2018, within seven years of the reforms announcement, it surprised many. The shift from stiff resistance to reforms to sudden mergers appeared paradoxical. Did it represent a quantum shift in the strategic calculus, heralding a demilitarised FATA (Federally Administered Tribal Areas) at last?

Nawaz Sharif had already been ousted from office and replaced by his own party's Shahid Khaqan Abbasi. The civilian government was besieged, and general elections were only a few weeks away.

The people of the tribal areas were growing restless with the militarisation of their region and its status as an abode for militants. The educated tribal youth openly decried being treated as cannon fodder in the strategic games played in their area. By 2018, an indigenous movement of the tribal youth, the Pashtun Tahaffuz Movement (PTM), had sprung up, giving voice to the muted turbulence of their spirit.

They demanded, "not development, but peace and human rights, an end to using our land for dubious strategic purposes, end to enforced disappearances." Denouncing militancy, they used slogans against army control that were unthinkable a few years before. PTM's power of logic, simplicity, and sincerity was irresistible.

The U.S. forces in Afghanistan were fatigued, and talks of negotiating with the Taliban for the US pullout filled the air.

The resultant mess in Afghanistan might give impetus to the nationalist sentiment in parts of Pakistan espoused by the newly emerged indigenous PTM.

Merging the tribal districts into the province for the sake of optics, if not in actual practice, seemed to fit into the security calculus. This might explain the astounding speed with which the areas were merged into the province through a drive led by the security establishment, not by civilians.

Thus, on Friday, 18 May 2018, the National Security Committee, not the Cabinet or Parliament, decided to merge the tribal areas into the province. A few days later, on 22 May, the Cabinet endorsed the Security Committee's decision and prepared a Constitutional Amendment Bill.

The next morning, on 23 May, the ministry of states and frontier regions moved a summary through the law division to Prime Minister Shahid Khaqan Abbasi. It stated, among other things, that "A Constitutional amendment to the effect has also been finalised."

On 24 May, the Constitutional Amendment Bill was tabled in the National Assembly and passed with just one vote more than the required two-thirds majority. Less than a week later, the National Assembly's term expired.

On 25 May, the Senate passed it with just two votes more than the required two-thirds majority.

As the merger involved a change in the province of Khyber Pakhtunkhwa's boundaries, it was mandatory that the Provincial Assembly also pass it. So, two days later, on 27 May, the Provincial Assembly passed it as well. It was a closed holiday, and the Provincial Assembly had to be specially called into session. It was its last act on a Sunday, as its five-year term ended the next day, 28 May.

A review of the verbatim proceedings of the federal and provincial legislatures showed there were no deliberations.

Finally, the President assented to it on 31 May.

The civil-military bureaucratic complex that had been opposing reforms now appeared to be pushing the process with electronic speed. It seemed too good to be true. Some said it was madness. But there was a method in the madness.

The 23 May summary to the PM also attached a draft regulation, "The FATA Interim Governance Regulation, 2018", ensuring the continuation of the centric rule of the tribal areas through civil-military bureaucratic machinery.

Promptly, the Prime Minister approved the summary and sent the regulation to the President, who signed it into law just hours before he himself was divested of the power to issue any regulation regarding tribal areas.

There was craft behind the speed with which the tribal areas were merged into the province. Instead of ushering in meaningful political, judicial, and administrative reforms and development of the merged districts, the regulations perpetuated military control of the areas. After the merger, sixteen members were elected to the Provincial Assembly, but the regulation could not be repealed.

The tribal areas may have been merged, but the mindset of "strategic piece of land" has not changed.

Chapter 6

The Guantanamo Bay prisons

The "FATA Interim Governance Regulation, 2018" and the subsequent "Action in Aid of Civil Power Regulation Ordinance 2019" were crucial instruments that further strengthened the army's grip over the erstwhile tribal areas. These regulations empowered the armed forces to detain individuals on vaguely defined charges without production before courts and keep them in opaque "internment centres" under military control in tribal districts.

Alarmingly, a mere statement by an army officer was deemed sufficient evidence for conviction. Little information about these internment centres was made public, leaving many questions unanswered. These pressing questions included:

- Where are these centres located, and how many exist?
- How many prisoners are held in each centre?
- What crimes are they accused of?
- How many have died in custody in these facilities?
- Have any trials in court begun?

The internment centres have, in effect, been used to institutionalise enforced disappearances in the country.

The Supreme Court, in its order dated 10 December 2013 in the case of Mohabat Shah vs the Federation, stated:

"Army authorities in PATA have removed 35 persons from the Malakand internment centre out of which only 7 persons have been produced. As far as the rest of them are concerned, their whereabouts would only be known to the army authorities. They had no authority to detain them illegally. The Chief Executive of the Federal Government, Chief Executive and the Governor of the Province of KPK are directed to immediately proceed with this case and ensure recovery of these persons within seven days and submit a report to the Registrar for our perusal. The persons who are responsible for the same should be dealt with strictly in accordance with the law."

During hearings in the Peshawar High Court in 2019, it also transpired that a number of forcibly disappeared persons had actually landed in these internment centres, virtually turning them into Pakistan's own Guantanamo Bay prisons.

Hundreds of security checkpoints continued to straddle the

tribal areas, particularly in North and South Waziristan, with people facing humiliation at these posts. Instead of being manned by the police, the military operates these checkpoints, bringing the army face-to-face with the people. The reasons for the military manning these checkpoints and continued army policing have not been explained.

Despite the merger, the tribal districts have remained a "no-go" area. A delegation from the Human Rights Commission of Pakistan (HRCP) that wanted to visit the victims of the Khar Qamar incident in 2019 for condolences was turned back.

The HRCP delegation was not even permitted to visit the Dattakhel camp near Bannu, where displaced tribal people from Waziristan were lodged. The officer in charge of the camp did not allow its members a glimpse inside. Instead, a young inmate of the camp, who seemed well-tutored in informing visitors that all was well inside, was brought in by the commander to brief the delegation.

The International Court of Justice (ICJ) warned that the Regulation "will lead to serious human rights violations and miscarriage of justice." It urged the government to "reject this dangerous, oppressive and counterproductive strategy and instead strengthen its judicial process and law enforcement in line with its domestic law and international human rights obligations." However, this warning has not been heeded.

When the Regulation was challenged in the Peshawar High Court on the grounds of being discriminatory, the government extended it to the whole province on 5 August 2019 – the very day when India annexed Kashmir and divested it of its special status.

The Peshawar High Court (PHC) subsequently struck down the Regulation as unconstitutional. Declaring the "internment centres" illegal, it directed the provincial police chief to take over their control.

Just as the provincial police were preparing to take over the illegal internment centres, a Supreme Court bench headed by Chief Justice Asif Saeed Khosa suspended the PHC order and decided to constitute a larger bench to decide the case.

During the hearing, the Chief Justice made noteworthy comments that generated headline news. The last hearing in the case was held in December 2019, a few days before Justice Khosa retired. Observing that the U.S. had established Guantanamo Bay prisons outside its jurisdiction, but here we were detaining people in a similar manner within our own jurisdiction, he made stinging criticism of the centres. However, he did not stay the suspension of the PHC order by the court. His observations appeared to be primarily for public consumption, seemingly designed to enhance his reputation just days before he laid down his judicial robes.

Khosa retired, and three Chief Justices followed him, but the case has not been fixed for further hearing.

Guantanamo Bay-like prisons continue to operate under the watch of the army, with the merged districts turned into a black hole and strident militarisation persisting.

Chapter 7

Renaming the province Khyber Pakhtunkhwa

Changing the name of the erstwhile North-West Frontier Province (NWFP) to reflect the linguistic and cultural identity of its people had been a cherished dream of Pashtun nationalists for long. However, centrists rejected calls for the recognition of the Pakhtun cultural identity as unpatriotic and anti-state.

The Awami National Party (ANP) and other nationalist parties had waged a long-drawn political struggle to change the province's name but to no avail.

President Zardari appreciated that the name "North-West Frontier Province" represented only a geographical identity, not its people's cultural and linguistic identity. He understood that a people's urge for the recognition of their cultural identity is irresistible.

Zardari believed that the Pakhtun belt had suffered immensely at the hands of militants, with a large number mysteriously finding refuge in the tribal areas. He thought strengthening Pakhtun nationalism was needed to counter the militants' ideology and threat. Renaming the province to reflect its people's cultural and linguistic identity was the first step towards this goal.

In preparation for his address to the UN General Assembly in 2008, his first as head of state, Zardari made a bold move. The initial draft of his speech revolved around the usual topics of Kashmir and Palestine. However, at the last minute, Zardari replaced the old name "NWFP" with "Pakhtunkhwa" in the final text, writing it in his own hand. This change came even before the 18th Constitutional Amendment was passed.

Renaming the province was an emotive issue. The non-Pashto-speaking population, particularly in the Hazara division, resented it, and protests erupted.

Initially, the Pakistan Muslim League (Nawaz) PML-N opposed changing the name to Pakhtunkhwa and nearly faced an internal revolt over the issue. However, weathering its internal storm, it eventually voted for the change in the National Assembly during the 18th Amendment Bill, agreeing to the name "Khyber Pakhtunkhwa" instead of simply "Pakhtunkhwa".

Although the National Assembly passed the bill on 8 April 2010, the battle for renaming the province was not yet over. The bill still needed to pass through the Senate a week later, on 15 April, where it was bound to meet stiff resistance due to the composition of the upper house.

The political face of General Musharraf, namely the Pakistan Muslim League (Quaid-e-Azam) PML-Q, had 21 members in the Senate. Its leading figures, the Chaudhries of Gujrat, had declared their opposition to the name change, linking it to the creation of a separate Hazara province—a demand that had already sparked public demonstrations. This linkage threatened to subvert the Khyber Pakhtunkhwa Bill.

Because of internal differences within his party, Nawaz Sharif became ambivalent when the bill came up in the Senate. He was now undecided whether to support or oppose it. The Hazara chapter of PML-N, which traditionally fared better in the Hazara Division than other parties in general elections, opposed the name change.

Protests in the Hazara Division over renaming the province turned violent, resulting in six deaths and scores of injuries. PML-N called a party meeting to consider the situation, with Nawaz Sharif stating that rushing the bill through Parliament in haste was a "mistake".

Three days before the Senate session, on 12 April, President Zardari called a meeting of the party's core group. The violent protests in Hazara had not only threatened the new name of the province but also risked unravelling the entire 18th Amendment. Urgent action was needed to defuse the situation.

Zardari called for a list of senators from all parties and reviewed it to identify potential opponents of the bill. He also inquired if any senator had demanded something in return for supporting the bill, indicating his readiness to accept such demands.

A senior party leader, Syed Khurshid Shah, said that the required Senate numbers for passing the bill would be complete if the Saifullah group supported it.

Zardari acknowledged that Anwar Saifullah Khan was

unhappy as he had not been made provincial governor. He explained that he wanted to appoint him but Asfandyar Wali and the ANP strongly opposed it. During the meeting, the President called Anwar Saifullah Khan to assure him that he was waiting for an opportune moment to make him governor.

"You know I do not say yes if I do not intend to do it," he told Anwar Saifullah Khan.

After the conversation, the President informed the meeting that the Saifullah group would support the bill in the Senate.

Maulana Fazalur Rehman and JUI had demanded the post of chairman of the Council of Islamic Ideology (CII). For the PPP, this was a tall order. The appointment of a conservative rightist to this constitutional post was against its progressive outlook. Several party leaders opined that a hardline conservative Moulvi as chairman of CII would send the wrong message.

The President brushed aside these arguments, saying, "Don't worry; we will handle him when it comes." He asked Khurshid Shah to convey his approval to Maulana Fazalur Rehman. Thus, the post of CII chairman was bartered to secure support for renaming the province.

Zardari believed that Nawaz Sharif would be a greater loser than the PPP if the bill were rejected at that stage. Seeing my surprise at this observation, he turned to me and said, "*Aap ko koi khabar nahi.*" (You don't know anything.)

Zardari acknowledged that Asfandyar Wali was desperate but had not threatened him with consequences if the renaming wasn't done. Asfandyar Wali was convinced that Zardari was doing his best to push it through. He believed that the PPP's support would bring the two parties closer together and strengthen secular forces against the Taliban and Al Qaeda.

"When I first called the Frontier Province by the name of Pakhtunkhwa in my address at the UN, many people were surprised," Zardari said.

Naming a former ISI chief, Zardari recounted that the intelligence chief had warned that renaming the province would make the Pakhtuns look towards Afghanistan instead of Pakistan.

"I disagreed and told him that Pakistani Pakhtuns owned properties and businesses in Pakistani cities, in Islamabad, Lahore and Karachi, not in Afghanistan. Islamabad, not Kabul, is their centre of gravity."

Emphasising the need to recognise the Pakhtun cultural identity, he said, "Imagine how I would feel if, denying me identity, I was addressed only as '*Oai.*'" He asserted that the Pakhtuns have a right to have their identity recognised, adding, "They deserve better."

There was some discussion on whether the PPP alone should fight the battle in the Senate for renaming the province or ask Asfandyar Wali to lobby with other political parties. Zardari said that Asfandyar Wali would encounter problems as some people would make unrealistic demands that he would not be able to meet.

Finally, the bill also sailed through the Senate, and the North-West Frontier Provincc was officially renamed "Khyber Pakhtunkhwa".

Chapter 8

FATA reforms chronology

1976 – Zulfikar Ali Bhutto appointed the first committee on FATA reforms under Major General Naseerullah Babar, then IG Frontier Corps. The committee recommended merging the province's areas.

1997 – Introduction of adult franchise in FATA.

March 2004 – Benazir Bhutto established the PPP FATA Reforms Committee, the first of any political party to do so.

September 2004 – Formal directions issued by Benazir Bhutto to PPP legislators to invoke parliamentary instruments demanding reforms in FATA.

November 2004 – Senate passed a unanimous PPP Resolution on FATA/FCR (Frontier Crimes Regulations) reforms.

August 2005 – The Senate adopted a report from the Committee of Human Rights calling for reforms in the FCR.

2006 – Petition filed in the Supreme Court by Benazir Bhutto seeking political reforms in the tribal areas.

2006 – As Patron-in-Chief of the Shaheed Bhutto Foundation (SBF), Benazir Bhutto directs the foundation to engage tribal people in proposing a comprehensive package of reforms.

2008 – In his first address to Parliament, Prime Minister Yousaf Raza Gilani promised to repeal the draconian FCR.

April 2008 – A cabinet committee under Law Minister Farooq Naek was set up to propose FCR reforms. The cabinet approved the cabinet committee's recommendations.

August 2008 – Shaheed Bhutto Foundation started engaging with a cross section of hundreds of tribesmen from Bajaur to South Waziristan. The process resulted in a grand Jirga that unanimously adopted a resolution demanding specific reforms, the first of its kind.

January 2009 – President Zardari invited the Tribal Jirga to the Presidency to firm up reform proposals. The Jirga unanimously demanded reforms in FCR and several other changes.

August 2009 – The reform package was finalised. It was decided that the President would announce it at midnight on

Independence Day 2009.

Independence Day 2009 — President Zardari was suddenly asked to refrain from announcing the reform package by the security establishment just three hours before the actual announcement.

March 2011 — Representatives of major political parties called on President Zardari. Expressing disappointment that the reform process had been halted, they demanded early reforms and mergers in the province and pledged to support the President.

May 2011 — U.S. Navy Seals carry out a daring operation and take out Osama bin Laden hiding in the military cantonment, Abbottabad.

Independence Day 2011 — President Zardari, disregarding opposition, puts his signature on two far-reaching orders:

1. Amendments in the FCR (2011).
2. Extension of the Political Parties Order 2002 to the Tribal Areas to permit political engagement of the masses by political parties.The door for reforms opened for the first time in over a hundred years since the 1905 FCR.

Independence Day 2012 — President Zardari announced local governments in the tribal areas.

April 2018 — "The Supreme Court and High Court (Extension of Jurisdiction to Federally Administered Tribal Areas) Act, 2018" passed. It extended the jurisdiction of the Supreme Court of Pakistan and the Peshawar High Court to ex-FATA.

May 2018 — The 25th Constitutional Amendment was passed to merge tribal districts in the province of Khyber Pakhtunkhwa.

May 2019 — The National Assembly passed the 26th Constitutional Amendment to allow for the increase in the number of general seats in the National Assembly from 6 to 12 and the number of seats in the Khyber Pakhtunkhwa Assembly from 16 to 24 for the merged districts. Mysteriously, however, the Constitutional Amendment Bill passed by the National Assembly was never placed on the agenda of the Senate. The struggle against militarisation and colonisation of ex-tribal areas continues as the region still remains a black hole.

Chapter 9

South Punjab Province — Zardari's calculus

In 2012, during a routine meeting of allied parties at the Presidency, the issue of rising religious extremism in southern Punjab emerged as a critical topic. Participants described it as a "serious fault line of the state".

The discussion centred on the Seraiki people of South Punjab, who had long endured deprivations and had been demanding a separate province. It was argued that ignoring this demand could create space for religious extremists to hijack a genuine political issue, exploiting it for their own objectives and bolstering their narrative. Political parties needed to find a way to prevent militants from co-opting the demand for a separate province, which was gaining traction among the Seraiki people. Additionally, a strategy was needed to neutralise the centrists opposing the division of Punjab.

Zardari stated that he was conscious of these concerns. He explained that, as an initial step, the Pakistan People's Party (PPP) had created a separate chapter for South Punjab and named Makhdoom Ahmad Mahmood its President. He added that a motivation for nominating Yousaf Raza Gilani as Prime Minister was also that he was Seraiki-speaking and came from Multan, South Punjab.

Zardari choreographed the steps for carving out a separate province of South Punjab but did not advertise them openly. He asked the Law Minister Farooq H. Naek to move a resolution in the National Assembly for the creation of a new province in South Punjab.

However, a resolution passed by the National Assembly was not the first step in carving out a new province. Article 239 (4) of the Constitution states:

"A Bill to amend the Constitution which will have the effect of altering the limits of a province shall not be presented to the President unless it has been passed by the Provincial Assembly of that Province by the votes of not less than two-thirds of its total membership."

So, what was the purpose of getting a resolution passed in the National Assembly?

The Pakistan Muslim League-Nawaz (PML-N) was the ruling party in Punjab and was averse to a division of the province. A resolution passed by the National Assembly would put pressure on the PML-N. It would not be easy for them to reject a popular demand, and they would have to respond to the National Assembly resolution. This would set the ball rolling.

On 3 May 2012, the National Assembly of Pakistan unanimously passed the following resolution:

"This House hereby resolves that in order to address the grievances and to secure the political, administrative and economic interests of the people of the southern region of the province of the Punjab and to empower them in this regard, it is expedient that a new province to be known as the Province of Janoobi Punjab be created from the present Province of the Punjab."

It also stated: "This House thus calls upon the Provincial Assembly of the Punjab to present a Bill in the Punjab Assembly to amend the Constitution in accordance with Article 239(4) of the Constitution of the Islamic Republic of Pakistan, 1973, for passage which would have the effect of altering the limits of the Province of the Punjab, thereby creating the Province of Janoobi Punjab."

Shehbaz Sharif led the PML-N government in Punjab. They could not ignore the aspirations of the people of South Punjab. Accordingly, they moved and passed two identical resolutions in the Punjab Assembly. Through one resolution, they called upon the federal government to set up a National Commission for carving out a new province of South Punjab, and through another, they called to "restore the previous Bahawalpur province".

The President then sent the resolution passed by the National Assembly and the two resolutions passed by the Punjab Assembly to the Speaker of the National Assembly, Fahmida Mirza. He requested her to form a multi-party Parliamentary Commission under the Constitution "for the purpose of creating one or more province(s) in Punjab".

After setting this process in motion – indeed, even before it – Zardari maintained a low profile and studied silence in public. He attempted to create the perception that this was an initiative of elected Parliaments rather than his own.

Chapter 10

Zardari's plan misfired

Soon after receiving the presidential communication, Speaker Dr Fahmida Mirza formed a Parliamentary Commission comprising all parties "to look into all issues associated with making separate province(s)." It comprised six members each from the Senate and National Assembly to be nominated by the chairman of the Senate, the Speaker of the National Assembly, and two members from the Provincial Assembly of Punjab to be nominated by its Speaker.

The Parliamentary Commission was also tasked with proposing suitable amendments to the articles of the Constitution necessary for creating a separate province.

Senate Chairman Mian Raza Rabbani nominated Haji Adeel of ANP (Awami National Party) and me, both from Khyber Pakhtunkhwa, to the commission. The other four senators were from other provinces. The six MNAs nominated by the Speaker of the National Assembly were members of different political parties, making it a multi-party commission representing all provinces.

The chair of the Parliamentary Commission was to be elected by its members in their first meeting.

Senator Haji Adeel was widely respected, possessed great political acumen, and had a history of struggle for economic and political issues of smaller provinces.

Zardari wanted Haji Adeel of the ANP to chair the commission, believing it should be led by someone from a smaller province and not the PPP. Senator Haji Adeel was also more than ready to head it and seemed the most suitable candidate.

Zardari tasked the senior Party leader from Sindh, Syed Khurshid Ahmed Shah, with accomplishing this. Although Khurshid Shah was not a member of the commission and could not vote, he had a great personal rapport with parliamentarians across the political divide.

Shah quietly campaigned with commission members to vote for Haji Adeel before they met to elect their chairman. He also came to the commission's first meeting, saying it was a historic day and, though he was not its member, wanted to "witness" the proceedings. All members welcomed him. Haji Adeel was on board.

According to the plan, I was to propose the name of Senator Haji Adeel for the chairmanship.

As the meeting started and the secretary of the commission, following the procedure, invited members to propose someone from among themselves as chairman, I immediately proposed the name of Haji Adeel, almost sure that it would go through without any discussion.

However, the proposal was met with silence. No one objected to it, but no one seconded it either. The prolonged silence of the members was rather strange. Khurshid Shah was restless in his seat.

Finally, Maulana Abdul Ghafoor Haideri of JUI (Jamiat Ulema-e-Islam) broke the silence. But instead of seconding my proposal, he proposed my name for chairmanship. For some reason, the JUI did not want the ANP to head the commission. One by one, other members of the Parliamentary Commission seconded Ghafoor Haideri and endorsed me as the chairman.

I pleaded that as the President's spokesperson, I was too busy to undertake additional responsibilities, but my pleas were rejected. The commission's secretary invited me to take the chairman's seat and conduct the meeting.

I looked towards Khurshid Shah. He was speechless.

Zardari learned about it on television news before I reached the Presidency and called me. He was deeply dismayed. He said the opposition would not let the commission work, and the whole project would collapse.

"You are my spokesperson," he said, "The opposition will now say that this is a Zardari project and oppose it." His plans had received a severe setback. I tried to explain, but he did not listen.

"We should have managed the election of Haji Adeel," he said. For once, his plan had misfired. His frustration was palpable.

However, the commission undertook the task assigned to it. It invited written proposals from the general public, held personal hearings, and invited all National Assembly and Senate members from South Punjab for their views. Over two thousand communications from the general public and experts were received and examined.

Within a few months, it completed the task. Calling for a separate province of South Punjab, the commission submitted its report to the Speaker of the National Assembly and the Prime Minister in January 2013.

It proposed that the new province comprise the divisions of DG Khan, Multan, and Bahawalpur, as well as the districts of Mianwali and Bhakkar from the existing province of Punjab. Together, they constituted more than a third of the population and more than half of the province's land mass. Only one province, not two, was to be carved out. Despite extensive research, there was no evidence that Bahawalpur ever had the status of a separate province at any time in the past.

A comprehensive Constitutional Amendment Bill was also finalised to implement the proposal. It proposed about a dozen amendments to various articles of the Constitution to create one new "Junoobi Punjab-Bahawalpur" province.

In March 2013, the 24th Constitutional Amendment Bill sailed through the Senate, marking a major step toward creating a new province.

Zardari was pleased but knew that the plan for a separate province of South Punjab would not eventually materialise.

South Punjab Province - not to be

Although the Senate had passed the Constitutional Amendment Bill to create the "Junoobi Punjab-Bahawalpur" province, Zardari was not very sanguine about it.

After all, he was not allowed to announce the reform package for FATA in 2009 after it had been finalised and he was about to announce it.

The Constitutional Amendment Bill passed by the Senate was not tabled in the National Assembly. The PPP did not have the required majority in the Lower House, but there were also other reasons.

Much later, when Zardari was no longer President, he disclosed in a Party meeting that Army Chief Kayani opposed the new province but gave no details.

It is difficult to fathom why Kayani opposed the new province, and one can only make a guess.

The centrist mindset in Pakistan has always opposed decentralisation, viewing it as a divisive force. Does the military's centrist mindset explain Kayani's alleged opposition to the South Punjab Province?

Did he think that the division of Punjab would result in some political chaos, aggravating the security situation in the province and making it easier for militants and religious extremists to exploit?

In 2009, the successful military operation in South Waziristan almost eliminated the TTP threat. The militants moved from South to North Waziristan and were soon joined by the Punjabi Taliban, Lashkar-i-Jhangvi and the Ilyas Kashmiri group. They also took effective control of some areas. Although Kayani did not undertake military operations against them, he was under pressure at that time to launch a decisive operation against the Punjabi Taliban in North Waziristan.

Did Kayani fear that an operation against the Punjabi Taliban in North Waziristan would increase incentives for them to directly attack him in Punjab on the one hand and undermine the state's ability to use them for projecting state power beyond borders on the other?

Whatever may have been the reasons, General Kayani opposed the South Punjab Province, Zardari thought.

Chapter 11

A tool in the hands of the deep state

President Zardari once confided that Army Chief General Kayani was opposed to the division of Punjab. Whatever the real or imaginary reasons for Kayani's opposition, the issue of a Seraiki province has been employed by the deep state as a tool for political engineering.

On more than one occasion, Zardari himself had fallen prey to the deep state's machinations.

Days before the 2018 general elections, eight PML-N MNAs defected to Imran Khan's PTI, alleging that the party had failed to create the South Punjab Province. The deep state had herded them into the PTI fold under the guise of supporting South Punjab. Sentiments about South Punjab were whipped up to engineer defections towards Imran Khan.

After the 2018 elections, a strong parliamentary opposition emerged, threatening Imran Khan's journey to the Prime Minister's House. All opposition parties, including the PPP, decided to field joint candidates for the constitutional offices of Prime Minister, Speaker, and Deputy Speaker. They also agreed on a formula for this purpose.

Khan's sponsors in the deep state were alarmed at the emergence of a joint opposition to Imran and decided to prevent it. They played the South Punjab Province card to whip up sentiments and stall the formation of a united opposition against him.

It transpired that the deep state dangled the lure of a South Punjab Province to persuade the PPP to dissociate itself from the joint opposition project that was in the making in Parliament.

Zardari invited all the newly elected parliamentarians of the Party to Zardari House in Islamabad. Speaking candidly, he said he was ready to risk trusting the deep state in the hope of creating the South Punjab Province. He spoke only in general terms without specifying how the PPP's renewed bid for carving out a new province would be successful. No one asked for details. Everyone was stunned.

He told the Party parliamentarians: "*Hum nai South Punjab ki baat kee thee. Hum sooba banana chahte thai. Ab establishment bhi yahi kehti hai. Agar yeh South Punjab banatai hain tau humari vindication hogi.* (We have been talking about the South Punjab Province. We wanted to make it a province. Now, the establishment says the same thing. If they [the establishment] really make South Punjab a province, it will be a vindication of our position.)

He reminded them: "*Hum ne pehlai bhi Gilani sahib ko ijazat dee thee.*" (Even earlier, we had given permission to Gilani Sahib [to work on creating the new province]).

He then vowed, "*Hum jehan tak jaa sakain gai tau zaroor jaaingai.*" (We will go as far as we can.)

Zardari acknowledged that Imran Khan had been brought into power through engineered elections by the deep state but warned against confronting the military establishment directly. He said: "*Yeh difficult election tha. Har qism ka harba istemal kia gia and khul kar wo quwwatain saamnay aai hain. Iss manadate ko hum grudgingly maantai hain. Jamhooriat chalana hai iss ke daairay me reh kar.*" (This election [2018] was a difficult one. The powers employed all kinds of tricks openly. We grudgingly accept this mandate [given by the elections]. We will practise democracy staying within the available parameters.)

Advising the party to accept the harsh reality, he once again asked the parliamentarians to refrain from taking on the military establishment head-on.

"*Hum apne mulk ko Afghanistan, Libya aur Yemen jaisa nahi banana chahate. Ab election ho gia hai. Har koi apni chaal chale ga.*" (We do not want our country to become another Afghanistan, Libya, or Yemen. Now, the elections are over. Everyone will play their cards.)

Zardari reversed the decision of forming a joint opposition to Imran Khan, saying that the PPP should not play second fiddle to PML-N and should oppose Khan from its own platform. He said: "*Hum opposition karaingai lekin apni kursion per baith kar aur apnai darakht ke neechai. Apni leadership ke teht karaingai, kisi aur ke tehet nahi karaingai.*" (The PPP will be in the opposition but will play the game on its own turf. We will sit [in the Assembly] on our own benches [separately] as opposition, under [the shade of] our own tree, our own leadership, not under the leadership of anyone else.)

The key messages of his astounding address were:

1. If the establishment has decided to create the South Punjab Province, let us collectively work towards it.
2. No confrontation with the deep state.
3. The PPP will sit on the opposition benches as a separate entity and not as a camp follower of PML-N.
4. Revitalise the Party in Punjab and accept the 2018 election results, even if grudgingly.

Zardari may or may not have been right in his prognosis, but at least he was candid. He claimed to be willing to go far in the quest for creating the South Punjab Province and was prepared to trust the deep state.

Party leaders were left red-faced, particularly those who had negotiated the agreement on joint candidates of opposition parties for all constitutional posts.

However, neither Imran Khan nor his sponsors in the deep state were sincere about creating a separate province of South Punjab. During the over 40 months of his government, not a single step was taken towards fulfilling his manifesto promise. Zardari had misjudged the situation.

Come April 2022 and the vote of no-confidence against Imran Khan, the deep state employed the South Punjab card once again.

South Punjab PTI MNAs now ditched Imran Khan en masse as readily as they had ditched Nawaz Sharif in the 2018 general elections. Singing from a common songsheet, they now accused Imran Khan of failing to keep his promise and defected to the parties in the opposition grouping, Pakistan Democratic Movement (PDM).

Defections from PTI in the name of the South Punjab Province ahead of the no-confidence vote against it in April 2022 were indeed part of the political manipulations played by the deep state.

No political party has played South Punjab as a pawn on the political chessboard as craftily as the deep state has.

Zardari may not escape blame for trusting the deep state's false promise about the South Punjab Province as a "vindication of our (PPP) position". But who's to blame more: Zardari for trusting the deep state or the deep state for ceaselessly playing double games?

Section Nine

SOME MYSTERIES

Chapter 1

A mysterious political party

In early 2018, a series of mysterious political developments unfolded in quick succession. Zardari was no longer the President, but as President of the Party, he had to react to these events and steer the Party's course. His responses to these mysterious political challenges were no less mystifying.

Zardari made almost all important decisions by himself, often without meaningful consultations, which baffled many. At times, even Chairman Bilawal was surprised. Zardari consistently asked doubters in the party to trust him, saying, "Trust me, I have not and will never mislead you."

Balochistan's administration and politics had long been under the effective control of the establishment. Mysterious political developments began playing out in Balochistan first. Wittingly or unwittingly, the PPP under Zardari also played a role in these developments in the province.

Mysteries did not cease. In November 2017, the workers of a hardliner religio-political outfit called Tehreek-i-Labbaik Pakistan (TLP), brandishing bamboo and iron rods, effectively blocked the federal capital Islamabad from the twin city of Rawalpindi defying the government's persuasions and threats. The protestors were mysteriously supported by some elements, including some media outlets that brought them food and other items. It was finally called off when the government agreed to sign a humiliating surrender agreement with its leaders. Worse still, some uniformed officers distributed money among the workers to facilitate their return to their homes. It rattled the PML-N government, ultimately forcing Prime Minister Nawaz Sharif to quit. Taking suo motu notice of it later, the Supreme Court severely indicted state institutions and oversight authorities for letting the people down.

The Nawaz Sharif Government was still reeling from the shock of the Faizabad dharna when, in January 2018, his Party's government in Balochistan, led by Sanaullah Zehri, disappeared in no time at the hands of his own party members, without any apparent provocation.

First, Home Minister Sarfraz Bugti, known for enjoying the

backing of the deep state, resigned from the provincial cabinet. Simultaneously, opposition parties moved a no-confidence motion in the Provincial Assembly against the Chief Minister. Some PML-N members also revolted against their Party's Chief Minister. Within a short time, Chief Minister Sanaullah Zehri's government evaporated as he resigned.

The PPP also supported the no-confidence move against Zehri. There was no formal discussion in the Party, and Zardari had taken the decision. He probably hoped to win some seats from Balochistan in the Senate.

The PML-N, having lost its base in the Provincial Assembly, failed to secure a single Senate seat in the elections two months later. Whatever the motivation for the no-confidence motion, the PPP also failed to get a single Senate seat from Balochistan. It was also unable to win a single seat in the Provincial Assembly in the general elections held in July. The decision to support the no-confidence motion against the PML-N Chief Minister had cost the Party dearly.

Later, Sarfraz Bugti, at the centre of the Game of Thrones in the province, also became a senator and was sworn in as interior minister in the federal caretaker government of Anwarul Haq Kakar in August 2023. Abruptly, he resigned from the federal cabinet in December of that year to contest Provincial Assembly elections strangely on a PPP ticket, ultimately becoming the province's Chief Minister in March 2024 under the PPP banner.

Even stranger happenings were to unfold in the province. In March 2018, a new party called the Balochistan Awami Party (BAP) sprang up mysteriously almost overnight from almost nowhere. All the dissident PML-N MPAs joined it. The mysterious party went on to get six of its nominees elected as "independent" candidates from the Balochistan Assembly. It was unprecedented. Only mysterious elements within the state could have pulled off such a feat.

More mystifyingly, BAP named Sadiq Sanjrani and Anwarul Haq Kakar, two of the "independent" senators, as its candidates for the two top Senate offices of chairman and deputy chairman.

As subsequent events showed, an inexperienced, independent 40-year-old Sadiq Sanjrani was elected as the chairman of the Senate. He had no association with any political party.

The Party-less Sanjrani and his six associates refused to join any mainstream political party to lend some element of respect to political processes. Sanjrani went on to defeat the joint nominee of all major political parties who had a majority in the Senate. The election of a non-Party person as Senate Chairman was a defeat for the political parties and democratic principles. The Senate was thus set to be run by hidden puppeteers from behind the scenes.

Mysteries abounded. In the past, Imran Khan had dismissed calls for political accommodation with the PPP, saying, "How will I face myself in the mirror if I ever joined Zardari?" Taking a U-turn now, he said that if Zardari supported Sanjrani for the post of chairman, he would support Zardari's nominee for the post of deputy chairman. Who had persuaded Khan to take this U-turn was also an enigma.

PML-N leader Nawaz Sharif, on the other hand, announced he would support Raza Rabbani if the PPP nominated him. Rabbani possessed strong credentials and broad support within the Party. However, the rival PML-N's unilateral nomination was sure to be resented by the PPP leadership. It scuttled Rabbani's chances, if there were any.

Closed-door consultations among only a few began in Zardari House. Real estate tycoon Malik Riaz, former Deputy Speaker of the National Assembly and erstwhile PPP member Haji Nawaz Khokhar were very active.

In the small group discussions, Bilawal favoured Raza Rabbani. Calling Rabbani's election "Plan A", he asked that a "Plan B" be also made. This indicated that Raza Rabbani was unlikely to become chairman of the Senate. Despite his support, Bilawal also suspected that.

For Bilawal, the prospect of an independent senator, supported by BAP, getting elected as chairman was anathema, hard to stomach. His "Plan-B" was that the PPP would support

BAP's candidate only if the six "independent" senators from Balochistan formally joined the PPP. In addition, he wanted the PPP to be given at least the position of deputy chairman of the Senate. He did not want to support a BAP nominee as chairman unless the "independents" had formally joined the PPP. That was the least he thought necessary to save the Party from the embarrassment of being viewed as partaking in the Byzantine games being played by the establishment. He knew that alone and by himself, he could not hope to stop the deep state's Byzantine complex and devious tactics. His best bet was to prevent the Party from being placed in an awkward position and to search for some middle ground and quid pro quo.

Malik Riaz stepped out and talked with someone on the phone. He returned, saying that Imran Khan had refused to allow a PPP chairman under any circumstances. He was willing to give the post of deputy chairman to the PPP provided it agreed to the nominee of BAP for the chairman's post. It was not known who he spoke with on the phone to assert himself so authoritatively.

The PPP faced a difficult situation. It was hard to explain why it bargained for the position of deputy chairman when it could easily get Rabbani elected as chairman. There was also no guarantee that Imran would not renege on it despite having agreed to a PPP deputy chairman. After all, he was known for making U-turns and somersaults.

Chapter 2

The Senate chairman—but who?

A day before the newly elected senators took their oath, Zardari called a meeting of senior Party leaders at Zardari House, Islamabad, to discuss the election of the Senate chairman. In addition to Zardari and Bilawal, former Prime Ministers Yousaf Raza Gilani and Raja Pervaiz Ashraf and other senior leadership attended the meeting.

The discussion centred on the mysterious emergence of the Balochistan Awami Party (BAP), which had seemingly sprung up overnight with the backing of the deep state. It was clear that BAP's candidates for the top slots to run the House business would likely be beholden to their not-so-hidden backers. A BAP-supported senator as chairman would undermine Parliament, with the Senate potentially being run according to a script choreographed by the deep state. This scenario threatened to compromise the prospects of free and fair general elections scheduled for July that year.

A serious question that needed addressing was: What would be the political fallout for PPP if it aligned either with the deep state's creation, BAP, or with the opposition PML-N? With PML-N support, Raza Rabbani would win, but this alliance would be seen as PPP aligning with Nawaz Sharif. Did this suit PPP's political calculus?

Amid such concerns, Zardari asked Yousaf Raza Gilani for his assessment.

Gilani stated that the Party trusted Zardari's leadership and would accept his decision. Quickly realising the inadequacy of his remarks and the need for discussion, he suggested that legal luminaries like Aitzaz Ahsan should first give their views. Raja Pervaiz Ashraf concurred with Gilani. Aitzaz interjected, "The issue is not about trusting the leadership's decisions. The issue is weighing the pros and cons of our options to make an informed decision."

Nawaz Sharif had already announced his support for Raza Rabbani if the PPP decided to nominate him. The discussions revolved around the advantages and disadvantages of aligning with PML-N and nominating Raza Rabbani for the position of chairman.

Zardari, who had previously suggested in party meetings that Rabbani was too rigid, expressed reservations about his nomination. He argued, "Nominating Raza Rabbani would send out the message that PML-N and PPP have joined hands. The perception of supporting Nawaz Sharif would be the kiss of death for the PPP in Punjab."

He continued, "The issue is not as simple as it might appear to you. It's more than a mere numbers game. We can muster the numbers, but is it desirable and will aligning with Nawaz Sharif advance our political agenda?"

Zardari elaborated that electing Rabbani as chairman with PML-N backing would make the PPP appear to endorse Nawaz's current anti-establishment and anti-judiciary narrative. He questioned the authenticity of Nawaz's stance: "Nawaz's current narrative is unreal, temporary, and driven by political expediency. If it were indeed permanent and a real change of heart, I would support him. Are you sure that Nawaz has truly changed in adopting his new anti-establishment narrative?"

He urged party leaders to consider the consequences of aligning with Nawaz at that juncture. "What if Nawaz changes his hardline narrative and leaves the PPP in the lurch? Isolated and left alone, the PPP will lose. Ultimately, Nawaz will join hands with the establishment," he warned. Zardari thus framed the question: "Should we align with Nawaz or not at this point in time?"

Zardari then raised another concern: "Rabbani plans to give a Constitutional ruling on the trichotomy of powers and embarrass the army and the judiciary. Although he has withheld and not announced the ruling yet, he is brandishing it. Is this the right approach?"

It was clear that with some flexibility, the PPP could easily win the chairman's position. Surprisingly, no one in that meeting insisted that Rabbani was the best choice. Bilawal offered a candid perspective. While agreeing with his father that the PPP should not appear overly confrontational towards the establishment and judiciary in nominating its candidate, he also opposed bending backwards to appease the deep state. Mincing no words, he asserted that the PPP must protect its core political interests.

For Bilawal, nominating Rabbani was the first choice, but he recognised it might not be feasible. He proposed an alternative: if Rabbani's nomination was not possible, then the Baloch "independent" senators must join the PPP in return for the party supporting their candidate for the position of senate chairman. "This should be the minimum," he stated.

Everyone agreed. Zardari asked that Bilawal's proposal be explored further. In essence, the task was to approach the mysteriously elected "independent" senators supported by the equally mysterious BAP and ask them to join the PPP in exchange for support in the election to the top Senate slots.

Chapter 3

Bilawal's Plan-B fails spectacularly

BAP leader Mir Abdul Quddus Bizenjo was already in Islamabad. Someone suggested inviting him to Zardari House to discuss the possibility of "independents" joining the PPP in exchange for political support in the elections of the chairman and deputy chairman of the Senate. However, due to the heavy media presence outside Zardari House, it was decided not to call him to the ongoing meeting.

Instead, the PPP decided to send some senior members to meet Quddus Bizenjo and other BAP leaders at Balochistan House in Islamabad for discreet discussions. Two PPP interlocutors were dispatched for this purpose.

Upon their return to Zardari House, the interlocutors reported that the six "independent" senators had agreed to join the PPP, but only after its candidate, Sanjrani, was first elected as chairman.

Bilawal pointedly asked, "What is the guarantee that they will indeed join the PPP after Sanjrani has been elected as chairman of the Senate with the PPP vote?"

The interlocutors stunned the meeting with their disclosure: there were no guarantees at all that the "independents" would join the PPP even after Sanjrani's election. They had refused to provide any assurance and seemed confident of winning even without PPP support.

Given the numbers, the six party-less senators would have surely secured the position of chairman if they had joined the PPP. This alliance would have also provided some face-saving for the PPP, allowing them to explain to the public why they voted for a non-party, "independent" senator as chairman. The refusal of the "independents" to join the mainstream PPP until their nominee was actually elected as chairman—which was not possible without manipulations and floor crossing—was puzzling. Their confidence in Sanjrani's election as an "independent" chairman without PPP support was equally strange. Even more perplexing was the fact that the behind-the-scenes manipulators seemed unwilling to provide any face-saving opportunity for the PPP.

"Why then take the risk of supporting the "independents"

group, particularly when we can easily get Rabbani elected?" Bilawal asked pointedly. Zardari looked the other way.

The meeting grappled with the question: What to do now?

Someone proposed asking the "independent" senators to take an oath on the Holy Quran and promise to join the PPP after the election of the chairman and deputy chairman of the Senate.

Zardari rejected this idea, stating, "No, I do not want to bring the Holy Quran into political discussions."

He then announced that the PPP would support the Baloch group of "independents" even without the guarantee that they would join the PPP at a later stage.

A stunning silence followed.

Respecting his father, Bilawal did not speak further. Earlier, he had posed some challenging questions that remained unanswered, but he chose not to press the issue.

The refusal of "independent" senators from Balochistan to join the PPP in exchange for the Senate chairmanship was astounding. It raised the question: Who had assured the six "independents" that they would secure the post of the Senate chairman whether or not they joined any mainstream political party?

The interlocutors also revealed that during discussions at Balochistan House, Quddus Bizenjo frequently took brief breaks, leaving the room and then returning to resume the conversation. Apparently, he was seeking instructions from someone in another room. The identity of these background orchestrators remained unknown to the interlocutors.

When the elections for the chairman's office were held, the PML-N candidate Raja Zafarul Haq was defeated by "independent" Sanjrani by 11 votes, despite the numbers initially favouring the former.

Nawaz Sharif appointed a special team to investigate. The investigators reportedly claimed that two senators each from JUI-F and FATA (who had earlier announced joining PML-N), one senator from ANP, and three senators from the ruling alliance had voted against Raja Zafarul Haq.

While the identity of those from the ruling alliance who voted against Raja Zafarul Haq was concerning, the greater worry was the mockery this had made of democracy.

Earlier, the BAP, with only a few seats in the Provincial Assembly, had managed to remove Balochistan's Chief Minister Sanaullah Zehri from office.

Having conquered the provincial Balochistan government and its assembly, the manipulators in the deep state had now also conquered the Senate. The election of an "independent" senator from Balochistan with no roots in any political party as chairman gravely undermined democracy. The subsequent conduct of business in the Upper House of Parliament demonstrated that its reins were being pulled from the outside, bringing no glory to the House.

Democracy had been gravely undermined, and the political parties, including the PPP, were made to eat humble pie.

It was speculated that the deep state may have threatened mainstream political parties with a discreet message that the last JIT (Joint Investigation Team) had not yet been formed, forcing them to do its bidding. The deep state won a pyrrhic victory. All mainstream political parties had lost, and there was nothing for any party or leader to cheer about.

A cartoon published in the English daily *Express Tribune* a few days later depicted Zardari riding the PPP horse and kicking it in a polo match, symbolising the internal strife within the party.

Chapter 4

A mysterious Senate resolution

Arbitrary conditions for disqualifying politicians from holding political offices were introduced during a military dictator's rule in 1962. PPP's founding Chairman, Zulfikar Ali Bhutto, changed the law in 1975, removing these arbitrary conditions.

In 2000, General Musharraf resurrected the disqualification provisions to ban selected politicians from politics. Relying on this resurrected law, the Supreme Court in July 2017 disqualified Prime Minister Nawaz Sharif from being elected as a member of Parliament in the Panama Papers case. He thus ceased to hold the office of Prime Minister. Later, through another court ruling, Nawaz Sharif was also disqualified from holding the Party head's office.

In October of that year, the PML-N government passed the Election Act 2017, reversing the Musharraf-era law to clear the path for re-electing Nawaz Sharif as Party head.

Opposition parties, including the PPP, opposed it, accusing the PML-N of bulldozing person-specific legislation to benefit its leader, Mian Nawaz Sharif. The PPP's opposition was ironic, as it was under its first chairman that the clause disqualifying politicians arbitrarily had been removed.

A few days after the Election Act 2017 was passed, a mysterious Parliamentary resolution surfaced in the Senate. It was not sponsored by any political party but signed by some senators. The resolution was very poorly drafted, casting doubt on the professionalism of the Senate's conduct of business.

A senator from FATA came to me and confided that he and some other fellow senators from the tribal region had been handed a copy of a resolution and asked to submit it to the Senate secretariat after signing it.

He showed me a copy of the draft resolution. It called for the repeal of the section in the Election Act 2017 that had paved the way for Nawaz Sharif's election as Party head. The draft's poor language showed that it was not the work of someone with even rudimentary knowledge of parliamentary instrument drafting.

When I asked who had drafted it and which political party had sponsored it, he disclosed that no political party but a senior officer of the security establishment had given it to him and other senators from FATA.

"I respect you like my father," he said and sought my advice, but also quickly added that he would have to do as he had been directed. He spoke with me as if to unburden something weighing heavily on his conscience.

A few days later, Zardari called an emergency meeting of some Party leaders in Zardari House. Aitzaz Ahsan, Sherry Rehman, Senate Chairman Raza Rabbani, and I were called to it. The agenda of the meeting was not known.

Zardari talked about the amendment to the Election Act 2017 that allowed the disqualified Prime Minister Nawaz Sharif to head his political party. Without any discussion, Zardri said it must be reversed and asked Raza Rabbani what he could do about it.

Rabbani said that the Senate had passed the bill but had not yet been assented to by the President. It had, therefore, not yet become law. After it was assented to and had become an Act of Parliament, an amendment could be moved to make any changes in the law. He said that laws could not be repealed or amended on the basis of mere resolutions. Any amendment would have to be moved in the form of a Bill, and that too after it had been signed by the President and enacted as law.

Those behind the mysterious resolution naively assumed that a law passed by Parliament could be amended through resolutions and motions. This indicated the low level of behind-the-scenes manipulators of the Upper House of Parliament. Zardari also asked why a resolution against a law passed by Parliament could not be moved in the Senate to undo the law.

Raza Rabbani said that apart from the fact that amendments are not done through resolutions, it would be odd even to move a resolution against the Bill that the Upper House had just passed. Having voted for it only a few days back, the senators would be accused of having passed a law thoughtlessly and without even reading it. It was also pointed out that the Bill had been challenged in the Supreme Court, and it would be best to wait for its verdict.

Zardari said that the matter being before the court was a good occasion to move the proposed resolution. It would strengthen the judiciary's ability to strike down the law.

I could not help but recall that just a few days back, I had been shown a draft resolution by a senator from the tribal areas. It was very poorly worded and looked highly mysterious.

Zardari was not surprised. He said that a copy of the resolution was available from a PPP senator he named, a confidant of Zardari, and asked that it be obtained from him. I rang up the senator and he promptly sent a copy. It was the same as what I had seen the day before.

Zardari asked that the resolution be re-drafted if it indeed was poorly drafted.

It also transpired that a few Karachi-based PPP senators had already signed it even before the Party issued any directions. Apparently, the senator named by Zardari had asked them to sign it without consulting anyone. These Party senators thought the Party's decision was conveyed through Zardari's confidant.

Later, a resolution was indeed moved by the PPP and passed by the Senate. Supported by other political parties, it said that anyone ineligible to be elected as a lawmaker should also be ineligible for becoming an office-bearer of a political party.

One could not but marvel at the mystery behind the Senate resolution.

Chapter 5

Enigmatic, mysterious statements

On 30 April 2018, the print and electronic media quoted Asif Ali Zardari as saying that Nawaz Sharif was "more opportunistic and cunning than I thought" and that Nawaz Sharif had "duped" him into making threatening "brick-for-brick" anti-General Raheel Sharif remarks some three years earlier, in June 2015.

Media sources attributed these comments to Zardari, claiming he had spoken to unnamed Party leaders in Lahore. The statements referred to a speech Zardari had delivered to tribal people in Islamabad in June 2015, where he had indeed warned the military establishment not to overstep its mandate. In that speech, Zardari had cautioned that if the Pakistan People's Party (PPP) took to the streets, not just Sindh but the entire country would come to a grinding halt.

Zardari's June 2015 speech had included pointed remarks about the military's role: "Army Chiefs come and go every three years, but the political leadership is here to stay. We know the country and know how to run it." However, he did not indicate what had prompted his anger towards the establishment in his speech. Soon after the speech, Zardari left the country and remained in self-imposed exile for 18 months.

In the April 2018 media reports, Zardari was also quoted as saying that Nawaz had used his June 2015 speech to mend fences with General Raheel Sharif, effectively abandoning Zardari. "We supported government efforts to strengthen democracy and civilian supremacy, but Nawaz Sharif stabbed us. Nawaz Sharif will suffer now as we will not join hands with him," Zardari allegedly stated.

The media reports further attributed several critical statements to Zardari:

- "While we remained engaged in politics, Nawaz was busy in trading. He sold us out on every occasion."
- The National Accountability Bureau (NAB) and other investigation bodies had become active in Sindh at Nawaz Sharif's behest.
- Nawaz Sharif had assured him that Pervez Musharraf

would not be allowed to leave the country, but he was actually making a deal to let him go without taking anyone into confidence.

Nawaz Sharif reacted angrily to these reported statements. He claimed he had communicated his "displeasure" to Zardari over his anti-army remarks in 2015 and cancelled a planned meeting with him the following day. Nawaz questioned, "Why did Mr Zardari not say at the time that I had asked him to issue this anti-army statement?"

Nawaz went on to defend his actions and criticise Zardari:

- In 2008, the PML-N had joined the PPP-led coalition on the conditions of impeaching General Musharraf, restoring the sacked judges, and repealing the 17th Amendment. Nawaz accused Zardari of not keeping his word, claiming that Zardari had said political agreements were not the words of the Quran and Hadith.
- Nawaz stated that Zardari had visited him in Raiwind along with another national political leader, insisting that all Musharraf's acts be validated by Parliament, but "I refused straight away."
- Regarding the NAB's activity in Sindh, Nawaz claimed that both Zardari and Dr Asim Hussain knew very well that it had become active on the orders of the Director General of Rangers, not his.

Some Party leaders denied that Zardari had made the statements attributed to him. They insisted that Zardari's statements were only issued by his official spokesperson, and the media office had not released this particular statement.

As Zardari's spokesperson, I [the author] called a press conference to disown the interview attributed to Zardari as false. I did not seek his permission to do so. However, Zardari somehow learned of my planned press talk and called to say, "Farhatullah, you ignore it." Consequently, the scheduled press conference was cancelled.

This turn of events left me puzzled. Did Zardari actually speak "off-the-record" with the media outlet, or did he ask someone to plant the story, attributing it to "unnamed party leaders?" Was it a case of deliberate ambiguity? What purpose did it serve? It remained a mystery.

Chapter 6

Enigma inside a mystery

In February 2016, a statement purportedly issued by Zardari was even more puzzling than usual. Terming General Raheel Sharif's decision to refuse an extension in service as "premature", Zardari reportedly said that the decision could turn Pakistanis' hopes into despair and jeopardise the fight against terrorism.

"At this critical juncture, continuation of the army leadership is necessary to stem the tide of terrorism. And when the time comes, the political leadership must make a decision taking into account national interest and security situation," he had supposedly stated.

The statement stunned everyone when it hit the headlines on TV channels. It contradicted Zardari's initial response a month earlier, in which he had hailed the announcement of General Raheel's retirement plans. Zardari was not known for having any special liking for the Army Chief or holding him in high esteem. In fact, in the past, he had warned of a "brick for brick" response, apparently threatening General Raheel Sharif.

Why, barely a month after welcoming Raheel's retirement plans, would he now call for the continuity of his leadership of the army? The words used in the statement made it look formal and deliberate: "Our party considers General Raheel's decision premature, which can turn people's hopes into disappointment."

Totally unaware of the statement, party leaders were not in a position to confirm or deny it. They could only say, which they did, that the spokesperson had not issued the statement from the party's official platform. Party leaders also said that an investigation would be carried out to determine who had issued the statement and why. If there was indeed some undisclosed mechanism whereby one of the close aides was tasked with issuing such statements behind the back of the media office, no one could tell.

The formulation "our party considers..." was particularly puzzling. No meeting had been held to discuss the issue at any party forum.

Several hours later, Zardari called Hamid Mir, the host of Geo News' flagship talk show "Capital Talk", to deny the statement. Mir tweeted: "Asif Ali Zardari just called me and expressed total ignorance about his statement. He said, "Me or my Party never issued any statement."

But the damage had been done.

Even more surprisingly, a day later, a PPP MPA filed a resolution in the Punjab Assembly seeking an extension in the services of General Raheel Sharif. The resolution stated that General Raheel's services were commendable and termed his retirement "premature". It further claimed that the situation in the country demanded that the Army Chief not retire. "This House asks the federal government to give him [General Raheel] extension in service in the national interest," the resolution read.

No investigations were carried out into the two statements attributed to Zardari. The PPP MPA in the Punjab Assembly who had submitted the resolution did not explain who had authorised him to do so. The party also did not seek an explanation.

Enigmas were shrouded in mysteries. Zardari's capacity for enigma was mystifying indeed.

Chapter 7

Zardari and WikiLeaks

In 2006, Australian editor, publisher and activist Julian Assange founded WikiLeaks, an organization specialising in publishing troves of highly classified diplomatic cable exchanges between U.S. diplomats in different world capitals and the State Department, as well as diplomatic documents of Saudi Arabia. Their publication created a storm in diplomatic and political circles throughout the world.

In November 2009, WikiLeaks posted on its website highly uncomplimentary remarks purportedly made by Saudi King Abdullah bin Abdul Aziz about President Asif Zardari, calling him the biggest obstacle to Pakistan's progress.

Zardari may or may not have been upset, but he showed no signs of it. Responding to the leak, the foreign office, on its own initiative, described the report as "mischievous, misleading and contrary to facts." The report was discussed in one of the daily media briefing sessions with Zardari.

In a similar situation, when the President of a friendly country allegedly made uncomplimentary remarks about Benazir Bhutto, she decided against responding publicly and agreed with her foreign policy advisor that "there will be time to set the record straight."

Zardari thought otherwise. He did not want to set the record straight now or at any time in the future.

He directed that a press release be issued saying that, regardless of the so-called leaks, the President respected the Saudi monarch as "an elder brother" and that nothing would be allowed to harm Pak-Saudi ties.

The Saudis were very pleased with his reaction.

In December 2010, some leading national dailies headlined purported WikiLeaks that seemed to glorify Pakistan army generals, demonise Indian generals, and claim that India, indeed, was using its foothold in Afghanistan against Pakistan.

Following are some quotes from the purported WikiLeaks highlighted by some leading national dailies of the country:

• "The Inter-Services Intelligence (ISI) chief Ahmed Shuja Pasha's extension in service was termed as a good omen in one such cable, and it was added that his further presence on the scene would enhance the agency's abilities to combat anti-terror war."

• "An earlier cable ruled out any direct or indirect involvement of ISI in 26/11 under Pasha's command while Mumbai's dossier, based on prime accused Ajmal Kasab's confessional statement, was termed funny and 'shockingly immature.'"

• "The cable confirmed the active presence of ISI in India but refused to confirm any involvement of ISI in any terror incident across India and did confirm intelligence collection by its agents and operatives."

• "Another cable stated that Indian involvement in Afghanistan was increasing considerably and all was going on with the consent and knowledge of President Karzai and his administration. The cable further reads that growing Indian influence and presence in Afghanistan was focused towards Pakistan and China, both simultaneously."

• "WikiLeaks revealed that a cable sent from a U.S. mission in India termed former Indian Army Chief General Deepak Kapoor as an incompetent combat leader and rather a geek."

• "His (General Deepak Kapoor's) war doctrine, suggesting eliminating China and Pakistan in a simultaneous war front, was termed as 'much far from reality.'"

• "Another cable indicates that General Kapoor was dubbed as a general who was least bothered about security challenges to the country but was more concerned about making personal assets and strengthening his own cult in the army. The cable also suggested that a tug-of-war between Kapoor and the current Indian Army Chief had divided the Indian Army into two groups."

• "Another cable indicated the involvement of top Indian Army leadership in engaging Hindu extremist militants to carry out certain terror operations to keep Indian Muslims on the back foot and to keep pressure on neighbouring Pakistan's army and intelligence agencies, particularly the Inter-Services Intelligence."

Lauding it editorially, a leading English daily said in part:

"The whistleblower website WikiLeaks has ruffled many a

feather for exposing the inner feelings of important personalities on the world's political stage. [Washington] knew very well that the Indians were stoking the fires its war on terror had lit in FATA and were helping the disaffected people of Balochistan to rise against Pakistan. The Americans never tried to pull up its real strategic partner [Pakistan] to save it from public humiliation. On the other hand, Pakistan, the 'key ally' in the war on terror, was always pressed to 'do more' and eliminate the sanctuaries of the so-called Quetta Shura in the province's capital."

Senior newsroom staffers privately said that they had been advised by official sources to play up these WikiLeaks. The leading English daily *Dawn*, however, was suspicious and did not publish these reports.

Days after WikiLeaks' disclosures hit the headlines, the *Guardian* of Britain published a report by its correspondent stating that the purported WikiLeaks documents were fake and not true.

"An extensive search of the WikiLeaks database by the *Guardian* by date, name and keyword failed to locate any of the incendiary allegations," it said.

"The controversial claims, published in four Pakistani national papers, were credited to the Online Agency, an Islamabad-based news service that has frequently run pro-army stories in the past. No journalist is bylined," the *Guardian* said.

"The lopsided media coverage highlights the strong influence of Pakistan's army over an otherwise vigorous free press," the *Guardian* report further said.

Noting that the story was bylined to "agencies", the *Guardian* said the term "agencies" in Pakistan means both a news agency and a spy outfit.

Following the exposé, the newspapers which had published the purported WikiLeaks issued a clarification and apology.

A newspaper tendering the apology said that the story was released by the Islamabad-based news agency "Online" and was published with the confidence that it was a genuine report.

However, this was not the case. It was a planted story, the newspaper admitted.

"When contacted, the news agency and some of the editorial staff were themselves unclear about the source of the story and said they would investigate the matter," the newspaper further said.

The news agency also regretted filing an inaccurate story, apologised for it, and sacked the reporter under whose byline it had been published.

Through mysterious plants, fictitious WikiLeaks cables were used for propaganda purposes.

The *Guardian* described it as "the first case of WikiLeaks being exploited for propaganda purposes."

During a media brief session with Zardari, the fake WikiLeaks were discussed in some detail. The question arose: How stupid do some state officials really think Pakistanis are? The remarks once made by the late Zamir Niazi that the Pakistani media was becoming a hub of agency men willing to lie and cheat to protect and promote their patrons in the establishment were recalled.

Zardari chuckled at how the leaks had been exposed as a lie but did not utter a word. He had a big laugh.

He had often been saying in Party meetings: "*Deewaron ke bhi kaan hote hain.*" (The walls also have ears.)

Chapter 8

Zardari and the military

Zardari did not subscribe to the view that Pakistan's existential threat came from across its borders. Rather, he believed that the numerous fault lines posing existential threats to the country, such as militancy, ethnicity and poverty, lay within its borders. Indeed, he said as much while addressing a gathering of senior former bureaucrats whom he had invited to the Presidency for a brainstorming session. The press release of his address received wide media coverage and was also applauded by some foreign dignitaries who met him in those days.

However, some time afterwards, Zardari told me I should not have highlighted his address at the meeting. He said it was not well received by the army leadership.

The generals had no love for him. According to WikiLeaks' revelations in early 2009, Army Chief General Ashfaq Parvez Kayani discussed with the Americans the possibility of "persuading" President Zardari to resign - replacing him with ANP (Awami National Party) leader Asfandyar Wali Khan. General Kayani also said he would keep Prime Minister Yousaf Raza Gilani in place.

In another cable, then U.S. Vice President Joe Biden recounted to Britain's then Prime Minister Gordon Brown a conversation with Zardari a year before. Zardari had told him that Kayani and the ISI "will take me out", according to the cable. The cables also showed that Zardari had made extensive preparations in case he was killed. Indeed, he kept weapons in his bedroom in the Presidency. A leading anchor person who had called on him in the living area of the Presidency witnessed the arsenal and wrote about it in a column.

The generals believe that the military alone can save the country from "corrupt politicians" as well as from the "existential threat" from across the borders. They seem to believe they alone have the right to determine the contours of crucial state policies. A major reason for their dislike of Zardari was rooted in his disdain for this view. Tensions between Zardari and the army leadership for most of his tenure have been no secret. Coup rumours have often been circulating and, tongue in cheek, gleefully regurgitated by media persons close to the establishment. Zardari, however, never took them seriously. His posture, whether natural or assumed, was as if he couldn't care less.

While Zardari was no puppet of the military, it cannot be denied that he went to great lengths to keep the generals in good humour and not displease them. His readiness to go the extra mile to keep the army leadership happy was extraordinary, but it also disappointed many.

Here is a description of some instances that demonstrated his generosity in accommodating the demands of the army leadership, regardless of the fallout:

In February or March 2010, media reports emerged that General Kayani had extended the service of a few lieutenant generals without seeking government permission. This critical decision, which had profound implications for the institution, received only brief news coverage with little subsequent discussion. Such matters were not minor procedural issues and should have required government approval. The Prime Minister was unaware of these extensions. By not seeking prior sanction, Kayani effectively positioned the military as a state within a state. During a media briefing, President Zardari dismissed suggestions that the matter needed to be addressed with the Army Chief.

The National Institute of Modern Languages (NIML) was established in 1970 to train government officials in various languages. As numerous military officers also received training at NIML, the institute was under the control of the GHQ. When Musharraf took power, he transformed the institute into a university in 2000 through an ordinance, renaming it the National University of Modern Languages (NUML). The ordinance designated the President as the chairman of its board.

In March 2011, a presidential ordinance altered the command and control structure of NUML. The Army Chief, rather than the President, was made chairman of NUML's board of governors.

This ordinance contradicted the principles of the Higher Education Commission (HEC). It stipulated that the chairman of the university's board of governors would appoint only senior serving or retired army officers as vice-chancellor (VC) and rector of the university.

As chancellor, the President's role was purely ceremonial, limited to presiding over university convocations. However, it appeared that some elements sought to deny President Zardari even that ceremonial function. The education ministry pushed the ordinance through hastily, disregarding the opposition from the parliamentary education committee. No clear explanation was provided for this hurried change. Without raising any questions, Zardari signed the ordinance on the same day it was presented.

In July 2010, the PPP government gave a three-year extension in service to the Army Chief General Kayani, who was due to retire in November of that year. It was unprecedented in many ways.

Even before the decision was taken, media reports circulated that Kayani would be given an extension. Secretary of State Hillary Clinton was due to visit Pakistan, and it was speculated that she would convey the U.S. Administration's desire to give Kayani an extension. During media briefing sessions, whenever I mentioned persistent media reports, the President kept quiet and did not utter a word. There was no way to find out what he really thought.

The late Arif Nizami of the *Nation* was invited to lunch by the President in those days. Talking about it, he said that General Kayani had called him personally on the phone, asking him not to publish reports that the U.S. Administration wanted Kayani to be given an extension.

On the eve of Hillary's visit, the highly respected party leader Makhdoom Ameen Fahim told a journalist, "Kayani will get the extension now."

Amid such speculations, Prime Minister Yousaf Raza Gilani announced the extension decision on television on 22 July 2010, just as Hillary had concluded her visit to Pakistan and met the

President and the Prime Minister.

The timing of the announcement was curious. If Kayani had indeed been averse to a perception that the U.S. wanted his extension, the announcement's timing could not have been worse for him. Or was it done on purpose? It is difficult to say.

The President was in Karachi when the Prime Minister announced the decision. He phoned and asked about the public reaction to it. When I said that, by and large, the public reaction was negative, he said that it was a "bold decision" and that all such decisions would have both positive and negative comments. Alluding to the PM's remarks in his speech that he had spoken with the President about it, he said it was necessary to show that the Party stood by the decision.

During a chat on one of his foreign visits, Defence Minister Chaudhry Ahmad Mukhtar said he opposed giving an extension to the Army Chief. The proposal to create a new post of commander-in-chief and appoint Kayani to it had also been mooted, but it was finally not accepted. Mukhtar thought that the creation of the new post and the extension to Kayani would come to haunt us in the future.

Kayani had been appointed Army Chief by General Musharraf, who, in turn, had been giving himself an extension upon an extension for the eight long years that he had remained at the helm.

Commenting on the extension decision, the *Dawn* newspaper on 24 July editorially said:

"Like it or not, the extension does not reflect well on the army as an institution. ... Whatever Gen Kayani's intimate familiarity with the present state of affairs and whatever his unique understanding of the situation, a strong institution should be able to withstand the retirement of one man, however experienced."

"Regular, scheduled changes in leadership are in fact meant to keep institutions vibrant and strong. That there are 'special circumstances' at the present time is not fully convincing either. Externally, the uncertainty in Afghanistan, the intransigence of India, the unpredictability of the Americans

— all these circumstances have existed before, and the country has survived them."

"The public does not know yet, perhaps it never will, if the decision was a total capitulation or the result of a quid pro quo."

Years later, when he was no longer President, Zardari told a Party meeting that Kayani wanted an extension for only 12-18 months. He said he told Kayani that the Army Chief was not like the police chief to be given piecemeal extensions for a year or two. He had, therefore, decided to give him an extension for the full term of three years, he told Kayani.

After he left the Presidency, I once asked Zardari whether it was wise to give Kayani an extension. He replied, "I will take you out on a sea voyage in a boat off the Dubai coast where no one can listen to our talk about it." Zardari alone knows the compulsions behind giving Kayani an extension.

Whatever means he adopted, Kayani secured an extension for himself, even if it was not in the institution's best interest. Institutional interests have hardly been given preference over personal ambitions.

Section Ten

ZARDARI BOUNCES BACK

Chapter 1

Zardari returns from Dubai

The media's reaction to the President's illness and travel to Dubai was almost bizarre, bordering on a frenzy. Every media pundit claimed to know the "real reason" for his going to Dubai. Some asserted he had fled to escape the "Memogate" scandal for good, never to return. Others insisted he was playing games, at which he was a past master. Some claimed, quoting unnamed doctors, that Zardari was permanently disabled.

Nearly everyone thought Zardari was a closed chapter.

Grist was also provided to the rumour mills by blogs associated with credible foreign media houses. A blog linked to the prestigious Foreign Policy magazine in the United States added to the hysteria. It headlined a report that Zardari was on his way out. Quoting former U.S. officials, it claimed that President Zardari had sounded incoherent during his conversation with U.S. President Barack Obama about NATO's killing of 24 Pakistani soldiers in Salalah. The blog suggested Zardari was incoherent because the noose was tightening around his neck.

The blog also claimed that the U.S. government had been informed that President Zardari might resign due to ill health, though it did not specify who had provided this information. Those who suspected that Zardari was the mastermind behind the Mullen Memo readily believed suggestions that the army was about to send Zardari home.

His detractors believed an "in-house change" was finally occurring in Pakistan. They thought it was only a matter of days before the Memogate scandal would devour President Zardari.

When informed of the media hype suggesting the President had fled and would never return to the country, Zardari sent a text message from Dubai to his political secretary, Jamil Soomro. Naming a particular TV anchor, the President asked Soomro to convey, "I am coming back and soon."

Though he may still have been unwell, in the few days of rest—first at the American Hospital and later in his house in Dubai—he had regained some strength and was ready to resume another round of the fight.

Soomro informed the TV anchor, who broke the news, but no one believed it. Everyone preferred to believe Zardari had fled for good.

Returning as suddenly as he had left the country two weeks earlier, the President landed in Karachi in the early hours of Monday, 19 December. Two days later, he returned to Islamabad at night. Going to Dubai had been merely a pause in the battle, not a retreat from the battlefield.

Back in Islamabad, he resumed normal functions: receiving credentials from ambassadors, signing legislation into law, and meeting with the coalition partners' leaders. He looked fatigued, but it was business as usual.

Chapter 2

No state within a state

A day after the President arrived in Islamabad, Prime Minister Gilani launched two verbal salvos on 22 December.

Addressing a function to mark the birth anniversary of the Quaid-e-Azam, he asked all state institutions to stay within constitutional parameters. Later the same day, addressing the National Assembly, he said, "If the army considers itself a state within a state, then it is unacceptable."

"We have to come out of this slavery. If we remain slaves to this system, then there is no need for the Parliament," he declared.

Rejecting media reports that visas were issued clandestinely by Haqqani at the instance of Zardari to secret U.S. agents, he asked, "Who gave a visa to Osama to live in Pakistan for six years?"

He had cut deep into the military fort and chinked its shining armour.

The President called a meeting to brief Party leaders on why it had become unavoidable for the Prime Minister to make such statements. This move indicated that the Prime Minister had spoken with the President's knowledge and approval.

To provide context, the Prime Minister told the Party leaders at their meeting that, according to standard procedure, the GHQ and ISI were required to submit their replies to the Supreme Court in the Memogate case through the federal government. The Army Chief knew this and had agreed to it in his conversation with Gilani.

However, the army and ISI chiefs submitted their replies directly to the Supreme Court, bypassing the Prime Minister's office. Their statements contradicted the federation's stance.

"I was shocked," Gilani said.

Gilani informed the Party leaders of another reason for his statements.

Upon the President's return from Dubai, the Army Chief telephoned him to inquire about his health. Learning about the telephone conversation, journalists reported that the tension between the President and the Army Chief was over and it was business as usual.

Kayani, however, was not happy with the media's interpretation of his phone conversation with the President.

For him, it was not business as usual, and the Memogate issue remained unresolved. He telephoned the Prime Minister, saying that he wanted to issue a clarification. Gilani asked that the draft clarification be shown to him before it was issued. Kayani agreed.

Gilani said that while he was still talking with the Army Chief on the phone, television channels were reporting an unusual statement by the army's media wing. It read:

"The telephonic conversation between the President and COAS lasted approximately one minute in which he enquired about the health of the President. Hence, attributing anything more to this telephonic conversation is unfounded and unnecessary," a curt ISPR statement said.

Moreover, the defence secretary, a retired army general, refused to authorise the attorney general to represent the ISI and the army in the Supreme Court. He told the court that the army and ISI operations were not under the federal government's control.

"This was an act of defiance," Gilani said.

"I decided to deliver hard-hitting speeches and state that a 'state within a state' was not acceptable," Gilani told the Party meeting.

The Party leaders lauded the Prime Minister. The President rose in his seat as a mark of appreciation and respect. It was not business as usual. Zardari signalled that he was ready for another round.

Chapter 3

The army reacts — Zardari defiant

Reacting sharply to the Prime Minister's statement that the army and ISI chiefs had acted illegally in submitting replies in the Memogate scandal, the army issued a terse statement. It declared that those remarks could have "very serious ramifications with potentially grievous consequences."

"There can be no allegation more serious than what the Honourable Prime Minister has levelled against Chief of the Army Staff and Director General ISI and has unfortunately charged the officers for violation of the Constitution of the country," said the army's statement.

"This has very serious ramifications with potentially grievous consequences for the country."

In response, the Prime Minister sacked Defence Secretary Lt Gen (retired) Khalid Naeem Lodhi, who was considered close to the Army Chief. He appointed a female bureaucrat, Nargis Sethi, as the new defence secretary.

The Party meeting also decided to invite applications for the Senate elections despite these still being three months away in March. This early call for applications was unusual, but Zardari wanted to convey the message that fresh elections were out of the question and that the same assemblies would elect the Senate.

During the meeting, a staffer slipped a note to the President. It stated that General Kayani, addressing a military darbar, had just said that the army supported the democratic process and the government. Surprisingly, no one applauded as it was read. The Army Chief's apparently positive statement was ignored as inconsequential and not worth noting.

The press release of the meeting that day also ignored the Army Chief's statement. Instead, it stressed Parliament's supremacy and asserted that all institutions were answerable to it.

The President then asked that the Prime Minister's statements be particularly welcomed and that solidarity be expressed with him.

After the meeting, Rehman Malik suggested privately that a mention should also be made that the PPP did not want a clash with the army.

"Why, is it necessary?" I asked.

"I am telling you, it is absolutely necessary," he insisted.

I relayed this suggestion to the President and Prime Minister. Both rejected it emphatically, stating there was no need to say that the PPP did not want a clash with the military.

A suggestion was made to introduce resolutions in all assemblies demanding that pictures of past dictators be removed from official buildings. The President remained quiet on this matter, and no decision was taken. It was left open-ended.

The meeting also discussed apprehensions of a possible military takeover in the wake of the humiliation on 2 May. According to WikiLeaks, General Kayani had told the U.S. ambassador in Islamabad that he might "reluctantly" consider putting pressure on Zardari to resign.

The mood in the meeting was defiant. The President declared that in the event of any misadventure by the army, it would be the judiciary and the army who would be the losers, not the PPP. He also lauded the resolution passed by the Punjab Assembly against any such misadventure.

Following the meeting, the President met with heads of coalition parties, including Asfandyar Wali Khan, Munir Khan Orakzai, Chaudhry Shujaat, and Chaudhry Parvez Elahi. They all assured the President of their support.

Chapter 4

The "cat-and-mouse" game

Osama bin Laden (OBL) was shot in the head on Pakistani soil, his body whisked away and dumped into the sea in the wee hours of 2 May by U.S. Navy Seals. The announcement was made neither by the GHQ (General Headquarters of the Pakistan Army) nor the foreign office but by the President of the United States, Barack Obama. Embarrassed, the army and intelligence leadership were fuming, but they could hardly do anything to salvage their hurt ego.

The U.S. had decided not to inform anyone in Pakistan about the raid. No one in the country had any knowledge, not even the premier intelligence agency that prided itself on being among the best in the world. Those who boasted of full preparedness at all times were exposed as never before.

Just a few days before the raid, Army Chief Kayani, addressing cadets at the Pakistan Military Academy (PMA) in Kakul, had flexed his muscles against the militants and declared that they would have no place to hide. His embarrassment must have been the deepest.

To mask their humiliation, hollow claims bordering on the ridiculous were made by "defence analysts" that the operation was known at some level of top military leadership. Inspired news reports quoting "top level official sources" claimed that Pakistan was on board about the OBL operation at some official level.

The national psyche, which equates patriotism with support for the military, was pressed into service to retrieve some of the badly damaged credibility.

A trusted former judge of the Supreme Court, reputed for washing the establishment's dirty linen, was appointed chairman of the Abbottabad Inquiry Commission. When all else failed to retrieve honour, guns were turned against Zardari, all blazing.

The OBL fiasco presented an opportunity to establish a Truth Commission, but it was missed. Had it been established, not Zardari but some sacred cows would have had their faces tarnished. Those who always sought to paint themselves as white-washed heroes might have been revealed as villains, and the supposed villains might have been revealed as heroes.

It also provided an opportunity for the nation to overhaul the intelligence agencies, address the growing imbalance in civil-military relations, and introduce a measure of accountability in the military. It offered a chance to put their own house in order and end the intimidation and overthrow of constitutional governments by over-ambitious Bonapartist generals.

Whatever the reasons, Zardari missed this opportunity. In addition to a huge loss for the nation, he also paid a heavy personal price.

Thus, Memogate was invented to find scapegoats, distract attention from the military and intelligence leadership's failure, and cover up their humiliation. That was why blazing guns turned against Zardari.

In his memoirs *In the Line of Fire*, Musharraf unwittingly called his duplicity in the war against militants a "cat and mouse game".

Memogate was the latest in the series of "cat-and-mouse games" played by Musharraf's successors in uniform against the civilian and political leadership of the country ever since its creation.

Epilogue

Recovered from an illness that had sent him into a tailspin and forced him to seek medical treatment in Dubai in early December 2011, Zardari returned to Islamabad three weeks later, all smiles and ready to face his powerful detractors.

By late November 2011, the storm unleashed in Pakistan by the Memogate scandal had already claimed its first victim, Husain Haqqani.

In December, the army and ISI chiefs, along with Nawaz Sharif, took their case against President Zardari to the Supreme Court. This was no ordinary ambush of the President; it was akin to a suicide attack on the supreme commander of the armed forces. The attackers—namely the army and ISI chiefs, the opposition leader, and the chief judge—survived, leaving the supreme commander wounded but still breathing and nurturing hope for yet another round.

The attackers had won, but it was not even a pyrrhic victory. Looking back, they were defeated, though they failed to realise it at the time.

Pakistani-American businessman Mansoor Ijaz had long been accusing the ISI of being a rogue institution, urging successive U.S. Administrations to declare it as such. He repeatedly called upon them to dismantle the ISI, citing its support of jihadis attacking American troops in Afghanistan. In 2011, reflecting Ijaz's views, Mike Mullen, chairman of America's Joint Chiefs of Staff, famously called the Haqqani network of Taliban in Pakistan's tribal areas the "veritable arm of the Pakistani ISI". This alleged connection of the ISI to the Haqqani network strained relations between Pakistan and the U.S.

Yet, in their pursuit of Zardari, the army and ISI chiefs found themselves in the awkward position of embracing their nemesis, Mansoor Ijaz. By claiming the Memo was genuine and implying it had been written at Zardari's behest, they inadvertently boxed themselves, not Zardari, into a tight corner. In their eagerness to confront Zardari, they failed to recognise how foolish they appeared. The irony of embracing Mansoor Ijaz was entirely lost on the generals, even as Mike Mullen, the intended recipient of the alleged Memo, dismissed it as not credible.

When Zardari collapsed in the first week of December that year, he refused treatment in medical institutions under General Kayani's control. The harder Kayani pushed for the President to be treated in army medical institutions, the more firmly Zardari refused. Could there be a greater display of distrust towards the Army Chief by his supreme commander? It was a silent indictment, but its jarring significance was also lost on the Army Chief.

Upon Zardari's defiant return to Islamabad, Prime Minister Gilani dealt a blow to Kayani that must have left him reeling. On 23 December, he questioned on the floor of Parliament how Osama bin Laden had lived in a military cantonment for so long while the whole world was searching for him. "We are being asked by the judicial [Abbottabad] commission about issuance of visas (to Americans). But I want to ask how Osama bin Laden lived here for the past six years? On what type of visa was he living here?" Gilani said in remarks that haunted Kayani and the ISI chief. He also warned that a "state within a state" was unacceptable.

A fortnight later, in the second week of January 2012, Prime Minister Gilani was quoted in China's *People's Daily Online* stating that Pakistan's Army Chief and head of intelligence had acted unconstitutionally by making direct submissions to the Supreme Court about Memogate behind the government's back. This was broadcast as General Ashfaq Kayani was visiting China, leaving him fuming.

Gilani had also removed the defence secretary, General Lodhi, a confidant of Kayani, for writing to the Supreme Court that the government had "only administrative, but not operational, control of the army".

The next day, the military hit back, saying, "There can be no allegation more serious than (the army and ISI chiefs violating the Constitution)."

"This has very serious ramifications with potentially grievous consequences for the country," the military statement said, without specifying what these might be.

It further claimed that General Kayani had "followed the book" and had passed its response via the defence ministry to the Supreme Court according to the law. Kayani wanted Zardari to ask Gilani to retract. Zardari was not obliging.

Zardari was undoubtedly badly bruised in the fight that had been picked against him. To say that he was a superhuman who remained unaffected would be a grave misrepresentation. However, it is also true that by the end of the conflict, his detractors in the state institutions, political opposition, judiciary, and media had lost much more than he had.

The Memogate scandal was soon consigned to the dustbin of history as Zardari went on to complete his five-year term amid significant achievements.

During his tenure, he peacefully removed a military dictator from the Presidency in August 2008.

Less than two years later, in April 2010, he restored the 1973 Constitution and transferred most powers to Parliament.

In April 2011, he filed a reference in the Supreme Court without fuss or fanfare, urging it to revisit its 1979 verdict executing former Prime Minister and his father-in-law, Zulfikar Ali Bhutto, even as the Court was then headed by his nemesis, Chaudhry Iftikhar.

In 2013, he oversaw a general election and the peaceful transition from one civilian government to another. That year, he also administered the oath of office to his political rival, Nawaz Sharif, as Prime Minister and exited the Presidency with a guard of honour.

A few weeks before leaving the Presidency, he also laid the foundations for CPEC (China-Pakistan Economic Corridor).

He lived to see the day in March 2024 when the Supreme Court issued its mea culpa verdict, acknowledging that the trial of Prime Minister Zulfikar Ali Bhutto forty-four years ago was "unfair and lacked due process, both at the trial stage and in the endorsement of the verdict by the appellate court." This rare acknowledgement by the judges that Bhutto's execution was a judicial murder brought many, including his son Bilawal, to tears when he spoke with the media that day.

A few days later, he went on to be re-elected President—a distinction never before earned by a civilian President.

In time, Nawaz Sharif also publicly acknowledged his blunder in moving the Supreme Court against Zardari in the so-called Memogate case.

Overwhelmed by guilt, Sharif's accountability czar, Saifur Rehman, who had previously sent Zardari to jail on corruption charges, reportedly begged forgiveness, admitting he had wronged the former President.

A few months into his second term as President, Zardari signed the Constitutional Amendment (26th Amendment) in a bid to end the strident politicisation of the judiciary. His nemesis, former Chief Justice Iftikhar Chaudhry, now living in obscurity in Islamabad not far from the Parliament House, must have watched this development with horror.

While the judges finally showed humility in accepting Parliament's right to make legislation and declaring mea culpa in the Zulfikar Ali Bhutto case, the powerful military did not show any humility nor give up its indulgence in politics. Zardari keeps his inner thoughts closest to his chest and may be hoping that someday the powerful army will also bow before the people. It may be his dream, but he remembers his wife, Benazir Bhutto, telling a famous international conference in Cairo in 1994, "Everyone has a right to dream."

In the final analysis, the life of Zardari, painted as a villain, brings to mind Dostoevsky's famous novel *Crime and*

Punishment. In it, the central character, Raskolnikov, believed that the woman named Sonya was a sinner. Upon discovering the truth about her—that Sonya was not a sinner—he leapt towards her, kissed her feet, and asked for forgiveness. In that profound encounter, Raskolnikov acts as if he "worshipped the triumph of human endurance, and the strength of the human spirit, which could withstand so much and bear so much."

Those who, in the words of General Musharraf, have played "cat-and-mouse" have lost their game to human endurance. Even if they have not yet sought forgiveness, Zardari couldn't have asked for more. He had the last laugh.

Index

D

E

F

G

H

I

J

K